A History of Fortification

FROM 3000BC TO AD1700

A History of Fortification

FROM 3000BC TO AD1700

by

Sidney Toy
F.S.A., F.R.I.B.A.

PEN & SWORD MILITARY CLASSICS

This Book is Dedicated to
FIELD MARSHAL VISCOUNT MONTGOMERY OF ALAMEIN
K.G., G.C.B., D.S.O.
in honour of and in gratitude for his supreme achievements
in the field both in attack and defence.

First published in Great Britain in 1955 by
William Heinemann Ltd.

Published in this format in 2006 by
Pen & Sword Military Classics
an imprint of
Pen & Sword Books Ltd
47 Church Street
Barnsley
South Yorkshire
S70 2AS

ISBN 1-84415-358-4

Typeset in 9/10.5pt Sabon by Mac Style, Nafferton, E. Yorkshire
Printed and bound in England by CPI UK

Pen & Sword Books Ltd incorporates the Imprints of Pen & Sword Aviation,
Pen & Sword Maritime, Pen & Sword Military, Wharncliffe Local History,
Pen & Sword Select, Pen and Sword Military Classics and Leo Cooper.

For a complete list of Pen & Sword titles, please contact
Pen & Sword Books Limited
47 Church Street, Barnsley, South Yorkshire, S70 2AS, England
E-mail: enquiries@pen-and-sword.co.uk
Website: www.pen-and-sword.co.uk

Contents

Preface

Modern researches point strongly to the conclusion that the art of fortification had reached a high state of development even at the dawn of history. Powerful military works, dating from the remotest periods, have been found in Asia Minor, in Greece, and in the basins of the Tigris, the Euphrates, and the Nile. In the development of the art through the ages it is also clear that the peoples of these countries in their continuous conflicts with each other, and later with the legions of Rome, learnt and adopted the methods of attack and defence of their foes, and in the course of time their military works came to resemble each other more and more.

With the rise of the Romans the development received a fresh impetus, and in the process of extending and consolidating their conquests the Romans built fortifications which, while being monuments of inventive genius and skill each adapted to its particular purpose, were also at any given period, of great uniformity in fundamental principles of design.

For many centuries following the fall of the Roman Empire the nations of Western Europe were so much involved in continuous strife in the open field that the development of the art was confined largely to the Empire of the East. But from about the eleventh century of our era progress in this respect again became general among the leading nations of Europe and the levant. For it was the especial concern of every great leader to be familiar with the latest methods of attack and defence, since his safety and the safety of his followers depended upon his ability to forestall any surprise line of assault; and the Middle Ages afforded abundant opportunities for travel. The pilgrimages to Jerusalem, which took place from the fourth century, the Crusades, and pilgrimages to Rome, Compostella, Cologne and other holy places provided great scope for investigation. Again private journeys, both at home and abroad, were made frequently by ecclesiastics and laymen; and it is abundantly clear from their works that during these expeditions they kept their faculties alert, and that on their return they made good use of their observations. In the development of fortifications there were naturally variations of form in the several countries, consequent on differences of climate, available material and national characteristics. Early advances were also made in one country, and a tardy adherence to traditional practice is observable in another. But none the less the progress was, in the main, general. A survey and study of many of the castles of Europe, the Levant and elsewhere has led the author to the conclusion that no clear grasp of the history of military architecture can be obtained from the study of examples in one country alone, and that more general treatment is essential to a proper understanding of the subject.

The object of this work is to trace the development of the art of fortification generally from the period of the earliest historical examples down to the forts designed for defence by artillery, noting in their order the salient features of the military works themselves as well as the siege operations employed against them. Since the design of the fortifications, the details of structure and the methods of attack and defence were, in essence, the same whether related to a town, a castle, or even a camp, the developments are noted in order wherever, they occur, and the fortifications described and illustrated are chosen from among those in which the original features are most perfect. For further illustrations and details of the fortifications in England, Scotland and Wales described in this volume, the reader is referred to the author's *The Castles of Great Britain* (1953, second edition 1954).

In the main the castle is considered in its military aspect, as a fortress, and its domestic arrangements only in so far as they are ancillary to its functions as a fortification and are necessary in a residence.

When technical terms are used, in order to avoid pedantic and discursive arguments, those such as "shell-keep" have been chosen as being at once descriptive and familiar. To avoid confusion, the word "storey" is used throughout to mean one of all the stages into which a building is divided, including the basement, the first storey being the lowest.

An earlier work by the author on the subject. *Castles* (1939) was published shortly before the outbreak of war. The stock of copies of that book soon became exhausted, and, while the issue of further editions was prevented by the diversion of effort in other directions, the national appeal for metal resulted in the melting down of all the blocks and printer's type of the work. The book had therefore to be set up anew, and advantage has been taken of that fact by the issue of what is practically a new work. The first book was restricted to consideration of fortifications in Europe and the Near East. In this work, while the early volume entirely re-written and revised is incorporated, a large amount of Continental and Levantine material has been added, and the scope of the subject has been so far extended as to embrace military defences in whatever country they are found.

There is no pretence here at anything approaching exhaustive treatment of a subject so wide in a space so limited; and no one is more conscious of the deficiencies and omissions of the following pages than the author. The material must of necessity be selective. But it is hoped that the work may be a useful contribution to an important and fascinating field of study.

The author wishes to express his thanks for valuable help to Sir Charles Leonard Woolley, M.A., D.Litt.; to Sir Mortimer Wheeler, M.G., M.A., D.Litt.; President, Society of Antiquaries of London; Professor Ian A. Richmond, M.A., LL-D.; Sir Alfred Clapham, C.B.E.; Professor K. A. C. Cresswell, F.B.A., D.Litt., whose plans of the Citadel of Cairo the author has freely drawn upon to augment his own measurements; and to A. R. Beal, Esq. He also gratefully acknowledges information obtained from some modern works on the subject, in particular the following: *L'Afrique Byzantine*, by Charles Diehl (Paris, 1896); *Manuel d'Archéologie Française*, by Camille Enlart (Paris, 1904); *Deuchen Burgen*, (Berlin, 1889) and *Die Burgen Italiens* ('Berlin, 1909), both by Bodo Ebhardt; *Military Architecture in England*, by Professor Hamilton Thompson,, C.B.E., M.A., D.Litt.; the Inventories of the Royal Commissions on Historical Monuments (London and Edinburgh); Arquitectura Civil Espanola, by Lamperez and Romea (Madrid, 1922); Les Chateaux de Croises en Terre-Sainte, by Paul Deschamps (1931); and the Monographs on Scottish Castles, by Dr. W. D. Simpson, O.B.E., M.A. He desires especially to thank the numerous governing bodies and private owners, at home and abroad, who kindly granted him permission to examine the buildings in their charge. All the drawings have been prepared and a large number of the photographs were taken by the author; and he has himself examined and surveyed most of the fortifications described.

14 NORTH AUDLEY STREET,
GROSVENOR SQUARE,
LONDON, W.1.

SIDNEY TOY.
October, 1954

Acknowledgements

The author and publishers gratefully acknowledge the permission of the following to reproduce copyright photographs in this book.

The Times, for Carcassonne (1420) and Le Krak des Chevaliers

Messrs. Paul Popper Ltd., for The Great Wall of China.

Kenisley Picture Service, for Harlech.

Messrs. John Lane The Bodley Head Ltd., for two photographs of Peking, from *The Walls of Pekin* by Osvalt Siren.

Country Life, for Tattershall.

Exclusive News Agency Ltd., for Monte Agudo.

Messrs. Hutchinson Ltd., for Tarragona, and two photographs of the Kremlin (2340).

Messrs. Atlantis Verlag, for Jerusalem (ioob), Kerak, Aleppo, and Babylon from their book *Palaestina* by Groeber.

Librairie Orienuiiste Paul Geuthner, for Saone, and Margat, from the book *La Syrie Antique et Médiévale* by Dussaud, Deschamps and Seyrig.

Verlag Ernst Wasmuth, for Peking and Tsinan.

Messrs. Aeronlms, for Tamworth, Waimer, St. Mawes, Restormel, Kenilworth, Farnham, Durham, Pembroke (l28b), Warwick, St. Michael's Mount, Dover, Portchester, Maiden, Caernarvon.

Harold G. Leask, Esq., for Trim.

Chapter 1
Ancient Fortresses

From the earliest times cities and palaces were surrounded by walls, often of enormous thickness and of great height, and having at their summits wide wall-walks with embattled parapets. Sometimes there were two, three, or more lines of such walls and a citadel within the innermost line; as in the ruined cities of the Hittites in Asia Minor.

Some ancient fortifications, remains of which still stand or have been uncovered by modern excavation, date from periods so remote and attain such high degree of perfection that it is not possible to assign the elements of the science to any definite age. The most ancient of the walls of Babylon, of Ur of the Chaldees, and of Troy all date from the third millenium BC; the fortifications of Atchana, near Antioch, from about 1900BC, and those of Ashur, the ancient capital of Assyria, from about 1600BC. The fortifications of Mycenae and Tiryns in Greece and of what is called the sixth city of Troy all date from the Mycenaean Age, about 1500 to 1200BC. When these defences stood upon a plain, as in Mesopotamia, they normally consisted of a mud-brick rampart, 26 ft. high, surmounted by a wall, built of burnt brick and bitumen, and were enclosed by a moat, canal or

Troy: Wall of the Sixth City.

river. When built on a hill, as at Mycenae and Tiryns, they were usually of stone, and the approach to them was by way of a steep ramp commanded by a tower at the head.

The gateways were often of great width and height and flanked by towers. Sometimes, as at Mycenae and Tiryns, they were reached by long approach roads under direct attack from the walls. At Alchana there is a triple gateway, and at Mycenae and Tiryns there are double gateways. The gateways at Khorsabad were of massive proportions, and the passages through them were of great length and were intersected by cross-chambers.

BABYLONIA
Babylon has been so thoroughly devastated, and the remains brought to light in modern times so fragmentary, that our knowledge of the city is largely derived from the descriptions given of it by Herodotus, Ctesias and Strabo; and these descriptions apply more particularly to the city as remodelled by Nebuchadnezzar the Second. The more ancient walls, dating about 2500BC, were, as found by modern excavation, 23 ft. 4 in. thick, and were strengthened at intervals of about 140 ft. by towers alternately of greater and less projection. They were defended by a moat.

About 600BC. Nebuchadnezzar strengthened these fortifications by increasing the thickness of the existing wall on the outside, digging a new moat, and constructing an entirely new line of defences, consisting of a wall and a moat, inside the old walls. The city was now protected by a double line of walls and moats, the outer moat being lined with burnt bricks set in asphalt. The full thickness of the outer wall, as measured from the ruins themselves, is 85 ft. 8 in. This dimension agrees closely with the measurement given by Herodotus.[1] The figures he gives for the height and extent of the walls must be taken simply as expressive of great proportions; exact measurements on such a scale would involve a complicated survey not reasonable to expect.

Babylon: The Ishtar Gate

The Ishtar gate at Babylon, crossing the sacred way near the palace, dates from about 600BC and still stands to a considerable height. Its walls are decorated in low relief with large figures of bulls and dragons, executed in glazed brickwork. The long passage through the gateway is intersected at three points by large cross-chambers.[2]

Nebuchadnezzar built a new wall round the Temenos ai Ur of the Chaldees. This was actually a cavity wall composed of outer and inner solid portions, each 3.25 m. thick, set 5.20 m. apart and connected at intervals by strong cross-ribs, the total thickness being 11.70 m., or 38 ft. 4 in. The wall is strengthened on both outer and inner faces by shallow buttresses, spaced at close intervals.[3] The four principal gateways are set back from the general face of the wall in such a manner as to form wide spaces in front open to attack from the walls on three sides. There were guardrooms on either side of the passage through the gateways.

EGYPT

At the southern extremity of Egypt, near Wadi Haifa, are the remains of three border fortresses, said to date from about 2000BC. They are all of purely military character. One of them, at the island of Uronarti on the Nile, was built of very thick walls supported at frequent intervals by massive buttresses constructed of brick with timber bonding.

The palatial buildings of Upper Egypt popularly known as temples, as those at Kamak, the Ramesseum, and Medinet Habu, all at Thebes, are enclosed by fortifications, often of great strength. The girdle walls around Kamak, actually three groups of majestic buildings, are largely destroyed, but their sites are clearly outlined. The dominating palace of Ammon consists of a long suite of halls arranged in line, preceded, on the side towards the Nile, by an open court and terminated at the far end in a complicated and intricate group of chambers which were probably devoted to domestic uses.

On the south side of the forecourt and running at right angles to the main suite of halls there is a temple, the temple of Rameses III. This building consists of a long open court flanked on either side by a row of statues of Osiris with a short hall and cells at the far end.

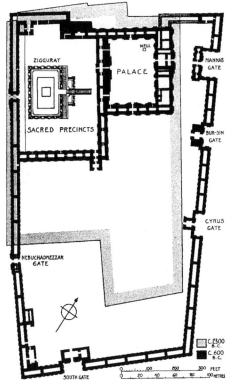

Plan of UR of the Chalders

The Great Hypostyle Hall, beyond the court, measures 340 ft. across by 165 ft. west to east. This stupendous structure consists of a nave, running west to east, flanked on either side by seven aisles. The nave, itself composed of a central and two side aisles with a colonnade on either side, is 73 ft. wide by 79 ft. high and its pillars are 11 ft. 4 in. in diameter and 65 ft. high. The capitals are surmounted by square abaci which in turn carry the longitudinal stone girders supporting the flat stone blocks of the roof. The nave has a clerestory consisting of stone slabs pierced by two tiers of tall vertical slots. The aisles are 51 ft. 3 in. high and their numerous pillars are 9 ft. in diameter and 42 ft. 8 in. high. In its pristine grandeur this fine hall with its great extent, gigantic pillars, 134 in all, its enormous height and sombre lighting must have been one of the most impressive buildings of any age or country.[4] In my photograph which looks across the hall, north to south, the aisle pillars are in the foreground and the nave with its clerestory and taller pillars, running at right angles to this avenue, in the mid-distance.

The Ramesseum, built about 1280BC, consists of a long rectangular suite of halls and courts, arranged one behind the other, surrounded by a girdle wall and entered through a massive pylon or gateway.

Medinet Habu: The Outer Pylons (Gateways)

Karnak: The Great Hypostyle Hall

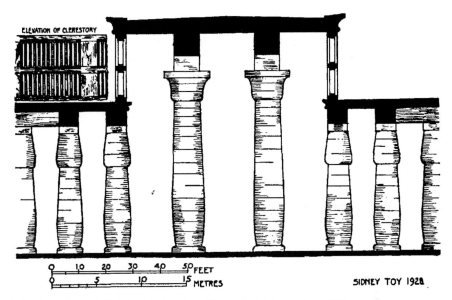

Karnak: The Great Hypostyle Hall. Section through the Nave and adjoining portion of Aisles

Tarragona: The Ancient Walls

Medînet Habu: Crenellations of the Outer Wall and part of the Outer Pylon

Medînet Habu was built about 1200BC, partly across the site of a smaller structure of about 1500BC. The new work consists of an extensive rectangular court surrounded by two lines of walls and having the palace in the middle, the court being entered at the south end through two gateways in line, one in each wall. The palace is similar in design to the Ramesseum. The outer gateway, which is defended by a guardroom on either side, is relatively small. The inner gateway, known as the Pavilion of Rameses III, is a powerful structure, three storeys in height and flanked by strong towers. Above the gateway are two tiers of chambers, and there are other chambers in the towers, with openings commanding the long entrance passage to the gate. Portions of the

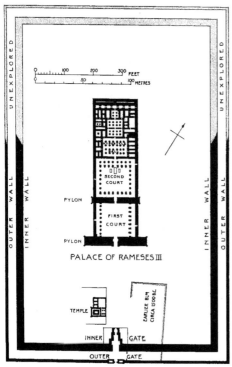

Plan of Medînet Haru

on all sides by a wall 79 ft. thick, with wall-towers at frequent intervals. The palace with its halls, courts and sacred precinct stands on the north side of the city, and partly projects beyond the line of the north wall, which is carried out around it. There is one gateway, in the north wall of the city and two in each of the outer walls. The gateways were all alike, and were formidable structures, each flanked by a tower on either side. They extended inwards 60 ft. beyond the inside face of the wall, and the passage through, intercepted at two points by large cross chambers, was about 155 ft. long. In front of each gateway there was a barbican, 150 ft. wide by 80 ft. long, with an outer gateway.

The city of Madaktu, as shown on a stone slab of about 650BC now in the British Museum, was surrounded by a single wall with wall-towers at frequent intervals and gateways, flanked by towers, at convenient points. It is also defended on one side by a wide river, which curves halfway round it, and on the other by a small stream or moat. There is a wide space between the walls of the city and the river, and on this ground are houses, interspersed with trees, and two castles. Both the castles stand close to the river, one of them rising directly from the ground and the other, a much larger structure, standing on a mound. Within the city are streets of houses, each house having one or two towers; and trees are planted in all parts.

crenellated parapet still remain on the summit of the inner gate and on the outer enclosing wall. The merlons of these parapets have semi-circular heads, similar to those shown on the bas-relief of Assyrian and Hittite cities.

ASSYRIA

On the stone slabs from the palace of Ashur-Nazir-Pal, at Nimrod, now in the British Museum, are represen-tations of cities besieged by the king about 800BC. These cities are defended by powerful walls, with wall-walks and embattled parapets, and are strengthened at frequent intervals by towers. Often there are two or even three lines of walls. The gateways are wide and high, have usually round, but sometimes flat, heads, and are flanked by a tower on either side.

The city of Khorsabad, near Mosul, of which there are extensive remains, was built 722–705BC. It is of rectangular plan, and was defended

Khorsabad: Plan of the City and Gateways

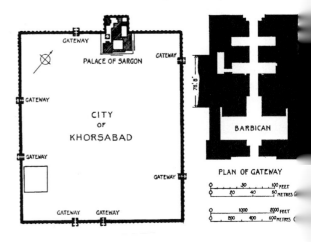

16

CITIES OF THE HITTITES

Of very early date also were the highly developed fortresses of the Hittites, that great people whose empire extended over the whole of Asia Minor, from the Aegean Sea to the borders of Mesopotamia. Ruins of their fortifications still exist, but it is more particularly to the incised drawings on the walls of Egyptian temples that we owe our knowledge of their appearance when complete.

A typical example is that of the city of Dapour, drawn on the south wall of the Great Hypostyle hall of the Ramesseum. The drawing dates about 1280BC.

The city is surrounded by two lines of curtain walls, and has a rectangular keep, or citadel, within the second wall. There is a large gateway in the outer wall, flanked by a tower on either side. Turrets rise from the inner wall, and all the walls and towers are surmounted by embattled parapets. The city is being stormed by the Egyptians, and the Hittites are fighting from the battlements of all three lines of fortification. Hoards (temporary wooden platforms) are projected out from the parapets of the inner wall and from the keep, and men are fighting from them. The weapons used are bows and arrows and lances. The Egyptians advance under the cover of long shields, rounded at the upper end and flat below, and the attack is by means of scaling ladders. Some of the Egyptians have evidently reached the battlements and are being hurled down by the defenders.

Hittite City: From the Ramesseum

Substantial remains of Hittite cities, defended by two or three lines of strong walls and having a citadel in the innermost line, still exist in various parts of Asia Minor, as at Sinjerii, Hamath and Carchemish. Sinjerii was circular in plan and was surrounded by a double line of walls. At Carchemish, on the Euphrates about seventy miles north-east of Aleppo, there were three lines of defences in succession, the Outer Town, the Inner Town and the Citadel, the Citadel being backed against the river. The walls of the Inner Town, where they have been excavated, are 5-8 m., or 19 ft., thick, and are built with vertical offsets like those of the Sixth City of Troy described below. The gates were flanked by towers, and the passages through them intersected by large chambers and halls.

TROY

At Troy the remains of nine cities, one buried beneath the other, have been brought to light, the earliest dating from about 3000 to 2560BC. The Second City, about 2500BC, was enclosed by a polygonal wall, and excavation has so far revealed two gates. The main gate had a long passage, with doors at two points, and was defended on one side by a large tower. The Sixth City is of the Mycenaean Age and is probably the Troy of the Homeric epics. The walls of this fortress are of great strength, and, with a very steep batter on the outer face, rise even now in places to the height of 20 ft. Along the faces of the wall, both inside and out, there are vertical offsets about 6 in. deep, running from the base to the full height of the wall and at intervals varying from 17 ft. to 27 ft. The panels of wall between the offsets are straight, and it is probable that this form of construction was adopted to avoid the curved surfaces which the contours of the curtain would otherwise require. Incidentally the buttress-like appearance which the long vertical shadows of the offsets impart to the wall greatly increases its effect of strength. There are three towers in the portion of the city so far explored, each of them defending the entrance to a gate, that at the north-east gate being built within the passageway.

The middle gate is formed at a point where one portion of the wall overlaps the other. The gate is placed on the inside face of the curtain, and the approach to it passes between the two

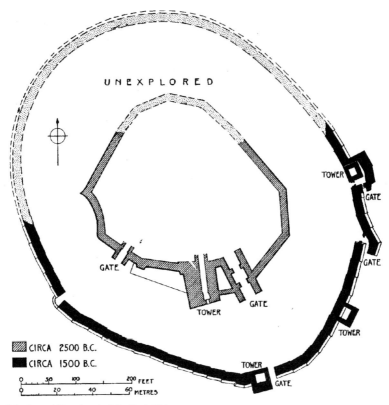

UNEXPLORED

TOWER
GATE
GATE
GATE
TOWER
GATE
TOWER
TOWER
GATE

CIRCA 2500 B.C.
CIRCA 1500 B.C.

0   50   100   200 FEET
0   20   40   60 METRES

Troy: Plans of the Second (Inner) and of the Sixth Cities

portions of the wall at the overlap, taking a right-angle turn in the course. The gate is therefore obscured from view from the outside.

GREECE

In Greece the fortifications of Mycenae and Tiryns both date from about 1500BC. The acropolis at Mycenae stands on a hill at the north end of the lower city. It is enclosed by a strong wall of massive hewn masonry, and is entered from the lower city by a ramp and a double gateway. The ramp is enclosed on either side by walls built of large blocks of stone, and is defended by a strong tower at the top, on the right-hand side of the gateway. The outer gateway, the Gate of the Lions, is built of monolithic jambs, which incline inwards as they rise, and a lintel composed of a single block of stone 16 ft. long and 3 ft. high in the middle. Upon the lintel stands a huge block of stone 10 ft. high bearing the figures, in low relief, of two lions facing each other on either

side of a column. Within the gateway there is a wide passage between two walls, and at the further end of the passage there was another gate, now destroyed. In the north wall there is a strongly defended postern from which a pathway leads down the hill to the open country. The ruins of the palace stand on the highest ground in the middle of the acropolis.

The hill on which Tiryns stands rises in two stages, first to a long level platform and then to another platform beyond and in line with the first. A wall of Cyclopean masonry, 26 ft. thick and originally about 65 ft. high, is carried round the edge of the lower platform, up the slope on both sides, and round the edge of the upper platform, thus enclosing a long and relatively narrow area running north and south. A cross wall, built along the upper edge of the slope between the two platforms, divides the fortification into a citadel, on the highest point, and a lower ward. The palace and principal offices stand within the citadel.

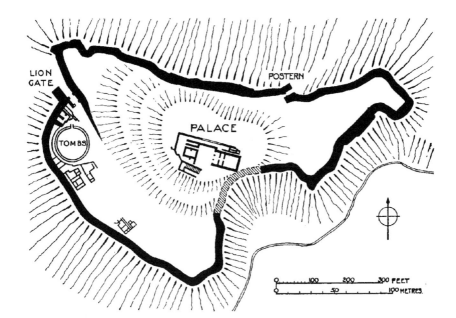

Mycenae: Plan of the Acropolis. After Perrot and Chipiez

Entrance to the fortress was by way of a ramp, or inclined path, which rises against the hill on the east side and leads to a gateway at the top. The ramp is commanded by a tower at the head, and is so placed that the right or unprotected side of an advancing force is exposed to attack from the defenders on the walls above. The gateway, which had a door at either end, opens on to the middle of a long passage running at right-angles to it, and

Plan of Tiryns. After Dorpfeld

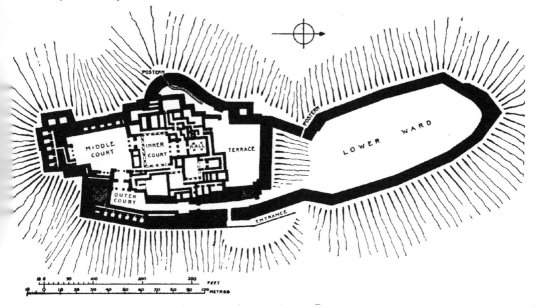

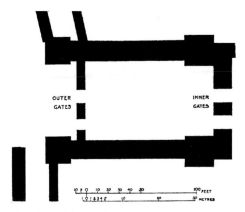

OUTER GATES   INNER GATES

Athens: Plan of the Depylon

having at one end the entrance to the lower ward and at the other the outer gate of the citadel. In order to reach the principal rooms of the palace (which are in the middle of the citadel) from this last gateway it is necessary to pass successively through another long passage, an open court, a second gateway, another court and a third gateway, each gateway being built at right-angles to that preceding it. There are two posterns, both in the east wall; one at the foot of a long flight of steps down from the citadel and the other near the south end of the lower ward.

At Athens the acropolis is built on the summit of a precipitous hill which stands within, and is completely surrounded by, the city. In the Mycenaean Age a huge wall of Pelasgic masonry, about 20 ft. thick, fragments of which still remain, was built on the top of the hill. About 480BC. this early curtain was replaced by a wall enclosing a larger area and having a gateway at the west end, the only accessible point. At the same time a wall, with gateways on the ancient roads, was carried all round the city. The gateway at the principal approach to the city, called the Thriasian Gale, was rebuilt about 350BC and renamed the Dipylon, or double gate. The Dipylon was built on the principle of that to the entrance to the acropolis at Mycenae, having outer and inner gates with an open passage, or court, between them. Here, however, there were twin gates at either end of the court. Both pairs of gates were flanked by towers, and the court was enclosed by high walls on either side. An enemy who had entered the outer and was checked by the inner

gates would be under attack from all sides of the court.

It was largely due to the strength of the Dipylon that Athens was able to resist the attack by Philip the Fifth, King of Macedonia, in 200BC. Finding that his design to take the city by surprise had failed, Philip decided on open attack, and advanced towards the Dipylon. An Athenian force went out to meet him, and great numbers of citizens stood upon the walls of the city to watch the conflict. Philip, observing this crowd of spectators, and desirous of making a parade of his prowess, advanced with a small body of horses, forced back the Athenians and rushed the outer gates. The fight was now confined within the limits of the court between the two barriers; and the king owed his safe retreat to the fact that the defenders on the towers and flanking walls feared to attack the melee below lest they should strike their own men. Henceforth the citizens kept within the inner gates of the Dipylon, and Philip, not wishing to be entrapped a second time, drew off his army.[6]

Many other cities of Greece retain remains of their ancient walls and defences, the fortifications of Messene, at the south-west of Peloponnesus, dating from the fourth century BC, being particularly extensive and interesting.

RHODES

A development in military construction occurred at Rhodes in the building of the ancient wall of the city about 400BC. On the side towards the city this wall formed an arcade of tall arches, vaulted just below the wall-walk. The arched recesses were 15 ft. wide by 10 ft. 6 in. deep, and were spaced 15 ft. apart. The portion of wall at the back of the recesses was 4 ft. 6 in. thick, and the full thickness of the wall 15 ft.[7] This scientific method of construction was followed later by the Romans and the Byzantines. Its advantages are threefold: a great saving of material; in the event of a breach being made the damage was localized and its repair facilitated; and the arches were useful for the accommodation of forces.

The strength of the fortifications of ancient Rhodes and the military skill of its defenders were put to severe test in the memorable siege of the city by Demetrius Poliorcetes in 305BC, and the victory was with Rhodes. Demetrius high. There are gates and towers of the same character and period. One of these gates, near the modern 'del Rosario,' is built of massive masonry, and has sloping sides like an Egyptian Pylon. Following the capture of the town by the Romans in 218BC the walls were repaired and heightened, and the whole fortifications were again restored by Hadrian about AD 120.

CHINA

Among the ancient defensive works existing in practically all parts of the world the Great Wall of China demands note. The Great Wall is a strong defensive line stretching along the northern borders of China, and built to protect that empire against the incursions of the Mongolians and Tartars. The main wall, never actually measured, is some 1600 miles long from Shan-hai-Kwan on the east to Chia-yu-Kwan on the west. There are fine gateways at each end of the wall and at points along its length. Outside the gateway at each end is an inscribed stone, set upright. Rectangular towers, standing astride the wall and projecting out on both sides, are built at intervals of about 200 yds. apart. The Pa-Ta-Ling gate at the Nankow Pass, and the Chia-yu-Kwan gate at the western end of the wall are each protected by a powerful and extensive barbican. The wall runs sinuously over mountains, valleys, ravines and rivers, tortuous in some places and at others ascending and descending almost precipitous hills. At two points along its length shorter subsidiary walls branch off from the south side and run eastward from the main structure.

The building of the wall is traditionally ascribed to Shih Huang Ti, a powerful monarch who ruled over China during the years 246–210BC. But there are strong indications that the wall was already in existence in his time; indeed it is highly probable that much, if not all, of the megalithic basement on which the superstructure stands in many places relates to periods long anterior to that emperor's days. There can be no doubt, however, that Shih Huang Ti was responsible for great works of reconstruction, fortification, and perhaps extension, of the wall, for he employed on this particular task vast numbers of workers, who were largely composed of convicts, prisoners of war and students who had incurred his displeasure. At later times, particularly during

Rhodes: Walls of the Ancient City

had brought against the city the most powerful siege engines of his time, including *petrariae* (heavy stone-throwing engines) and battering-rams, each of the latter being 150 ft. long and worked by a team of a thousand men. He had assailed the city from the harbour by floating batteries, and from the land by his renowned Helepolis, or huge siege tower. Yet, despite his skill and resources, the king was compelled to raise the siege after it had been carried on relentlessly for a whole year.

SPAIN

The Iberians who inhabited Spain from about 1500 B.C. lived in walled towns, as at Tartessus, Massia, Artagena and Tarragona, and much of their megalithic work still remains above ground or has been revealed by recent excavation. The Phoenicians and Carthaginians, who settled in Spain about the seventh century BC, and the Greeks, about the sixth century BC, all left examples of their works, particularly the last, for the first two were principally occupied in trading activities. The walls of Tarragona are of great height and are in places 20 ft. thick. Their lowest courses, in which both 'cyclopean' and 'polygonal' masonry occur, probably date from about 1000 to 1500BC. Those of cyclopean masonry are built of unhewn blocks about 12 ft. long by 6 ft.

the Ming Dynasty, AD 1368–1644, extensive works of restoration and reconstruction were carried out. Today the wall is in various conditions of repair. In the length towards the east, north of Peking (the portion most usually visited and photographed), it is practically intact; indeed in such good condition that it was used for the transit of troops during the recent Second World War. At some points towards the west it is in great disrepair, and in places stands in fragments only.

Its construction also varies along the line, but generally it consists of a core of earth and gravel, faced at the base with large stones, in places huge granite boulders, and at the superstructure with ashlar or brickwork. It has a considerable batter on both sides, is about 25 ft. thick at the base and 17 ft. at the summit, and is from 25 ft. to 30 ft. high. The wall-walk on the top is 13 ft. wide, and is paved with stone. The parapets, originally crenellated on both sides (as they still are in places), stand 5 ft. above the walk. The wall-towers project out on both sides of the wall and rise 12 ft. above the walk. In addition to the wall-towers, there are other and taller towers which stand well within the wall, and are spaced at long distances apart. These last served as observation posts. Having regard to its great length, its substantial character and construction, and the extremely difficult and varied terrain it traverses, here twisting in and out, there climbing steep declivities or crossing deep gorges, the Great Wall of China must be considered as among the most skilful works of the military engineer of any age.

SOUTH AFRICA

Scattered throughout Southern Rhodesia are numerous prehistoric buildings of which neither the period of their construction nor the precise original purpose is at present known. They have been examined on several occasions, and, as the result of investigations carried out in 1929 by Miss G. Caton-Thompson, were said to be of mediaeval character, dating from the tenth to the sixteenth century. The most thorough and scientific survey of the buildings was that made by Mr. R. N. Hall, F.R.G.S., who also pronounced the work to be of mediaeval periods. A piece of timber taken from the ruins and subjected recently to chemical analysis, is said to date from the early years of the seventh

century of our era. Further investigation regarding the date of these buildings is to be desired.[8]

The principal ruins are at Great Zimbabwe, Mashonaland, and may be divided into three groups known as the Elliptical Temple, the Acropolis, standing on a granite hill 250 ft. high, and the Valley of Ruins, stretching north and south between the other two. The Valley of Ruins is an extensive field of buildings, most of which were apparently dwellings, in various stages of decay. While some of them are in a very fragmentary condition, others are more complete, and have thick, well-constructed walls. The acropolis stands on an outcrop of massive granite boulders, and the position is fortified by a most skilful incorporation of the maze of soaring rocks into strongly-built walls, making adroit use of such spaces as exist here and there between the rocks. The elliptical building stands in the valley, and is the most substantial and complete structure of the whole site. It is an oval enclosure, 290 ft. across its major axis, measured externally, surrounded by a powerful girdle wall of varying thickness, from 10 ft. to 16 ft. at the base and tapering as it rises to the summit. The wall is built of squared local granite, well coursed and set without mortar, and even now in its ruined condition rises in places to the height of 34 ft. For about half its circumference, running round eastward and southward from the north-east to the south-west, the girdle is doubled by an inner wall of the same height, and at the main entrance on the north-east these two are again flanked by two other walls. On the outer face of the south side of the girdle wall, running round from point A to B on the plan, there is a decorative band formed of two rows of stones set zigzag in hollow grooves and separated by one course of masonry.

The main entrance was strongly defended. The first passage on the left was probably for those issuing to obstruct access to the outer gate, which was approached by six steep steps up with another step at the far end; then a passage on either side, another step and an assailant arrives at an open space strongly defended all round. The internal structures are not such a confused maze of buildings as they may at first appear to be, but are obviously designed on an organized plan. There are two especially defended spaces – one at the north,

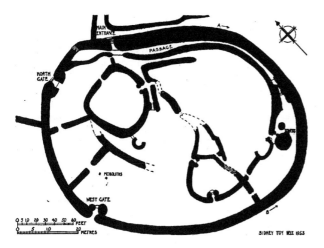

Great Zimbabwe: Plan of the Elliptical Building

the stronghold on the east, dominating the neighbourhood from the top of the hill, the fort; and the buildings stretching along the valley between the citadel and the fort, the dwellings and communal structures of the general community.

AMERICA

In the western hemisphere, particularly in Central and South America, are many ancient monuments, the date of which it is difficult to determine, owing largely to the complete severance of the peoples of the two hemispheres from prehistoric times to the sixteenth century of our era and to the absence of historical documents of die native races of America. The earliest existing document of these peoples is that known as *The Book of Chilam Balam*. This work was written after the Spanish conquest by the natives in their own language, and is simply a collection of their traditions, legends and myths. An extensive study of the ruins, many of which have been brought to light by recent excavation, has resulted in the production of a system by which the dates of these buildings are correlated with our own periods, pottery found on the sites figuring largely in the derivation of this sequence. Most of the buildings consist of pyramidal temples, colonnaded halls, palaces and private houses; and by this method of dating the earliest of them are of the first six centuries of our era. There are, however, some defensive works which appear to be of much earlier periods.

There is no doubt that the native races of pre-Columbian America are Mongolians. The prevalent theory of their presence in this land is that, at some remote period, their ancestors migrated across the Behring Strait and the Aleutian Islands from Siberia to Alaska, and gradually penetrated southward until they occupied the whole continent, and that the cultures of the various tribes into which they were split were indigenous. It is not impossible that as the result of further and more extensive investigation a clearer light will be thrown on this subject. Meanwhile, bearing in mind that on this side of the Atlantic works ranging in

standing clear of the outer walls and overlooking the main entrance, and the other, at the south, formed at a widening of the space between the outer walls and following their contours. The first is roughly square, is strongly fortified and was probably the head-quarters of the enclosure. Approach from the main entrance to the space on the south was by way of a long narrow passage between two lofty walls with a strong gate at the far end. The gate, in common with all entrances into this south space and with some other gates in the enclosure, was defended with a kind of drop-gate or portcullis, the grooves for which are to be seen on either side. Within the south space are two towers, side by side – one about 18 ft. dia. at the base and the other 8 ft. Both taper as they rise, and both have lost their upper parts. The largest one in its ruined state is 31 ft. high, and was probably a lookout and signal tower. Apart from these two spaces, the enclosure was divided into several large and smaller areas separated from each other by strong walls.

It is obvious, therefore, that for whatever purpose this structure was built to serve it was strongly fortified both against assault from without and, in the event of the girdle wall being penetrated, against attack from within. Indeed the whole three groups together form a well-designed disposition of parts for the outpost of a fairly large community, the oval structure on the west being the actual citadel, occupied by the rulers, officers and administrative bodies;

date from prehistoric times to those of our day are found in one city, a comparison of building technique in both hemispheres may be useful.

The western wall at Acapana, Tiahuanaco, Bolivia, is built with tall boulders set upright at short intervals apart, with rough-coursed rubble between them, in much the same manner as in some of the prehistoric forts in the eastern hemisphere. The walls of Allamay-lambo, some of those at Machu Picchu, and in particular the northern walls of the fortress of Sacsahuaman, Cuzco (all three in Peru) bear strong resemblance in structure to the megalithic base of the oldest parts of the Great Wall of China, to the prehistoric walls of Cosa, in Italy, and to the Mycenaean walls at Athens and Tiryns. At Yucatan, Mexico, are vaults constructed of series of corbels, bedded flat, with the narrow gap at the apex spanned by single stones, in all respects similar to those (also of the Mycenaean period) at Assos and Tiryns. All these ancient structures in America differ greatly in character from the buildings with which they are surrounded, and may well indicate rather the lingering traditions of the Old World than irrelative development in the New. Strong support is borne to this suggestion by a recent discovery in a pre-Columbian monument at Palenque, Southern Mexico. Here a large stone slab, forming part of the floor of the temple surmounting a pyramid, was found to conceal the access to a vault. On removal of the slab a stairway appeared which descended down through the body of the pyramid to a second floor, in which another movable slab proved to be the entrance to a burial chamber. Indeed, the structure has not only the form, but the purpose, of an Egyptian Pyramid.

WEAPONS, SIEGE ENGINES AND METHODS OF ATTACK AND DEFENCE

The weapons in use about 1280BC, as shown on the stone slabs of the Ramesseum and other temples in Egypt, are bows and arrows and lances. Scaling ladders were used to reach the wall-walks. By 880BC the art of attack and defence had made great progress. The Assyrian

Cuzco: North Wall of the Fortress of Sagsahuaman

bas-reliefs of that period show men rushing to the attack of a fortress with a lance in one hand and a shield, either round or rectangular, in the other. Archers advance under cover of mantlets, held in front by attendants – sometimes one attendant, grasping the mantlet in one hand and holding a sword in the other, to two archers. Mantlets were light screens constructed on a wooden frame and of sufficient height and width for protection.

The defenders fought from the battlements of the walls and towers of their fortress and from hoards projecting from the battlements, shooting and hurling a rain of arrows, stones and firebrands at the enemies and their engines.

The walls were attacked either by battering-rams or by men sapping at their base with crowbars. The rams, shod with iron and often in pairs, were set up in a strong timber framework, which worked on wheels and was entirely covered with raw hides as a protection against fire. The whole machine was mobile, and those working it were under cover. In order to check the ram, the besieged endeavoured to grapple its head in the loop of a chain which they lowered down from the wall; and the besiegers on their side seized the chain with hooks and tugged at it with all their might.

There were also siege towers which were built of timber, covered with hides and mounted on wheels. They were of two or more storeys, and from the top storey men fought on a level with those on the battlements of the fortress. Diades, who flourished under Philip, King of Macedonia, 360–336BC, claimed to have invented ambulatory towers which could be dismantled and taken about from place to place in pieces.[9]

The bas-relief showing the siege of a city by Ashur-Nasir-Pal, King of Assyria, about 880BC, now in the British Museum, gives a vivid picture of these operations. On the right is a combined battering-ram and siege tower. Of the two men mounted on the tower one is an archer and the other holds a mantlet in front of both with his left hand while he throws a stone with his right. The ram, worked by those under cover within the engine, has already broken away some of the stonework of the wall, while men in pairs are busily engaged in sapping at a lower level. Pairs of men, each consisting of an archer and a man holding a mantlet in one hand and a sword or dagger in the other, appear to form the main body of the attack. Men falling from the walls probably represent those who have been slain by the attacking forces as well as those who, having climbed up to the battlements, have been ejected by the defenders. The defence is from the battlements, the main weapons being bows and arrows. A chain, let down from the wall, has gripped the head of the battering-ram, while two men below, with iron hooks, are straining every muscle to disengage it. Others on the wall are

Siege of a City by Ashur-Nasir-Pal, c. 880BC

Siege of Lakish, c. 750BC

A bas-relief in the British Museum vigorously depicts this attack on Lakish, the tiers of scenes being tilted up for convenience of representation of the various subjects. Archers, stone throwers, slingers and lancers are in full action on both sides, and battering or boring-rams are at work tearing down the walls. There is a profusion of torches and stones thrown out on the enemy, who protects his engines from fire by copious douches of water. Ladders, not shown in position, are represented symbolically as implements used in attack. Women and children, with their effects in bundles on their backs, are being evacuated from the city, and prisoners, taken by the enemy, are being impaled within sight of those on the walls. The principles of attack and repulse by means of mines dug beneath the walls of fortresses had reached a high state of development by the end of the sixth century BC. At the siege of Barca in Libya, about 510BC, the Persians excavated underground tunnels that reached to the walls.

Among the Barceeans there was a skilled worker in brass who took a brazen shield and, carrying it round within the wall, applied it here and there at places where he, thought the workings might be. Where there were no mines the shield was silent, but at places near mining operations the shield made a vibrating sound. By countermining at these points the Barcaeans broke into the enemy's works and slew the men they found there.[10]

Mines excavated by besiegers usually commenced some distance from the walls, and had either the objective of effecting direct entry by tunnelling beneath the wall and into the fortress, or that of making a breach in the wall itself. The second, perhaps a later phase, is referred to by Polybius. The procedure was to excavate a large cavity in the base of the wall, propping and strutting with timbers as the work proceeded. When the cavity was large enough the timber was fired, the men withdrew and, if the work had been well done, on the consumption of the wood the wall above collapsed.[11]

By the end of the fourth century BC petrariae had been introduced and great strides had been

throwing down stones and torches on the assailants and their engine. Meanwhile women on a turret appear to be making frantic appeals to the enemy for mercy.

Fire played an important role in an assault, and flaming torches were thrown both by besiegers and besieged. Torches hurled at a fortress and water thrown down from the walls to quench them are shown on the reliefs of 880BC. But during the following century the use of these powerful weapons, especially by the besieged, was greatly intensified. In the assault on Lakish by Tiglath-Pileser the Third, about 750BC, immense numbers of flaming torches were thrown from the walls of the city on the advancing troops and their siege engines. Men with long-handled ladles, working under the protection of small turrets on the top of the engines, fought against the fire by pouring water over the affected parts. In this attack hand slings were used by both sides. Intimidation by resort to 'frightfulness' was pursued remorselessly, some of the prisoners being tortured or flayed alive, and others impaled in sight of their friends in the city.

made in the design and development of battering-rams and siege towers.

NOTES

1. Herodotus, *Clio*, 178.
2. *Vide A History of Babylon*, W. L. King.
3. *Vide* 'The excavations at Ur,' C. L. Woolley, *The Antuquaries' Journal*, Vol V, 1925.
4. The underpinning and setting upright of some of the pillars being then in progress, my survey was greatly assisted by the ladders and other means of measuring heights placed at my disposal. The old foundations of the pillars are of stone; in underpinning the deflected pillars the stone was being removed and the new foundations constructed of brick, manufactured on the spot.
5. Levy, *History of Rome*, XXXI, 24.
6. 'Philon de Byzance (fortifications),' *Revue de Philologie*, Paris, 1879.
7. *Vide Great Zimbabwe*, R. N. Hall, 1905; *The Zimbabwe Culture*, G. Caton-Thompson, 1931.
8. Vitruvius, *de Arthitectura*, XIX.
9. Herodotus, *Melpomene*, 200.
10. Polybius XVI, ii.

Chapter 2
Fortifications of Greece and Rome 300BC to 200BC

During the third century BC the art of war made rapid progress, due in no small measure to the inventive genius of that brilliant mathematician and engineer, Archimedes. Born in 287BC, Archimedes' lived at Syracuse and designed many powerful engines of war for its ruler Hiero the Second. He also effected many improvements in the fortifications of the town. So successful were the measures of defence adopted under his directions that the combined assaults of the Roman army and navy on the town in 215BC were repulsed again and again, until the forces drew off and substituted blockade for attack. Polybius, referring to these events, writes: "Such a great and marvellous thing does the genius of one man show itself to be when properly applied to certain matters. The Romans had every hope of capturing the town if one old man of Syracuse were removed,"[1]

It is clear, however, from the tactics adopted and the engines used by the Romans, by Hannibal, and by Philip the Fifth of Macedonia, that the progress of the art during this century was general. In their attack on Lilybaeum in Sicily in 250BC the Romans had all their siege engines destroyed by fire hurled at them from the battlements. They then determined to accomplish by famine what they had failed to do by assault, and dug a ditch and put up a stockade all round the city. They also built a wall round their own camp – a precaution which, if not common at the time, hereafter became the general practice.[2] At the siege of Capua in 212BC the Romans, advancing from three different points, completely surrounded the city by their works, which consisted of a rampart and two ditches, with strong forts at intervals all along the line.[3] Some towns were defended by two or three lines of moats. At Sirynx in Asia in 210BC there

were three wide and deep moats, each defended by a stockade.[4]

The Romans possessed a strong navy, including ships equipped with grabs and other mechanical devices. In the fleet taking part in the siege of Syracuse in 215BC were vessels, called sambucae, which could be brought up to the sea wall and, by means of ladders raised up by ropes and pulleys, could land their men directly on to the battlements of the town. To counter the attack from these and other vessels of the Roman fleet, Archimedes ordered the construction of a number of stone-throwing engines of various sizes, the larger for long distant ranges and the smaller for short ranges. One night, under cover of darkness, the Romans brought their ships so close up to the walls as to be too near for even the shortest range engine. But the "old man of Syracuse" was not defeated. He pierced the curtain wall with loopholes, 4 in. wide by 6 ft. high, spaced at short intervals apart. Through these loopholes the archers, themselves secure behind the wall, so disabled the enemy that he retired.[5] It was more by stratagem than by force of arms that three years later Syracuse fell and its defender Archimedes fell with it.

Sometimes when one part of the curtain wall, under severe attack from battering-rams and mines, was in danger of collapse the defenders built up an entirely new wall within the city across the damaged part, as was done during the siege of Abydos in 201BC.[6]

Gateways received particular attention. They were closed by gates and later also by portcullises. It is not possible to give any definite date to the introduction of the portcullis, but it is referred to in a treatise on military tactics of the fourth century BC attributed to Aeneas Tacticus. This author writes: "If a large number of the enemy come in after these and you wish to catch them you should have ready above the centre of the gateway a gate of the stoutest possible timber overlaid with iron. Then when you wish to cut off the enemy as they rush in you should let this drop down and the gate itself will not only as it falls destroy some of them, but will also keep the foe from entering, while at the same time the forces on the wall are shooting at the enemy at the gate."[7]

The portcullis comes into prominence at the town of Salapia, Southern Italy, in 208BC during the Second Punic War.

Hannibal, having got possession of the signet ring of Marcellus who had been surprised and slain in ambush, attempted to use it to obtain entry into Salapia unopposed. In the name and with the seal of Marcellus, Hannibal wrote a letter to the citizens informing them that they were to expect him on the following night, and that the soldiers in the garrison were to hold themselves in readiness for any service he might require of them. But the Salapians had been forewarned that Marcellus was dead and that no credence was to be given to letters written in his name. Preparing, therefore, for an enemy, they dispersed their men along the wall and placed a particularly strong guard at the gate at which they expected Hannibal to appear.

The Carthaginian vanguard consisted of Roman deserters, who in the Latin tongue ordered the guard to open the gate, as the consul had arrived. With a great pretence of excitement and haste the guards proceeded to obey. The gate (cataracta) worked up and down like a sluice gate, and was operated by levers and ropes. It was indeed what was later called a portcullis. Eagerly the enemy passed through the gate, but when about 600 of them had entered the guards released the ropes and the gate fell with a crash, blocking all further entry. Thereupon, while the defenders on the walls rained stones, spikes and javelins on the enemies without, the citizens fell upon those who had entered, who, carrying their arms suspended from their shoulders, were taken completely by surprise; and Hannibal was forced to retire.[8]

SIEGE ENGINES AND SIEGE OPERATIONS

Great advance had also been made in the manner of conducting an assault on a fortress and in the design and construction of siege engines. In the attack on Syracuse in 215BC. Archimedes constructed powerful petrariae which were the prototypes of disappearing guns. These engines when not in action lay concealed behind the battlements; but when brought into play a great beam suddenly reared up into view, swung round on its axis and cast a stone weighing as much as 5 cwt. Balls of lead were also thrown by these engines.[9]

Ballistae (engines for throwing stones up to about 56 lb. in weight) and catapults (engines for throwing arrows and firebrands) were also used at this period, as were mantlets, often extended into long screens. The siege towers were sometimes of many storeys.

In the attack on Echinus by Philip of Macedonia in 211BC the king, having selected as his point of attack one section of the city wall with a tower at either end, proceeded to erect elaborate works against that section. He built two tall siege towers with battering-rams, one opposite to each of the wall-towers; and between the siege towers, connecting one with the other, he constructed a rampart of earth and a stockade. In the gallery behind the stockade he set his miners to work driving two tunnels towards the wall, while other miners were employed in digging a system of underground passages between the camp and this gallery, so that his men could pass to and fro safely. The siege towers were each of three storeys and, in addition to fighting men, contained catapults, fire-extinguishing equipment and, in the ground storey, men employed in clearing the way in front of the towers so that they could be moved forward. In addition to these works Philip had three batteries of ballistae trained on to the city, which finally surrendered to him.[10]

Many cities were carried simply by escalade. In their assault on Illiturgi in Spain, in 207BC, the Romans observed that the highest point of the city stood on a precipitous cliff, but was otherwise unfortified. By the use of spikes, which they drove into the cliff as they mounted, those behind supporting those above and those above pulling up their companions below, they swarmed up the cliff and took the city. The walls of New Carthage were carried by escalade in 210BC. As a defence against escalade especially made prongs were used to prevent the fixing of the ladders, and iron grapples were let down from the battlements, seizing the assailants and lifting them up the face of the wall.[11]

Grappling cranes were constructed by Archimedes during the siege of Syracuse. These cranes stood on the sea walls, and when a Roman ship approached let down an iron hand which clutched the ship by the prow and raised it until it stood upright on its stem. They then suddenly released it, and the vessel fell back into the water, to be either overturned or swamped. Men also were clutched from the deck of a ship and dropped into the sea by this engine.[12]

Difficult problems of transport were often encountered and solved. The genius of Hannibal in this respect was amply demonstrated during the siege of Taranto in 212BC. Taranto is built on a peninsula which protrudes across the mouth of its great natural harbour, called Mare Piccola, leaving only a narrow channel between the point of the peninsula and the land on the other side. The citadel was built at the point, commanding the channel, which at the time of the Punic wars was the only entry into the harbour. Hannibal had obtained possession of the lower city and had thrown up works between it and the citadel. But, finding the latter to be too strong to be taken by storm, he decided on a blockade. While, however, supplies were reaching the citadel by sea, a blockade could not be effected. His own fleet was at Sicily, and the ships belonging to Taranto were bottled up in the harbour, held in by those in command of the channel. Determined to get those ships out, Hannibal drew them from the water by means of engines, loaded them on to waggons, and had them transported across the neck of land and launched into the sea on the other side. They then sailed round opposite the citadel and completed the blockade.[13]

"Frightfulness " as practised by the Romans appears to have been actuated as much by the desire to intimidate as by vengeance Polybius says that following the taking of the city of New Cartilage "when Scipio thought that a sufficient number had entered he sent most of them, as is the Roman custom, against the inhabitants of the city with orders to kill all they encountered, sparing none, and not to start pillaging until the signal was given. They do this I think to inspire terror, so that when towns are taken by the Romans one may often see not only the corpses of human beings, but dogs cut in half and the dismembered bodies of other animals, and on this occasion such scenes were very many owing to the numbers of these in the place."[14] On the capture of Illiturgi by the Romans, Livy says: " They butchered all indiscriminately, armed and unarmed, male and female. Their cruel resentment extended even to the slaughter of infants."[15]

NOTES

1. Polybius, Bk. VIII, 7.
2. *Ibid.*, Bk. I, 42.
3. Livy XXV, 22.
4. Polybius X, 31.
5. Polybius VIII, 5.
6. *Ibid.*, XVI, 30.
7. Aeneas Tacticus, cap. XXXIX. Loeb Ed., 1933.
8. Polybius X, 33. Livy XXVII, 28.
9. Polybius VIII, 5.
10. Polybius IX, 41–42.
11. Livy XXVIII, 19/
12. Polybius VIII, 6, 7.
13. Livy XXV, II.
14. Polybius X, 15.
15. Livy XXVIII, 20.

Chapter 3
Fortifications in Europe and the Levant 200BC to 30BC

Military architecture had now become a special science, having schools at important centres, as at Rhodes; and during the two centuries preceding our era many treatises were written on the subject. Philo of Byzantium, who flourished about 120BC, wrote a treatise on mechanics and military architecture which, judging from the fragments still extant, must have been a most comprehensive work.[1] From this treatise we learn the principles of the art as taught and practised in the second century BC.

The plan adopted for any fortress, Philo writes, must be decided upon only after a careful inspection of the site it is to occupy, as the salients, inclination and curves of the curtain walls are determined by the nature of the ground on which they are to stand. He describes several plans, as the "ancient," the "saw-shaped," the plan with concaved walls, and the plan with double walls. Curtain walls should be at least 15 ft. thick, built in gypsum and well bonded; to prevent escalade they should be at least 30 ft. high. Sometimes the side of a fortification most exposed to attack is protected by two walls, spaced from 12 ft. to 18 ft. apart, and joined at the top by a vault or timber roof. Some curtain walls are embattled but have no wall-walks. In time of siege temporary platforms may be erected behind their battlements and removed as desired. Even if the enemy is able to scale these walls he will find at the top that he can proceed no further, and, being himself an easy target, he is faced with death or retreat.

The curtain wall should be 90 ft. from the houses of the town, thus providing a road for the easy transport of engines, vehicles, etc., the passage of reinforcements along the whole line of defence and, in case of need, a space for digging an internal intrenchment.

Towers must be of a form suitable to the position they occupy in the wall. If angular, they should be so set as to present a projecting angle in the centre, so that blows may be received at a salient angle. When round, the face stones should be cut from wood templates to expedite construction. Towers should not be bonded to curtain walls, or, owing to the inequality of weight, fissures will develop and endanger their stability. They should be protected by a basework, or bastion, to prevent the approach of sappers. Both walls and towers should stand upon solid foundations, and their upper courses should be set in gypsum and strengthened by iron clamps, run with lead. In positions most exposed to attack from siege engines the walls should be faced with hard stones or stones with salient bosses, and well tailed into the body of the wall. Timber ties of oak should be buried in the walls of both curtains and towers, the timbers being placed end to end and forming horizontal chains at vertical intervals of 6 ft. The presence of these ties greatly facilitates the repair of any part of the wall which may be damaged.

Posterns are often built on the sides to facilitate the making of sorties. They are so arranged that the soldiers when in retreat are not obliged to turn to the left, thus exposing their unprotected right sides; one file making a sortie from postern A will re-enter by postern B, and all the other files will adopt the same course. Some posterns will be constructed obliquely through the wall, while others have an elbow turning; but all should be so designed as to be out of range of stone-throwing engines and obscured from view from the outside.

Great attention should be paid to the outworks. There should be an advanced wall and at least three lines of ditches, the spaces between the ditches being protected by palisades and planted with thorns. In front of the advanced walls empty earthenware jars should be buried. These are placed in an upright position with their mouths upward, stopped with seaweed or imperishable grass and covered with earth. Troops may then pass over the jars with impunity, but the engines and timber towers brought up by the enemy will sink into them.

Vitruvius, writing about 30BC, says that the plan of a stronghold should not be square or have sharp angles, but should be polygonal, so that the movements of the enemy might not be obscured by salient corners. The fortification should be surrounded by uneven ground to make approach difficult; and the roads leading to the gate should be winding and turn at the gate, so as to expose the right side of an attacking force. Foundations should be of greater thickness than the walls they support, and the walls should be of sufficient width to permit of two armed men passing each other freely on the wall-walk.

Towers should be spaced not more than an arrow's flight apart, in order that the wall between them might be swept from end to end by the engines on either tower. The wall-walk from one section of the wall to the other must be carried across the inside of the tower by a timber bridge only. Then, if one section of the wall is carried by storm, that section can be isolated by removing the bridge in the tower at either end. Vitruvius agrees with Philo that walls should be consolidated with timber bonding – and recommends scorched olive wood – a material which, he says, is imperishable, and will remain unimpaired when either buried in earth or immersed in water.[2]

Among the most interesting military works of this period are the ruins of Pompeii. The fortifications of Pompeii have the rare historic value of immunity from alteration since AD 79, when the city was overwhelmed. It is obvious that all the defences are of a period anterior to that catastrophe.

The Herculaneum Gate dates from about 100BC. It has a wide central carriage-way flanked on either side by a footway, and is about 60 ft. long. The carriageway was closed by a portcullis on the outer side of the gate, and by wood doors on the city side. The footways were closed by iron doors on the outer and by wood doors on the inner side. The middle portion of the gateway formed a large hall, or court, which stretched across all three passage-ways.

The city wall is of various periods, from about 400 to 100BC.[3] As finished at the latter period, it was composed of outer and inner

Pompeii: Plane of the Herculaneum Gate and the City Wall and Section through the Wall

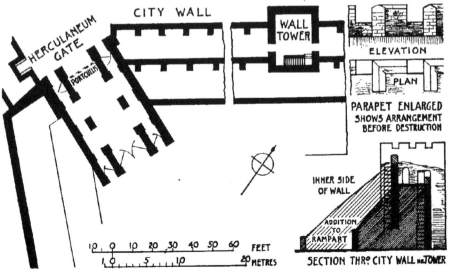

facings of stone and a core of earth. It was 20 ft. thick and about 32 ft. high to the wall-walk. On the inner side the wall was supported by buttresses, placed about 10 ft apart, and was backed by an inclined rampart of earth. The outer parapet has disappeared, but from the arrangement at the base of short buttresses projecting into the core of the wall at regular intervals it appears to have been provided with wing walls. Wing walls projected inwards from the left ends of the merlons of parapets and, according to Procopius, were for the protection of the left flank of the men firing through the embrasures, in the event of another part of the wall being carried by assault. Traces of such wing walls have been found elsewhere, and in AD536 they were introduced into the fortifications of Rome.[4] In lieu of an inner parapet there is a screen wall which was carried up to the height of about 14 ft. above the wall-walk, and protected the city from the missiles fired from siege engines. Rectangular towers, extending through the full thickness of the wall and projecting out on either side, are built at intervals along the line of this fortification. They are open to the wall-walk by doorways on both sides.

WESTERN EUROPE

The fortifications of the southern parts of Western Europe at this period had already reached a state of development as far advanced as those at Rome and the Levant. The ancient stone walls, towers and gateways of Tarragona in Spain, dating from periods long before the taking of that city by the Romans in 218BC, were referred to above; and from Caesar's account of his assault on Marseilles it is clear that the defences of that independent city were also powerful stone structures.' Further north the defences, though less developed, were still of great strength. In his campaigns in Gaul, 58 to 49BC, Caesar found that the Gallic cities were surrounded by walls, built of large stones and earth, and bonded by an ingenious system of timber ties. The outer ties were exposed on the face of the wall, alternating with tie courses of masonry. These walls, while not unpleasing in appearance, were fireproof, and offered enormous resistance to the assaults of his battering-rams.[5]

In Britain, before the advent of the Romans, he inhabitants lived in towns, built on hill tops or on level ground and defended by ramparts and ditches. Sometimes the sites chosen were defended by nature on two or three sides, as on a promontory. In that case it might only be necessary to throw up artificial works across the neck of the promontory. Otherwise the ramparts and ditches were carried all round, as at Maiden Castle, Dorset, one of the finest fortifications of its kind in existence.

Scattered throughout the north of Scotland and adjoining islands are a large number of forts, called brochs, dating from the first century BC and later, and now in ruinous condition.

Brochs are circular in plan, with walls from 12 ft. to 16 ft. thick, pierced by a low, narrow and tunnel-like door. The internal diameter is about 25 ft. In some cases the wall is carried up so high that the structure becomes a round tower consisting of two concentric shells, tied together at intervals by long stones. The outer shell is steeply battered, while the inner one is practically vertical. Chambers and stairways are formed in the space between the shells, the stairways as they rise concentrically with the walls giving access to tiers of galleries which are lit from the courtyard. The most perfect example of a tower broch is at Mousa, Shetland, which stands to the height of about 45 ft. Its outer wall is unbroken by any aperture save for the doorway on the ground floor, but four series of slits run up the inner wall. Chambers, stairways and galleries are formed in the space between the shells.[6]

Walls, built of timber and masonry, somewhat similar to those surrounding the Gallic towns, occur in Scotland and North Wales. The wall consists of outer and inner faces of masonry, spaced widely apart and tied together at intervals by timber beams, and an infilling of rubble and timber bonders. When skilfully constructed with a conservative use of timber and of infilling of the right material and well rammed, these walls can be fireproof, as Caesar found those in Gaul to be; but built crudely and in haste they can be destroyed by fire, as was such a wall at Masada.[7]

Most stones associated with timber and suitably arranged for the purpose can be fused in intense heat, the alkali of the timber acting as a flux. Many of the Scottish forts built of this composite material have been burned, and the most conspicuous part of the wall is the fused core, the faces having collapsed when the tie beams were burned through. Such are the vitrified forts. The vitrification was clearly not a process of construction, but the result of fire spread from the huts within or incendiary attack by an enemy without the fort.

In districts where timber was plentiful and stone scarce, large stakes densely intertwined with branches of trees and thorns were sometimes the materials used in the defences. Stone-built forts such as those at Cow Castle on Exmoor and Grimspound on Dartmoor are constructed without mortar, the walls consisting of a rubble core faced with large stones. In some forts there is a single enclosing wall, and in others two concentric walls with a short space between.

The strength of the gateways consisted largely in the difficulty of access. The entrance was placed near a precipice, as at Mount Cabum in Sussex, or was masked by cross ramparts involving sinuous passages of approach, as at Maiden Castle and Hod Hill. Or again the passage of approach was protected by an outwork on either side, as at

Blackbury Castle, Devonshire. Sometimes the principal enclosure, or citadel, was protected by one or two outworks, as at Winkelbury, Wilts., and Bury Castle, Somerset.

Maiden Castle stands on a site which was occupied as early as 2000BC. The eastern third of the site was fortified about 300BC, and the fortifications were extended westward to their present dimensions about 100BC. The castle covers an extensive oval area on the crown of a hill, 432 ft. above sea level, and is defended all round by several lines of ramparts and ditches. Recent excavations show that the ramparts consist of earth, chalk, clay and rubble, faced with stone and buttressed at intervals by upright timber posts. On the summit of the rampart is a series of pestholes, spaced at 4 ft. to 2 ft. 6 in. apart. These holes belong to a defence of a later period. The original wall, of which a portion still remains, was of stone[8].

SIEGE ENGINES AND SIEGE OPERATIONS
The engines of attack and defence were considerably improved during this period.

Maiden Castle from the air: Looking West to East

Philo of Byzantium speaks of having seen an engine, invented by Ctesibius, which threw stones by means of compressed air; and Vitruvius in the course of his treatise on the construction of siege engines describes a ram which, rotating in a channel by means of pulleys, acted as a boring machine. During the siege of Marseilles in 49BC the projectile engines in the city were so powerful that they threw iron-pointed poles 12 ft. long with such force that, having pierced through four rows of mantlets, were only brought to rest by burying themselves in the ground.[9] Sickleshaped hooks, fixed at the end of long poles, were used at the siege of Ambracia in 190BC for pulling down the battlements of the city.[10]

The tortoise was used by the Romans at the capture of Herac- Iciim in 169BC. Three picked maniples were employed. The men of each maniple held their shields above their heads, and closed up until the shields overlapped and formed a roof over the whole body. Under these shell-like covers, resembling huge tortoises, the maniples moved up in succession to the walls.[11] This manner of attack was used by Caesar in the Gallic wars. The name tortoise was also applied to an enclosed battering-ram, from the analogy of the moving in and out of its head, and to a penthouse on wheels.

Tall siege towers were in constant use. At the siege of Marseilles in 49BC. Caesar built a stationary tower, 30 ft. square and six storeys in height, under the very walls of the city and in face of a rain of missiles from its engines. The walls of the tower were of brickwork 5 ft. thick. When the lowest storey was built it was covered with a solid fireproof roof, which was not secured to the walls but rested upon them like a lid. The eaves projected considerably, and from them screens were hung on all sides, covering all the walls. By means of screws, the whole canopy, roof and screens, was now raised to the height of one storey, and the workmen proceeded to build the walls of that storey under its protection. This process was repeated in the same manner until the full height of the tower was attained.[12]

Penthouses, called variously *vinae*, *musculi*, and even *testudines*, were also in frequent use. A penthouse was a covered passage provided for the protection of men employed in sapping or undermining a wall, or in filling ditches. It was usually built of timber and covered with raw hides. At Marseilles Caesar constructed a penthouse between his stationary siege tower and a tower of the city he wished to undermine. The penthouse *musculus* was 60 ft. long, was built of heavy timbers and had a sloping roof with three coverings. The under covering was of tiles set in mortar, the next was of hides and the outer (to deaden the effect of blows from stone missiles) was of fire-resisting mattresses. Barrels, filled with resin and tar and set alight, were cast down from the wall on the penthouse, but they rolled off the sloping roof and were promptly removed with long poles and forks. Eventually, under the protection of their covered way and of the engines working in the siege tower, the sappers were successful, and brought down the tower they were undermining.[13]

Mining, while generally effective in reducing a fortress, sometimes failed, and the miners engaged in it were repulsed with considerable loss. At the siege of Ambracia in 190BC the Romans with their battering-rams broke through the wall again and again. But each time a breach was made they were faced by a new wall which had been built up hurriedly behind the old one. As a last resort they took to mining, hoping to carry out the work secretly. For many days they were able to dispose of the excavated earth unobserved; but the dump was eventually seen by the citizens, who at once took measures to discover the position of the mine. They dug a trench on the inside and parallel with the wall, lining the inside of the trench nearest the wall with very thin plates of brass. By the vibration of these plates at a certain part they were able to locate the mine, and by countermining broke into it. They arrived none too soon, for the enemy had not only reached the wall, but had dug out and underpinned a long stretch of it. A desperate but indecisive fight ensued, and the Ambracians, failing to dislodge the Romans by force, resorted to measures which proved more effective.

They procured a large corn jar, filled it with feathers, placed on the top of the feathers some pieces of burning charcoal and covered the mouth with a perforated lid. They then pierced the bottom of the jar with a hole into which they inserted a tube, passing the tube axially through the jar until it reached the charcoal. The jar was now placed in the tunnel with its mouth towards the Romans and all the space about it, with the exception of one hole on either side, was sealed up, the side holes being for the pikes they thrust through to prevent the enemy from approaching the jar. With a blacksmith's bellows they now blew into the tube on to the burning charcoal, gradually withdrawing the tube as the feathers caught fire. Soon a most nauseating and pungent smoke from the feathers was projected into the mine, and the Romans, unable to endure the repugnant fumes, were forced to abandon their works.[14]

NOTES

1. Phiton de Byzance, *op. cit.*
2. Vitruvius, *de Architectura*, V.
3. *Vide Monumenti Antichi R. Accodemia Nazionale dei Lincei*, Vol. XXXIII, 1929.
4. Procopius, *History of the Wars*, Bk. V, cap. XIV, 15.
5. Caesar, *De Bella Gallico*, VII, 23.
6. *Vide "Scottish Brochs,"* A.O. Curie. *Antiquity*, Vol. I, 1927.
7. Josephus, *The Jewish War*, Bk. VII, cap. VIII, 5.
8. Maiden Castle, Dorset. Report of Research Comm. Soc. of Antiqs., No. 12, 1943.
9. Caesar, *De Bella Civili*, Bk, 2, cap. 2.
10. Polybius XXI, 27.
11. *Ibid.*, XXVIII, II
12. Caesar, *De Bello Civili*, Bk. II, 8. 9.
13. *Ibid.*, Bk. II, 10.
14. Hero, from Polybius XXI, 28.

Chapter 4
Fortifications of the Roman Empire

The Romans governed for so long a period, penetrated and occupied their vast empire so thoroughly, and built so substantially, that there still exist throughout Europe, the Levant and North Africa extensive remains of their military works. It is only possible here to point out the principles of these fortifications and describe some of the prominent examples.

The camps built by the Romans when laying siege to a city had developed in the course of time into a plan so perfect that it was taken as a model for the permanent camps founded in various parts of the Roman empire, and also to some extent for the layout of new cities. These camps were normally rectangular enclosures, surrounded by a rampart or wall and generally by one or more ditches. There were usually four gateways, one near the middle of each side, the principal gate being called the *porta praetoria*. In the centre of the camp, facing the *porta praetoria*, was the administrative tent of the commanding officer – the *principia*, having on one side of it that officer's residence – the *praetorium*, and on the other the *horrea*, or strong store houses. Running right and left in front of all three was the *via principalisy* terminating at one end in the *porta principalis dextra* and at the other in the *porta principalis sinistra*. The *via praetoria* led from the *porta praetoria* to the *principia*, and in line with it, behind the *principia*, was the *via documana* which terminated at the far end in the *porta documana*. A fourth street ran parallel with the *via principia*, often terminating in a gate at each end. In addition a road ran all round the camp, immediately inside the rampart. The main portion of the camp was occupied by blocks of barracks.

Josephus, describing the Roman camps, said that the walls were strengthened by towers, and that engines for throwing stones, darts and arrows, were stationed along the defences

Aosta: Plan of Porta Praetoria

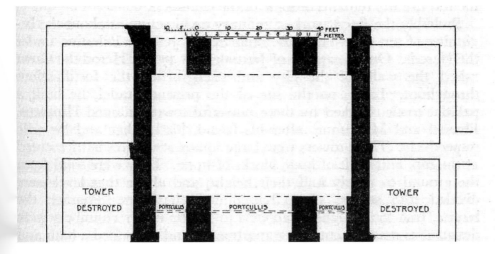

between the towers. "They also erect four gates, one on every side of the enclosing wall, and those large enough for the entrance of beasts and wide enough for making excursions if occasion should require. They divide the camp within into streets, very conveniently, and place the tents of the commanders in the middle, but in the very midst of all is the general's own tent, in the nature of a temple; in so much that it appears to be a city built on the sudden, with its market place and place for handicraft trades, and with seats for officers superior and inferior, where, if any differences arise, their causes are heard and determined. The camp and all that is in it is encompassed with a wall round about and if occasion requires a trench is drawn round the whole, whose depth is four cubits, and its breadth equal."[1]

One of the earliest permanent fortifications, of which there are substantial remains, constructed on this principle, is that of the city of Aosta, Italy, built by Augustus in 23BC on the site of a Roman camp. This fortress forms a rectangle 793 yds. by 624 yds., enclosed by a wall 21 ft. high and defended by square towers at the corners and along the sides. There were four gates of which two still remain. One of them, the *porta praetoria*, has three arched entrances of which the central is a carriage-way and the others footways and each entrance was defended by a portcullis. The gateway is 65 ft. long, and encloses a large hall extending across the width of all three arches.

At Rome, AD23, Tiberius built the Castra Praetoria at the north side of the city and outside the ancient Servian walls. The Castra Praetoria was a great rectangular fort, 481 yds. long by 415 yds. wide. It was enclosed by a battlemented wall 12 ft. high, and accommodated 10,000 men of the praetorian guard. The men lived in vaulted chambers, some of which were arranged back to back in long rows, each row being two storeys in height. Other chambers were built against the inside face of the enclosing wall, and probably formed the supports of the original wall-walk. When the outer city walls of Aurelian were built, AD271–275, the camp was included within the city, and its walls were raised to the height of 24 ft. In AD312 Constantine the Great disbanded the praetorian guard, broke up the camp, and pulled down the wall between the camp and the city; but the outer walls, being part of the defences of the city itself, were preserved. These walls still exist, and at the north and east sides of the fort are the remains of some of the chambers.

Probably the finest work of military architecture at about the beginning of our era were those built by the Jews in Palestine under the Herods. On his capture of Jerusalem in 37BC, Herod the Great raised the walls of the city and strengthened the fortifications throughout. Later, on the site of the present citadel, he built a palatial castle, flanked by three powerful towers, named Hippicus, Phasael and Mariamnc, after his friend, his brother and his wife respectively. These towers were large square structures battlemented at the top, and built of huge blocks of stone. They were solid from the ground to nearly half their height, and above that level were divided into storeys of well appointed chambers. Phasael, the largest, rose to a height of about 140 ft. Its upper chambers were designed as magnificent living apartments, and contained a bath and every requisite appertaining to a royal palace of the period. Josephus said that this tower in appearance resembled the celebrated Pharos of Alexandra.[2]

When Titus took and destroyed the city AD70 he spared these three towers on account of their great strength and, despite the destruction wrought by Julius Severus, AD133, and all the other vicissitudes it has undergone, there can be no doubt that the lower part of Phasael still exists in what is now known as the Tower of David. A typical stone of this megalithic structure, measured by the author, is 10 ft. long by 4 ft. high, and has a drafted margin from 4 in. to 5 in. wide.

Herod Agrippa the First, about AD41, laid the foundation of the outer defence or third wall of Jerusalem. The wall was 15 ft. thick, and was being constructed in so powerful a manner with enormous blocks of stone that Agrippa, fearing to excite the suspicions of the emperor, suspended the operations. But the work was resumed and completed after his death, AD44. The wall was 30 ft. high to the wall-walk, and was finished with battlements and strengthened at frequent intervals by large square towers. The towers were built of ashlar. They were solid to the height of the wall-walk, and rose in storeys of chambers 30 ft. above that level. On the top they supported cisterns for the storage of rain water. Foundations of this wall, with its huge blocks of stone, were discovered a few years ago.[3] At the north-west of the city, where the third wall turned southward, the Jews built a large octagonal tower, about 110 ft. high, which they called Psephinus.[4]

At the time of the Herods the cities of Palestine throughout were strongly defended, and at least one of them, Joppa, was protected by two lines of walls.[5] But among the most powerful strongholds in the country was that of Masada, built by Herod the Great about 30BC on the site of a more ancient fortress.

Masada stands on a plateau on the top of a high hill near the west shore of the Dead Sea, and has strong natural defences. The hill is precipitous on all sides, and the fortress on the top is inaccessible except by a narrow path which winds sinuously up on the west. The plateau on the top is roughly egg-shaped, having its major axis, about a third of a mile long, running north and south. Herod surrounded the whole plateau by a stone wall, about 10 ft. thick and 18 ft. high, and strengthened by thirty-eight towers, 75 ft. high and arranged at intervals along the curtain. On the western side of the enclosure, commanding the path of approach, he built a strong palace or citadel; and on the path itself, some distance down the hill from the fortress, he built a tower as an advance post. Within the fortress numerous dwellings and other buildings were erected, and, owing to the scarcity of water, Herod provided an extensive system of rockcut cisterns, which were excavated in various parts of the enclosure and provided the fortress with an abundant water supply.

The palace, virtually a donjon or keep, was rectangular in plan, and was built on principles at once of strength and splendour. It was enclosed by lofty walls, and had at each corner a powerful tower 90 ft. high. Internally the design was on a sumptuous scale. The walls and floors were covered with slabs of stone of various colours; there were pleasant cloisters for perambulation, and there was an elaborate provision of baths for various purposes.[6]

The fortress of Masada, both in design and purpose, resembled the mediaeval castle in a striking manner. In design, with its rectangular keep placed near the curtain wall of an extensive bailey, it has many mediaeval parallels – as at Arques and Falaise in France, and Rochester and Scarborough in England; while in purpose, like many of the castles of the Middle Ages, it was built entirely as an isolated fortress for the defence of one leader and his followers, and that at a period when all other strongholds were cities intended for the defence of large communities of people.

Not knowing what the future might have in store for him, Herod built Masada as a safe and impregnable retreat where he, and such forces as he could collect, would be able to hold out against almost any odds. With this contingency in view, he not only made the lavish provision for the water supply noted above, but also laid in vast stores of corn, wine, oil, pulse, dates and other fruits. In storing these commodities Herod's servants must have been in possession of preservative methods since lost; for the provisions when discovered AD70, a hundred years later, were said by Josephus to be quite fresh and good.[7] Herod also laid in great stores of iron, brass and tin, and of weapons of war of all kinds.

On the fall of Jerusalem, AD70, a large body of Jews held Masada for a long time against the forces operating under the procurator Flavius Silva. In order to prevent any escape, Silva built a wall all round the foot of the hill on which the fortress stood, and established forts (foundations of which still remain) at strategic points. Selecting an eminence immediately opposite the entrance on the west, he built a great mound and set a tall tower, plated with iron, upon the mound. In the tower he placed his siege engines, and from them poured such a hail of stones and darts at the fortress that the position of the Jews on the walls became untenable. Then, unmolested, he was able to bring up a large battering-ram against the wall. After some time a breach was made, and a portion of the wall completely overthrown.

But the resources of the Jews were not yet exhausted. Experience had shown that a wall built with timber bonding, being more resilient, offered greater resistance to attacks from battering-rams than those of solid stone. In great haste, therefore, they built, inside the breach, a wall constructed of a framework of timber and an infilling of earth. When the ram was brought against this new obstruction its blows had no other effect than of shaking the materials together and consolidating the whole work. However, the new wall had evidently been built with greater haste than skill. Too much timber had been used, and too little ramming of the infilling done. For the Romans, failing in their attempt to overthrow it, threw a great number of burning torches at the barrier, and, the timber work having caught fire, the wall was destroyed by being burnt down. Having achieved this result, the Romans retired for the night, knowing that the Jews were at their mercy and that there was no escape. The Jews, believing themselves to be faced with butchery and slavery, first killed their wives and children and then destroyed themselves.[8]

Probably the finest works of the later days of the empire are the fortifications of Rome itself. The Emperor Aurelian, AD270–275, extended the confines of Rome and surrounded the enlarged city by a powerful wall 12 ft. thick, and about twelve miles in length. Later, probably under Maxentius, AD306–312, this wall was raised to about double its original height. In heightening the wall the old wall-walk was covered in and retained as a lofty gallery with loopholes to the field, a second wall-walk with embattled parapet being formed above it. As finished, the wall was now some 60 ft. in height, and was strengthened at intervals of about 100 ft. with square towers of bold projection, and was pierced by eighteen gates. Repaired and strengthened at later periods, about two-thirds of the wall and nine gates still remain.[9]

Directly their rule was established, the Romans proceeded to build in all countries under their control systems of camps, frontier lines and cities.

On the German frontier they constructed a line of fortifications between the Rhine and the Danube which extended for a length of about 300 miles. The *Limes Germanicus*, as this frontier line is called, was probably completed in the early years of the third century AD, when previous works of Vespasian, Domitian and Hadrian were consolidated and strengthened. The frontier runs from Rhenbrohi, on the Rhine, to Hienheim, near Regensburg on the Danube, and is of two distinct kinds of works. The western portion, known as Pfahlgraben, or pale, consists of an earthen mound and a ditch; and the eastern portion, the Teufelsmauer (Devil's Wall), is a stone wall 4 ft. thick. Both sections are strengthened at frequent intervals by signal towers and by rectangular stone-built camps, some of the camps standing close to the rampart and others slightly back from it.

Limes of similar character were also thrown up along the eastern and southern boundaries of the Roman empire. Those in North Africa, built as a defence against inroads by the nomadic and predatory tribes of the desert and running along the southern confines of Mauritania, Tripolitania and Cyrenaica, are still in course of investigation. They are found to consist of lines of forts, large and small, connected by walls and ditches.

The native Gallic towns, as we have seen, were protected by stone walls of great resisting

Fréjus: Plan of the Porte des Gaules

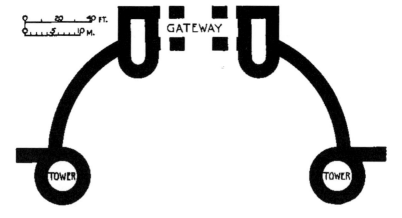

strength at the time of the Roman invasion in 58–49BC. But on the conclusion of hostilities the Romans built throughout the land their own system of military works. Extensive remains of these fortifications still exist at Fréjus, Nîmes, Autun, Le Mans, Senlis and elsewhere.

Fréjus, the Forum Julii of the Romans, was a colony of the Eighth Legion, founded in 31BC on the site of a more ancient town. It was an important naval station, and had a large harbour, now filled up by alluvial deposits. Among the most interesting remains of the fortifications, which date principally from the time of Augustus and are now in a most ruinous condition, are the Porte des Gaules and the Porte de Rome, both built on a similar plan.

The Portes des Gaules is the best preserved. The gateway is set at the back of a large semi-circular forecourt, the entrance to the court being guarded on either side by a powerful round tower. The gateway itself is flanked by a tower on either side and has three entrances, the central one for carriages and the other two for foot passengers. This is a particularly strong design, since an enemy assaulting the gate in the forecourt would be under attack from four towers as well as from the side walls, and would find himself exposed to missiles from behind as well as in front.

The Porte Augusta at Nimes dates from 15BC. It has four arched entrances, of which the middle pair are carriageways, each 13 ft. wide, and the others footways, each 6 ft. 6 in. wide.

The carriageways were defended by portcullises. The gateway is 52 ft. long, and between the outer and inner walls there is a large court which extended across the width of both carriageways. On either side of the entrances there was a large tower, semi-circular in front and square towards the town.

At Autun, where there are considerable remains of Roman walls, are two gateways, the Porte St. Andre and the Porte d'Arroux, of about the same period as that at Nimes and having the same arrangement of openings, here however, the passages are relatively short. Over the passages, in each gate, there is an arcaded upper storey, connecting the wall-walk of the curtain on one side of the gate with that on the other.

Porta Nigra, Trevcs, Germany, built later in the Roman occupation, has two entrances, one 12 ft. 10 in. wide and the other 10 ft. 4 in. wide, each of them being defended by a portcullis. This gate is of considerable depth, and between the outer and inner entrances there is a large court 57 ft. long by 26 ft. wide.

The Roman double gateways, which provided one passage for ingress and another for egress, had great advantages over single gateways from a traffic standpoint. It is probable that had the mediaeval gateways been built on this design many would have been preserved which have been destroyed as obstructions. But the advantage was confined to times of peace. In an assault, since they multiplied the points requiring defence, they

Nîmes: Plan of the Porte Augusta

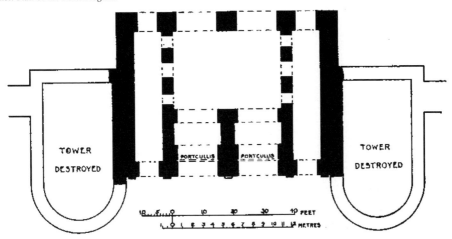

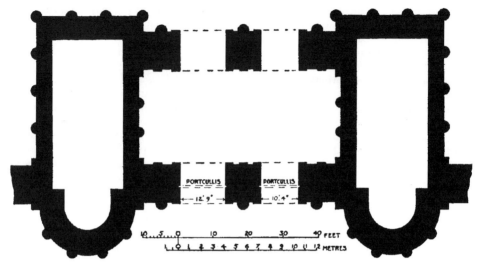

PORTCULLIS PORTCULLIS
12' 9"   10' 4"

10 5 0   10   20   30   40 FEET
1 0 1 2 3 4 5 6 7 8 9 10 11 12 METRES

Treves: Plan of the Porta Nigra

were a source of weakness, and in some cases one of the gateways was subsequently blocked by a stone wall.

At Senlis a considerable portion of the wall and sixteen walltowers, all dating probably from the latter part of the Roman period, are still standing, in some places almost to the full height. The masonry is of sionc, bonded at intervals with brick lacing courses two bricks thick. The towers are semi-circular, they are built solid up to the height of the wall-walk and

Senlis: Roman Wall and Tower

rise two storeys above that level. The lower storey of each tower is entered by a doorway on the wall-walk, and both storeys are lit by large round headed windows.

In Britain, following the Roman invasion of AD43, military roads and chains of forts were constructed in various parts of the country, legionary fortresses built at York, Chester and Gaerleon-on-Usk, and towns founded in London, Colchester, Leicester and elsewhere. In AD79 Agricola had advanced to the north of England, and appears then to have constructed the military road between the Solway and the Tyne, called the Stanegate. Two years later, having penetrated through the Lowlands, he built a frontier line across the isthmus between the Forth and the Clyde. This last consisted of a chain of forts, defended by stockades and ditches and connected by a military road. It was clearly a temporary fortification. About AD117 the Stanegate was strengthened by forts, but a few years later, 122–125, this line was re-formed by the building of Hadrian's Wall.

Hadrian's Wall was a formidable and permanent frontier, occupying a site of great natural defences. It lies to the north of the Stanegate, at distances from it varying from about one to three miles. The wall is constructed of stone with a concrete core, and is seventy-three miles long. For the greater part of its length it is about 7 ft. 6 in. thick; but a portion running for twenty-three Roman miles, between the point where it crosses the North Tyne and Newcastle, is about 9 ft. 6 in. thick. For the main part it stands on a very broad foundation, and it would appear that, as originally designed, the whole was to be ten Roman feet, or about 9 ft. 6 in. thick. But it is evident that the design was modified early in the course of the work. The height to the wall-walk was probably about 15 ft. For long stretches the wall runs along on the top of high ridges with precipitous falls on the north side; but on lower ground it is defended by a deep ditch with a level terrace, or berm, between the ditch and the wall.

There are sixteen forts along the line, spaced at intervals of about four miles, all built on the usual Roman model. Borcovicium, or Housesteads as it is commonly called, may be taken as a typical example.

Housesteads has a rectangular plan, rounded at the angles, and is enclosed by a stone wall, 5 ft. thick, backed by a clay rampart 15 ft. thick at the base. The wall is faced with coursed rubble and bonded at vertical intervals by a single course of stone slabs. On the north; where the frontier wall is on the cliff face, the wall of the fort is continuous with it. Square towers project internally from the angles and sides of the fort. There are four gates, each having a double carriageway and a tower on either side with a guardroom in the lower storey. Each carriageway was closed by a two-leaved door working on pivots. The stones, with the socket holes for the pivots and those in the centre against which the doors closed, still remain in position. The buildings within the fort were all of stone, and were divided by the *via principalis* and the *via quintana* into three sections, the middle section containing the *principia*, the *praetorium*, and the *horrea*. On the north of the *via praetoria* there was a long storehouse but otherwise the other two sections were occupied by blocks of barracks.

Directly inside the north gate there is a large water trough, built of stone slabs, and nearby a circular tile hearth, indicating a smithy. At the south-east corner of the fort there was a large latrine; it was a long and narrow structure, having a central passage with a row of seats on either side, built over a drain. A large tank adjacent, constructed of stone slabs, grooved and jointed with lead, supplied the water for flushing the drain.

At every Roman mile between the forts there was a mile-castle, a rectangular building measuring about 60 ft. by 70 ft. internally, projecting inward from the wall; and between the mile-castles the wall was again divided into three equal sections by two turrets, or signal stations, about 13 ft. square internally.

Plan of Borcovicium or Housesteads

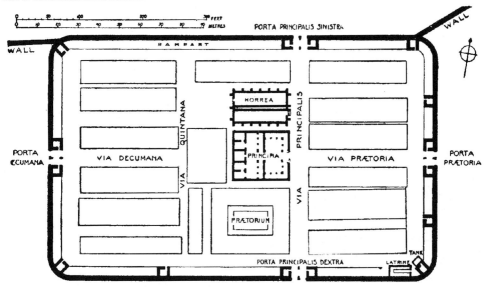

Hadrian's Wall could have offered no great resistance in the case of a massed attack, for there were no stairways to the wall-walk other than those at the forts, mile-castles and signal stations, and therefore no means of ready access to the battlements for the troops rushed along the road to repel an attack at an intervening point. But it was a serious obstacle to raiding parties, and might even hold in check for a short time large bodies while they were being outflanked by troops issuing from the north gates of the forts. It was also a continuous elevated sentry walk.

Between the Stanegate and the Wall there was a third frontier line, a flat-bottomed ditch 27 ft. wide, with a berm and a rampart on either side. This line runs along in straight stretches for the full length of the wall. It long remained a puzzle as to its purpose and date. As the result of the investigations carried out in 1935–36 it now appears to be definitely established that the Vallum, as this line is called, was formed at a period shortly after the building of the wall, and that its purpose was to protect the frontier garrisons against marauding raids from the south.

Following the conquest of the Lowlands the frontier was moved forward in AD143 to the line of Agricola's forts between the Forth and Clyde. A continuous rampart, called the wall of Antonius Pius, was thrown across the isthmus between Bo'ness on the Forth and Old Kilpatrick on the Clyde; additional forts were built and some of the old ones remodelled. The rampart is of sods for about three-quarters of its length, laid grass to grass and bonded like brickwork: the eastern quarter was of clay. Drawing a comparison between a rampart and a wall, Bede says: "For a wall is made of stones, but a rampart, with which camps are fortified to repel assaults of enemies, is made of sods, cut out of the earth and raised above the ground all round like a wall, having in front of it the ditch whence the sods are taken, and strong stakes of wood fixed on the top."[10] The Antonine Wall stood throughout on a strong stone platform, 14 ft. wide from face to face, and with a steep batter on both sides. It rose to the height of about 10 ft., and had a walk on the top about 6 ft. wide. It was defended for the greater part of its length by a ditch with a berm, varying in width from 20 ft. to 60 ft., between the rampart and the ditch. There are no mile-castles, but the forts, being only two miles apart, are much closer together than those on Hadrian's Wall.[11]

Colchester, built in the latter half of the first century of our era, and London may be taken as examples of Roman cities in Britain. Colchester has a rectangular plan with rounded corners. It was surrounded by a wall about 8 ft. thick backed by a rampart of earth 20 ft. thick, and apparently had six gates, two on the north, two on the south and one on each of the east and west ends. There were also two posterns. The wall was built of stone, roughly faced on both sides and tied at intervals with brick lacing courses four bricks thick. It was strengthend by internal towers. Semi-round towers, projecting externally, were added at a post-Roman period. Much of this work still remains, including the lower parts of the west, or Balkern Gate. The Balkern Gate had two carriageways and two footways. It projected out 30 ft. from the face of the wall, and was flanked on either side by a tower built on a quadrant-shaped plan. When complete this gate must have presented a most unusual and striking appearance.[12]

The curtain walls of London, built about AD140, incorporate at the north-west corner of the city a rectangular Roman fort, also of stone, built about forty years earlier. The city has an area of 330 acres, about three times that of Colchester. Portions of the land walls, on the north, east, and west of the city, which remain, have a plinth, and vary in thickness from 7 ft. to 9 ft. above the plinth. The walls are built of stone with lacing courses of brick. It is not known whether or not the wall was backed with an earthen rampart. All the gates are destroyed, but the foundations of one of them, Newgate, have been discovered. Newgate had a double gateway, each passage being about 12 ft. wide; and was flanked on either side by a square tower. The wall-towers, some of which were probably solid up to the height of the wall-walk, and the whole of the river wall were later Roman additions.

In the construction of their military works, as well as in the erection of public and private buildings, there can be little doubt that the Romans adopted the normal practice of employing native talent and labour. Tacitus, speaking of Agricola, says that he incited the natives to erect temples, courts of justice, and dwelling houses. He was also attentive to provide a liberal education for the sons of their chieftains, preferring the natural genius of the Britons to the attainments of the Gauls.[13] During the last century of their occupation of Britain the attention of the Romans was diverted from their northern frontier to their southern coast-line. From about the end of the third century AD the raids of the Saxons on the eastern and southern shores of England became more and more frequent and dangerous. The menace was so serious that the Romans built a series of forts, called forts of the Saxon shore, on the east and south-east coast. Extensive remains of these forts still exist, especially at Burgh, Reculver, Richborough, Pevensey and Porchester; that at Richborough, Kent, occupying the site of a fort of AD43.

Reculver, Richborough and Porchester are all rectangular forts. At Reculver the walls are 11 ft thick at the base, and rise in offsets to 8 ft. at the top. The walls of Richborough, which are of stone with brick lacing courses, are 11 ft. thick, and rise in places to the height of 125 ft. They are strengthened by round towers at the angles and square towers at the sides. A remaining gateway on the west has a single entry, 11 ft. wide, flanked by square towers. Pevensey is ovalshaped. Its walls still stand in places to the height of the wall-walk, 28 ft. above the ground. Both Pevensey and Porchester were fortified later by the Normans, who in each case built a castle within the Roman walls.

In these forts the wall-towers now project on the outside of the curtain instead of on the inside, as in the camps on Hadrian's Wall. This disposition gave greater range to the *ballistae* mounted on the towers, especially at the corners of the fort. At York, the defences of which were reconstructed at this period, a large polygonal tower or bastion was built at each of

Portchester Castle from the air (Castle in foreground at N.W. corner of the Roman Fort)

the west and south corners of the curtain. The lower part of that at the west corner, called the Multangular tower and now surmounted by a mediaeval storey, still remains. Here the projection is so great that an engine mounted on the tower would have a lateral sweep, outside the walls, of more than three-quarters of a circle. Internally the tower was divided by a cross wall, built to support the upper floor and the engine mounted upon it.

The last phase of Roman fortification in Britain was the extension of the Saxon shore defences northwards. In the last half of the fourth century the Romans built a line of signal stations on the headlands of the Yorkshire coast. Remains of these stations have been found between Huntcliffe and Filey. They were square towers built of stone, and were defended by an outer wall and a ditch, the outer wall having a bastion at each corner.

SIEGE ENGINES

The siege engines at this period were very powerful, and were used in large numbers. At the siege of Jotapha, AD68, Vespasian brought up a battery of 160 engines against the walls of the city.[14] In his description of Vespasian's army in marching order Josephus shows how the engines were transported from place to place. He says that the engines for sieges, and other warlike machines of that kind, were carried by mules, evidently in sections which could be re-assembled in the new position.[15] At the siege of Jerusalem, AD70, Titus used engines which threw stones of 1 cwt., striking with tremendous force objects a quarter of a mile away.[16] He also built three great siege towers, 60 ft. high and covered with iron plates.[17]

NOTES

1. Josephus, *op. cit.*, Bk. III, cap. V, 1–2.
2. Josephus, *op cit.*, Bk V, cap. IV, 3–4.
3. *The Third Wall of Jerusalem*, E. L. Sukenik and A. Mayer, 1930.
4. Josephus, *op. cit.*, Bk. V, cap. IV, 3.
5. *Ibid.*, II, VII, 31.
6. Josephus, *op cit.*, VII, VIII, 3.
7. Josephus, *op cit.*, VII, VIII, 4.
8. *Ibid.*, caps. VIII, IX.
9. *The City Wall of Imperial Rome*, I. A. Richmond, 1930.
10. Bede, *Eccl. Hist.*, Bk. I, 5.
11. *The Archaeology of Roman Britain*, R. G. Collingwood, cap. V, 1930.
12. *Vide The Castles of Great Britain*, p. 10.
13. Tacitus, *Life of Agricola*, cap. 21.
14. Josephus, *op cit.*, III, VII, 9.
15. *Ibid.*, III, VI, 2.
16. *Ibid.*, V, VI, 3.
17. *Ibid.*, V, VII, 2.

Chapter 5
Byzantine Fortifications from the Fifth to the Tenth Century

Following the withdrawal of the Roman legions from the out-posts of the Western Empire and the fall of Rome, the Western nations were left to defend themselves against their barbarous foes as best they might. For many centuries henceforth they were involved in a desperate strife of a kind which allowed little or no opportunity for the development of military architecture. It was in the Byzantine Empire that progress in this direction was made

Here, while the Persian frontier was maintained in the East, the advance of the Goths and Huns was held in check in the north and west. To ensure the protection of Constantinople from the onslaughts of the latter, a great wall, strengthened every sixty yards by powerful towers, was built in AD413 across the west, the land side, of the promontory on which the city stands. Having suffered severely from earthquake, this wall was repaired in AD447, when an outer wall was added and a wide moat dug before the outer wall. The walls are built of stone with a concrete core, and are bonded with brick lacing courses five bricks thick. The inner wall is 15 ft. 6 in. thick at the base, and rises to a great height. The outer wall, 6 ft. 6 in. thick, is constructed with a continuous series of internal arches. There are two wide terraces, or berms, one between the walls and the other between the outer wall and the moat. This noble fortification with its triple lines of defence, the inner and outer walls and the moat, repaired, and in some places altered, later, was a powerful bulwark of defence against the attacks of successive invaders; and even now, shattered by earthquake and neglected, is one of the most imposing and inspiring works of its kind in existence.

Walls of Constantinople

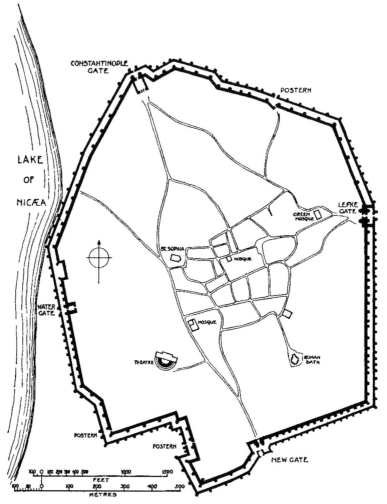

Plan of Nicaea

The fortifications of Nicaea in Asia Minor, though incorporating much work of later dates, are largely of about the middle of the fifth century. They have been ascribed, recently, to Justinian. But, apart from the fact that they resemble the land walls of Constantinople both in structure and disposition, it is not without significance that Procopius, in dealing with the subject at length, does not mention the fortifications in his descriptions of Justinian's works at Nicaea.[1] Nicaea is surrounded by a double line of walls, the inner wall of great thickness and height, and the outer lower and less substantial. Both walls are built of stone with brick lacing courses, and are strengthened by towers, placed at frequent intervals; the towers being so spaced that those in one wall stand opposite to an interval in the other.

A large residential tower on the south side of the city, higher and more powerful than the others, must have been a kind of donjon. It was against this tower, then occupied by the Sultan's wife, that the Crusaders concentrated their assault in the memorable siege of 1097; and it was not until attack after attack had been made upon it that the tower was eventually brought down, and then only by means of undermining the walls.[2] There are four gateways and three

48

posterns. The walls of Nicaea have withstood many attacks. They repelled the Crusaders again and again and are still in good state of preservation. Of the military works on the confines of the Byzantine Empire those of the fortress of Babylon of Egypt, now called Old Cairo, deserve special attention. This fortress, built in its present form during the latter part of the fourth or early part of the fifth century, stands on the right bank of the Nile at the head of the delta, and not only commanded the river at this strategic point, but also the passage across the river of the great caravan route from North Africa to the East. On the side of the fortress towards the Nile, and directly commanding the passage, are two circular towers, each 90 ft. in diameter and standing 66 ft. apart. These towers are of exceptional interest, not only on account of their unusual design and great size, but also because they stand close together and are designed to correlate with each other. They are constructed of small squared stone with brick lacing courses, stand on foundations consisting of large blocks of stone, and are bonded in with the curtain walls. Each tower consists of two concentric walls, spaced 15 ft. apart, and of eight radial ribs which connect the two walls and divide the intervening space into eight equal compartments. This is a particularly

Old Cairo: Plan of the Fortress of Babylon of Egypt

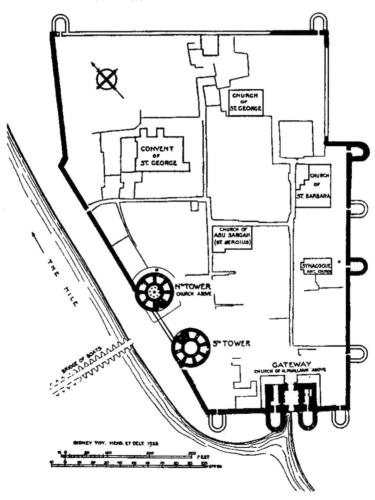

49

powerful and scientific method of construction, for, while the combined walls have the effective strength of a single wall 28 ft. thick, there is a great saving of material, and the tower is provided with spacious chambers in addition to a large circular room. The heavy ribs, radiating toward the centre, offer great resistance to attacks on the lower, while the compartments themselves are a source rather of strength than weakness; for if one of them, is broken into by a siege engine the damage is localized and its repair made relatively easy. One of the compartments in each tower, that immediately inside the curtain wall and facing the tower opposite, is occupied by a newel stairway.[3]

About AD 500 Anastasius, in his efforts to put a further check on attacks on Constantinople, built the "Long Wall," which, from a point on the Marmora forty miles west of the city, stretched northward across the land to the Black Sea. The wall was about fifty miles in length, and was strengthened by numerous towers. This emperor also fortified the city of Dara, in Asia Minor, on the Persian frontier of the empire.[4]

During the reign of Justinian great strides were made in military architecture. The Byzantine fortifications of this period are among the greatest works of military engineering known. Justinian not only strengthened existing fortresses throughout his vast empire but built numerous new ones. He rebuilt the fortifications of many large cities, strengthened those of others, and built or repaired numerous forts, his military works numbering 700. The building activity of the Eastern empire at this period is without parallel: the fortifications were scientifically and powerfully built, and to them the mediaeval engineers, both Christian and Saracen, owe much of their inspiration.

At Dara, about 140 miles north-west of Mosul, the fortifications of Anastasius, having been constructed hastily, proved to be weak and inadequate. Justinian repaired and strengthened them. He increased the height of the curtain wall by building a vaulted gallery, with loopholes to the field, upon the wall-walk along the whole line of the fortifications, and made another wall-walk with battlements above the gallery, so that there were now two fighting lines, one above the other. A second curtain wall was built outside the first, leaving a space of 50 ft.

between the two walls. The inner wall was 30 ft. thick at the base and, diminishing in thickness, rose to the height of 60 ft. The towers in this wall were 100 ft. high. The outer wall was smaller, but was also provided with towers, so placed that they stood opposite to intervals in the inner wall.

One of the towers of the inner wall, called the watch tower, appears to have been of greater importance than the others, and a kind of donjon. This tower was entirely rebuilt by Justinian.

In all his works Justinian gave great attention to the water supply of his fortresses. Dara obtained its supply from a stream which entered and passed out of the city through conduits in the wall, strongly guarded by iron bars. At the inlet the stream was protected by the mountainous nature of the country in this direction; but at the outlet the stream was a source of weakness, since it provided an abundant supply of water to an enemy encamped close to the walls. By the fortunate discovery of an underground passage, which could be entered by a shaft within the city and had an outlet many miles away, it was possible in time of siege to divert the stream into this subterranean passage and so cut off all the enemy's supply.

At Edessa water was obtained from a river which ran through the city, and which in time of flood caused great loss of life and destruction of buildings. Justinian, by cutting a deep channel through high ground on one bank and building a wall of enormous stones on the other, diverted the main course of the river round the walls. In this manner he not only saved the city from floods, but also provided a kind of moat for the hitherto unprotected walls. The part of the stream still allowed to follow the old course was carried through the city in a stone-lined channel.

At Theodosiopolis the walls were heightened by building a gallery over the existing wall-walk and a second line of battlements above, as was done at Dara. Here the wall-towers were so strengthened that each of them became virtually a keep in itself, and could be held independently.

The above works were on the Persian frontier of the empire. The other frontiers and outposts, from Egypt to the Danube, received equal attention.

Following the conquest of the Vandals by Belisarius, AD533–534, fortifications were built throughout the newly acquired territories in North Africa. Here it was particularly necessary to guard against the forces of revolt within as well as against the activities of enemies without the borders; and the military works were of great variety. They included fortified towns, such as Guelma, Thelepte and Bagai; open towns with fortified citadels, as Haidra, Mdauroch and Timgad; and isolated forts, as Lemsa and Ain Tounga. The first two classes were at once military stations and places of refuge in times of trouble for the civil population of the neighbourhood of the districtor city. The last were isolated castles occupying strategic positions, keeping watch over a plain, commanding an important valley, or guarding a pass. There were also outposts keeping watch at the borders. The Greeks had developed a scientific code of signalling from beacons, by means of which information as to the composition and character as well as of the numbers of an invading force could be signalled from station to station. Scattered throughout Algeria and Tunisia there are large numbers of these Byzantine fortifications, dating principally from the sixth century, many of them still in excellent state of preservation.[5]

These fortresses, though often rectangular, differ greatly in plan, some of them having a very irregular outline. The curtain walls are from 7 ft. 6 in. to 9 ft. thick, and, where the upper parts still exist are from 26 ft. to 32 ft. high. They are often arcaded on the inner face. The wall-walks are protected on the side towards the field by crenellations about 5 ft. high, and on the side towards the bailey by a low wall. They are approached from the courtyard either by flights of stone steps built against the inside face of the wall, or by stairways in the towers. Sometimes greater width is given to the wall-walk by corbelling on the inner side of the wall.

Towers of varying shapes, but most often square, project boldly out from the corners and sides of the curtain. They are usually of two storeys, the basement opening to the courtyard and the upper storey to the wall-walk on the curtain, the division between the storeys being either a stone vault or timber floor. Their battlements are reached by internal stairways. Sometimes the towers have no doorways to the wall-walk on the curtain, and are capable of being held independently.

The gateways are always defended by one and sometimes by two towers, one on either side. Often they pass through the lower storey of a tower, either going straight through or, entering through one of the lateral walls, take a right-angle turn within the tower before passing into the fort.

As at Nicaea and Dara there is often one tower which is larger, stronger and better fortified than the others. It occupies a position either at a strategic point behind and completely isolated from the curtain, or is in line with the curtain at the highest point in the fort or at a point particularly exposed to attack. This tower was in all essentials of its design and purpose the prototype of the rectangular keep or donjon of later times. It was the strongest building in the fortress, was capable of offering independent resistance, and was the place where the last stand was made.

Bagai, Algeria, is a good example of a fortified town. Here three of the wall-towers, projecting boldly out from salient angles of the curtain, are round, while the other towers are square. Occupying a commanding position on the north side of the town, there is a citadel, and within the citadel a powerful donjon about 85 ft. square. Haidra in Tunisia, and Timgad in Algeria, have well preserved citadels, each guarding an open town. In the former the curtain walls are built with internal arcades.

The citadel at Timgad forms a regular rectangle on the plan. There are towers at the angles and in the middle of each side, all of them square and all projecting boldly on the outside of the curtain. The principal gateway passes through a particularly large tower in the middle of the north wall, and was defended by a barbican. The barbican, which is of slightly later date, was entered through a lateral wall. The inner door of the gate was flanked on either side by a tower, now destroyed; and from each of these towers a mural passage runs through a lateral wall of the gate to the outer door, so that an enemy who had carried the first door, and was held up by the second, could be attacked from the rear by men issuing from the inner towers through the passages. In the south wall of the citadel there is a postern defended by the middle tower on that side.

Probably the best preserved of the isolated forts is that of Lemsa, Tunisia, a rectangular

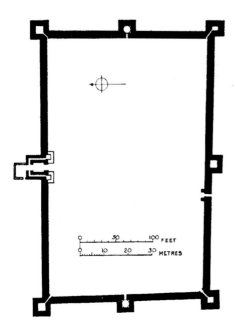

Timgad: Plan of the Citadel

Aïn Tounga: West Wall and Towers

castle with corner towers. Three of the walls stand to their full height, from 26 ft. to 32 ft., and retain their crenellations. Aïn Tounga, guarding a pass in Tunisia, is of trapezoidal plan, and has a tower at each corner, one of which (a strong rectangular building about 36 ft. by 40 ft.) is much larger than the others, and projects entirely on the outside of the curtain. The gateway passes through a tower near the middle of the south side of the fort, entering at one of the lateral walls and taking a right-angle turn in passing through.

The castle of Gastal, Algeria, forms a single rectangle with a round tower of bold projection at each corner and a square tower in the middle of one side.

In addition to the above types there are also numerous smaller forts scattered throughout Algeria and Tunisia, here guarding a narrow defile, there the approach to a village or important agricultural centre. These forts are plain square or rectangular buildings, having no corner turrets and only one gateway.

The fortifications of the Roman emperors on the Danube consisted mostly of single towers posted along the river, principally on the right bank. These towers, which had been destroyed by Attila in AD446, were rebuilt by Justinian in much stronger form, and many others were added at suitable points.

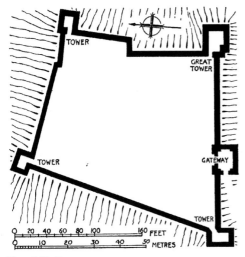

Plan of Aïn Tounga

At Episcopa, near Silivri on the Sea of Marmora, Justinian built entirely new fortifications, designed by one Theodorus Silentiarius, "a very clever man."[6] Here the wall-towers were of such bold projection that they commanded every point of the curtain between them. The gates were not designed in the usual manner between two towers in the wall, but each gate was placed at a point where the curtain took a short right-angle break inwards before continuing on the same line. The gateway was at the side, through the short wall of the break, and was therefore hidden from view. An enemy attacking one of the gates found himself in an angle of the fortifications, exposed to fire from the curtain wall on his flank as well as from the gate directly in front of him.

In fortifying the Dardanelles Justinian built a strong fortress at Elaeus near Cape Hellas at the western entrance to the Straits. Here he constructed a wall of great width and height, and dug a deep ditch in front of it. Upon the wall he raised two storeys of battlements, the lower one of which was vaulted and contained chambers for the garrison.

When Belisarius repaired the fortifications of Rome, after his capture of the city in 536, one of the improvements he made was the addition of wing-walls to the merlons of the parapets, like those at Pompeii referred to above. Remains of these merlons are still to be seen.[7] Belisarius also surrounded the wall with a moat.

The rise of Moslem power in the seventh century put the fortifications of the eastern empire to a severe test. Between AD637 and AD655 the Saracens had conquered Syria, Egypt and Persia; their fleets had swept the Levant and taken possession of Cyprus and Rhodes; and in AD668 they appeared before the walls of Constan-tinople and laid siege to the city. The siege lasted until AD675, when the Saracens were beaten off with great loss; but it would appear that the Byzantines owed their preservation as well to their use of that powerful weapon "Greek Fire" as to the strength of their fortifications.

Greek Fire (the precise composition of which is unknown, though sulphur, naphtha and quicklime seem to have been major ingredients) was a terrible weapon both on land and sea. On land it was made up into tubes, phials or pots, and either cast by hand or projected from engines at the end of arrows and bolts. On sea it was blown out of large copper tubes erected on the prows of vessels selected for the purpose. Water would not quench it but rather spread the fire hither and thither.

In AD716 Contantinople was again invested by the Saracens, who attacked the city both by sea and land. The siege lasted thirteen months, and ended in the utter destruction of the Saracen fleet by the fire ships of the emperor and the rout of their army at the land walls of the city by his allies.

From this period to the date of its fall in the fifteenth century the empire was constantly assailed from all quarters; but the traditions of skilful military architecture were well sustained throughout, particularly under the Isaurians and the Comneni.

NOTES

1. Procopius, *Of the Buildings of Justinian*, Bit, V.
2. William of Tyre.
3. "Babylon of Egypt," by the Author, *Brit. Archaeol. Journal*, 1937.
4. Evagrius, *Eccles. Hist.,* Bk. II, 37, 38, and Procopius, *Of the Buildings*, Bk. IV.
5. *Vide L'Afrique Byzantine*, C. Diehl, Paris, 1896.
6. Procopius, *op. cit.,* IV, 8.
7. Procopius, *History of the Wars*, V, XIV, 15, and *The City Wall of Imperial Rome*, I. Λ, Richmond, 1930, p. 72.

Chapter 6

Fortifications of Western Europe from the Fifth to the Twelfth Century

Throughout most of this period the countries of Western Europe had little or no respite for the establishment of permanent fortifications. Spain was overrun by the Saracens, who, but for their decisive defeat at Poitiers in AD732, would have overrun France also. Italy, Germany, France and England were all engaged in a continuous and desperate struggle for existence – either with other sections of their own peoples or against wave after wave of barbarous invaders. From the fifth to the tenth century the military architecture of those countries consisted largely in the repair of existing Roman fortifications or the building of others on the same plan. Even the military works of Charlemagne were designed on the Roman model.

Contemporary chroniclers confine their notices of buildings mainly to those of ecclesiastical or civil character, but here and there references to fortresses occur. In a poem written in the sixth century Fortunatus, Bishop of Poitiers, describes a castle built on a precipitous eminence on the banks of the Moselle, the foot of the hill being washed by the river on one side and by a stream on the other. The curtain was strengthened by thirty wall-towers; and a tower containing a chapel and armed with *ballistae* guarded the approach. The palace (*aula*) stood on the summit of the hill, and was of considerable size and magnificence.[1] Other references occur, but they are mostly vague in character; and, having regard to the paucity of remains and the facility with which the Normans overran northern and western France in the ninth century, the military works there at that period could not have been of great strength. Indeed so little faith was

placed in fortifications by Charlemagne and his immediate successors that permission was given to some bishops to pull down the walls of their cities, and use the material in building their cathedrals and churches.

But the raids of the Normans demanded that France should put itself in a state of defence. In AD862 Charles the Bald, King of France, ordered the construction of fortresses at all points to resist the invaders. The response to this order was immediate. The bishops began to repair and rebuild the walls of their cities, and nobles to build private castles. The multiplication of private strongholds became so great a menace to the authority of the crown that in AD864 Charles issued the Edict of Pistes, ordering the destruction of all fortresses which had been built without royal licence. But by a further edict of AD869 instructions were issued for the fortification of all towns between the Loire and the Seine.

In England, following the departure of the Roman legions the inhabitants continued to defend themselves behind the Roman fortifications of London, Colchester, Lincoln, York and elsewhere. But the successive raids of the Jutes, Saxons, Angles and Danes, the continuous and desperate strife between these peoples after their arrival and penetration of the country, and the constant passing of power into the hands of fresh nations of rovers were all factors inimical to the establishment of fixed defences. The conflict was ceaseless; and it was a war rather of pitched battles than of sieges. Both the Saxons and Danes constructed earthworks here and there throughout the country; but it was not until after the Peace of Chippingham in AD879 that Alfred the Great and, following him, his son and daughter were able to turn their attention to systematic fortification.

It was essential for the progress and development of the people that each community should be provided with adequate defence, and be secure at least from sudden attack. To this end Burns, or fortified towns, were built in suitable positions in various parts of the country. From AD910 to AD924 Edward the Elder and his sister, Ethelfleda. Lady of the Mercians, built over twenty such fortified towns, including Hertford, Tamworth, Stafford, Warwick and Towcester. They also repaired and strengthened existing defences, including those at Huntingdon and Colchester.

Of the character of these fortifications we have very little reliable evidence. The illustrations in Anglo-Saxon manuscripts which show towns surrounded by stone walls and towers are not helpful in this respect, because the illustrations themselves have been deliberately and meticulously copied from more ancient sources, and can have no local application. The Psalter Harl. M.S. 603, for example, dating about AD1000, contains illustrations which have been reproduced again and again as illustrative of Saxon buildings and life. But these drawings were closely copied from those in a manuscript of the ninth century, now in the Library at Utrecht and known as the Utrecht Psalter; and they again were copied from earlier classical types. And this is a typical example. The *Anglo-Saxon Chronicle* states tersely in respect of the towns that they were built or repaired, as the case may be; except in respect to Towcester, which the *Chronicle* states was encompassed with a stone wall.[2] Florence of Worcester speaks of old towns, constructed of stone, which by orders of Alfred the Great were moved from their old sites and handsomely rebuilt in more fitting places.[3] Therefore it may reasonably be inferred that where stone could be procured the fortifications of this period were of masonry. But where wood was plentiful and stone scarce they were probably of timber.

With the advent of the Normans to the court of Edward the Confessor, in the middle of the eleventh century, a type of fortification much employed in Normandy was introduced into England. In France as early as the ninth century, as we have seen, the nobles were building private castles. By the middle of the eleventh century a special form of fortification had developed, now known as the motte and bailey type, and consisting of a motte, or mound, varying from 10 ft. to 100 ft. in height and from 100 ft. to 300 ft. in diameter, and of one or more wards, or baileys, the motte and baileys being surrounded by ditches. Fortifications of this type are found in Germany, Italy and Denmark, but they are most profuse in Normandy and England.

The mounds are of three kinds: natural hillocks, partly natural and partly artificial, or wholly artificial, according to the nature of the sites they occupy. And it should be noted here that mounds are often described by writers as artificial before any investigation as to their composition has been made. The mound at Launceston Castle, hitherto referred to as artificial, was found, on excavation being made a few years ago, to be a natural hillock throughout.

Occasionally the mound stood alone

Plans of early Norman castles in England

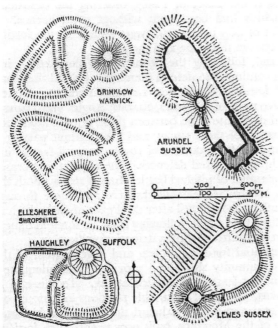

Launceston Castle: The Keep from the east

surrounded by its ditch, but normally it was protected by one, two or more outworks, or baileys, the baileys being arranged in such order, dictated by the character of the site, as would defend the keep on the mound. If there were two baileys, in some cases they were in line in front of the mound, in others on either side of it, and in others again side by side in front of the mound. A ditch was carried all round the fortification and also between the mound and the baileys and between the baileys. In some cases the mound stands entirely within the bailey, as at Bramber in Sussex and Skenfrith in Monmouthshire. At Arundel the mound stands exposed on one side in the centre of a long and relatively narrow bailey. At Lewes and Lincoln there are two mounds, and at Hedingham and Old Basing there are no mounds.

Castles such as these, placed in strategic positions, while being a source of danger to a weak ruler when held by truculent and disaffected lords, were of great value to a powerful king, such as William the First, when

held by trusted vassals. A few castles were built in England during the reign of Edward the Confessor, as at Ewias Harold and Richard's Castle, both in Hereford; but following the Norman Conquest they were spread profusely throughout the country.

If the mound was artificial, then the defences on its summit must have been of timber; and such a fortification is depicted on the Bayeux tapestry and described by Jean de Colmieu, writing about 1130.

Speaking of the flat open country south-west of Calais, Colmieu says: "It is the custom of the nobles of that neighbourhood to make a mound of earth as high as they can and dig a ditch about as wide and deep as possible. The space on the top of the mound is enclosed by a palisade of very strong hewn logs, strengthened at intervals by as many towers as their means can provide. Inside the enclosure is a citadel, or keep, which commands the whole circuit of the defences. The entrance to the fortress is by means of a bridge which, rising from the outer side of the moat and supported on posts as it ascends, reaches to the top of the mound."[4] Recent investigations have disclosed such a castle of the smaller type at Abinger in Surrey. Here on the summit of the mound there is a close row of post holes for the palisade and other posts, outlining a rectangular site in the middle for the keep.

Another chronicler, Lambert d'Ardres, writing of a wonderful timber keep built in the eleventh century (also in the flat country south-west of Calais) describes an elaborate structure of three storeys containing halls, chambers, a guardroom and a chapel. The ground storey was occupied by storerooms.[5]

In districts where conditions were favourable the keeps were built of stone. The keep of the castle of Brionne in Normandy, built about 1045, was of stone, as described by William of Poitiers, writing in the same century.[6] The keep at Langeais on the Loire, built at the end of the tenth or beginning of the eleventh century, is of stone. Of the Norman castles represented on the Bayeux tapestry, one is clearly built of stone, and stands on the ground; while two

others are represented much in the same manner as is the Westminster Abbey of the period, known to have been of stone. In some cases, as at Corfe Castle, Dorset, though the keep was of stone, the baileys were defended for many years by stockades.

At Durham Castle, built first about 1072, the keep on the mound was remodelled in the fourteenth century and largely rebuilt in 1838–40. It has been stated frequently that the original keep was of timber, but there is no evidence to that effect. The shape of the existing structure is similar to that of many shell keeps built in the eleventh and twelfth centuries, as at Tickhill and Lincoln; while it bears no sort of resemblance to keeps known to have been built in the fourteenth century, as at Dudley Castle. Such parts of the eleventh century curtain at Durham as remain, including that portion running from the chapel up to the top of the mound, are strongly built of stone; and there is every reason to believe that the original outer wall of the keep, parts of which

Durham Castle from the air

are incorporated in the existing structure, was of stone also.

In Prior Laurence's rhapsody on Durham Castle, written about 1150, he uses terms in his description of the keep (arx) which might well apply to many shell-keeps with outer walls of stone and internal divisions of timber.[7] He says that the level of the ground inside the keep was three cubits higher than that outside, and that the keep was embellished by noble projections gradually dying into the grim wall – a poetic description of buttresses which, as they rise, fall back by offsets into the general face of the wall. Owing to a mistranslation, *intus enim cubltis tribus altius area surgit* has been held to refer to the three terraces on the mound. But, apart from the fact that the three terraces on the mound were laid out by Bishop Cosin in 1670, what Laurence does say is that the ground level inside the keep was three cubits higher than that outside.

The work of rebuilding in 1838–40 was extensive; but on a close examination of the outer wall of the keep made recently I found that, while the upper pan of the wall had been rebuilt entirely, the lower part, though extensively repaired, had not been rebuilt. Here and there are large patches of original masonry, having stones deeply pitted with weatherworn holes and some stones set upright against the quarry bed, all similar to a wall in Barnard Castle in the same county, by common consent Norman work. On some sides of the keep are vertical joints where new masonry, differently coursed, abuts against the old work. The original outer wall of the keep was undoubtedly of stone, as one would expect. For it is most improbable that, while during the twelfth and thirteenth centuries ponderous and elegant buildings were being raised on the north and west sides of the bailey, the opulent bishops of Durham would have been satisfied with a timber keep, their last line of defence, until the middle of the fourteenth century and then build a structure three centuries out of date.

The perishable character of timber and its liability to destruction by fire and decay render it an unsuitable material for permanent fortification. From the earliest times fire has been one of the principal weapons of offence; and although even stone buildings are not proof against its attacks the damage done to them is partial and often repairable. With timber the destruction is total. The Normans must have been well aware of this fact, and the paucity of remains of castles of the early Norman period may be due in some measure to the pillage of stone for building purposes. At Topcliffe, Yorks., every stone has vanished from the site of what was the principal castle of the Percies for six centuries; and of the stone keep on the mound of Richard's Castle, Hereford, all but small fragments have disappeared. In some cases masonry may still lie buried beneath the soil. A mound on a hill at Lydney, Glos., hitherto considered an earthwork, was found, on investigation being made in 1929, to cover the foundations of a stone-built castle, dating from the twelfth century;[8] and the existence of hidden masonry on other sites is not improbable.

Timber, however, was of great value for temporary camps and forts which had to be constructed in haste. The Norman castles in England were founded to overawe and govern the districts in which they were built, and a large number of them must have been constructed hastily with such materials as were available. Many of them only served a temporary purpose, and were subsequently abandoned. A large number of them, judging by the ease with which they were destroyed (as at York, where charred remains of wood have been found on the artificial mound), must have been of timber. Many of the unlicensed or "adulterine" castles raised in haste in England during Stephen's reign, and destroyed after the treaty of 1153, were also probably of this material.

But where the mounds were natural hillocks, and where stone was in abundance and timber scarce, as at Launceston and Totnes, there can be no doubt that their flat summits were defended by a stone building, known as a shell-keep, from the first. It is probable also that some of these keeps which stand upon partly natural and partly artificial mounds were also built of stone from the first, the foundations going down to the virgin soil. At Skenfrith, where there is a round keep of the late twelfth century standing on an artificial mound, the foundations of the keep are carried down through the mound to the natural soil beneath.

The keep is that focal point of a castle to which, in time of siege, the whole garrison retired when the outer works had fallen. It was therefore the strongest and most carefully fortified part of the defences. It generally had a well, and contained all the offices, living and service rooms necessary to sustain a long siege. As originally built, it generally stood in line with the outer defences, so that while one side of it looked towards and commanded the operations in the bailey, the other side commanded the field and the approaches to the castle. The side open to the field also presented a line of escape. A shell-keep consisted of a ring wall, circular, ovoid or polygonal in plan. The living rooms (in the earlier examples often built of timber) were constructed against the inside face of the shell wall, either occupying the whole internal space, the roof timbers supported on the wall and a central pillar, or were ranged round a central courtyard. In many cases there was a square tower on one side of the shell, as at Arundel, Tamworth and Gisors.

There are a large number of shell-keeps in England, some of them dating from the eleventh and others from the twelfth century. Launceston, Tamworth and Restormel are examples. Gisors in Normandy and Pfeffengen in Switzerland are among those on the Continent.

The keep at Launceston is composed of an ovoid shell, dating probably from the eleventh century, and a round tower, built about 1240, inside the shell. The outer shell is 12 ft. thick and 30 ft. high, and has a deep battered plinth crowned by a round moulding. The wall-walk is reached by two mural stairways, one near the gateway and the other on the opposite side. A mural chamber, with a ventilating shaft in one corner, was probably a prison cell. The keep is approached up the steep and high mound (which recent investigation has proved to be a natural hillock) by a long flight of steps, formerly flanked by walls, and covered in by a roof. The foot of the stairway was guarded by a circular tower, and at the head stands the ruinous round-headed entrance to the keep, which was later protected by a portcullis. The transformation of this building from a mere shell to a powerful keep was probably the work of Richard, Earl of Cornwall and titular king of the Romans. The work consisted of the construction of the inner tower and of an embattled walk at the foot of the shell. Considering its commanding position, its three lines of defence, and its wide middle platform,

Restormel Castle from the air, looking West to East

Tamworth Castle from the air

this keep, when completed in the thirteenth century, must have been one of the most formidable in England.

Tamworth is probably another example of eleventh century work, at least in respect of the lower part of the walls, the upper part having been either refaced or rebuilt later. It has a multangularshaped shell, averaging 100 ft. diameter internally, and a square tower on the east which projects slightly on the outside of the shell. Here also the wall-walk was reached by two mural stairways, as at Launceston. On the east side of the mound on which the castle stands there is a deep moat, and the castle is reached by means of a stone causeway which is thrown across the moat from bank to bank. The causeway is built of herringbone work, and doubtless dates from the eleventh century.

In herringbone masonry the material comprising each course (flat stones or bricks) is not laid horizontally, but tilted up about 45 degrees. Bond is obtained by tilting the stones in each succeeding course in the reverse direction to that below it and sometimes by the insertion of one horizontal course at intervals, as at Tamworth. Two courses of such work present much the appearance of the bones of a herring. This method of construction is not in itself conclusive evidence of any particular period. It was used by the Romans, the Saxons, and was employed extensively by the Normans; it was used in Switzerland in thirteenth century work. Even within the last hundred years it has been adopted in places so far remote as the shores of the Bosphorus and the coasts of Cornwall. With the Normans, it was often associated with ordinary masonry; and at Colchester, while the outer walls of the castle and the lower part of the cross wall are built with the material laid horizontally, the upper part of the cross wall is built entirely of herringbone work. There is no reason to suppose, therefore, that the causeway at Tamworth is any earlier in date than the keep to which it leads.

The internal buildings of Tamworth Castle date principally from the fifteenth and seventeenth centuries. The living quarters having thus been kept in line with advancing customs, the castle has enjoyed almost continuous occupation from the time it was built to the present day. The original internal buildings were probably of timber, like those of the Round Tower of Windsor Castle, where the existing structures, dating in their present form from the fourteenth century, contain much timber re-used from older buildings.

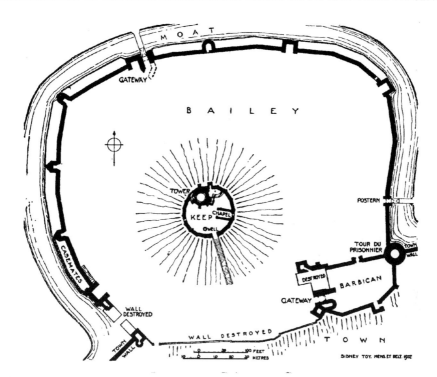

Plan of the Château de Gisors

Château de Pfeffengen

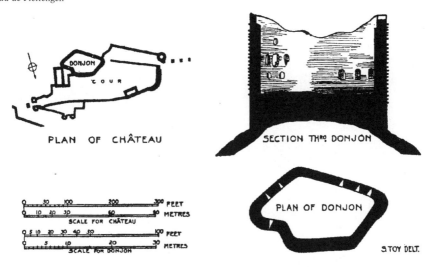

At Restormel the keep, dating probably from the first half of the twelfth century, was defended by a bailey which stood to the west of it, but the buildings of which have disappeared. The keep stands on a hill, and is founded on natural soil, but there is no mound other than that formed by the soil thrown up against its circular wall from the wide and deep ditch by which it is surrounded. Within the shell there is another wall concentric with it and surrounding a large court. The space between the shell and the inner wall, 18 ft. 6

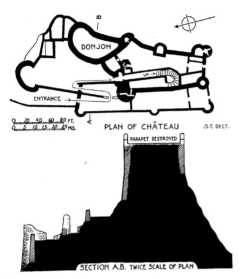

PLAN OF CHÂTEAU .S.T. DELT.

SECTION A.B. TWICE SCALE OF PLAN

Château de Dornach

in. wide, is divided by cross walls into several large rooms, two storeys in height. The ground floor contained the stores and cellars and the upper floor the halls and living rooms, with the kitchen, near the great hall, rising through two storeys. A square tower, later converted into a chapel, projects on one side of the keep.

The shell keep at Gisors dates from the early years of the twelfth century and from the first had a tower on one side, the foundations of which still remain. The tower was rebuilt in its present form about 1160; but the original structure was not of timber as has been suggested;[9] as shown by the existing foundations it was unquestionably of stone. The shell is multangular in plan, with pilaster buttresses at the external angles, and has an internal diameter of about 93 ft. It was approached up the mound by a steep flight of steps, originally protected by a wall on either side. In addition to the main wide entrance there are indications of a postern on the west side of the keep. On the east side of the shell are the ruins of a beautiful little chapel, built about 1175. There are also a well and the remains of a kitchen with large stonewash basin and drain. The wall was bonded by heavy timber ties about 10 ft. square and 15 ft. long. The holes left by similar ties were found in walls built at this period at Old Sarum.

Pfeffengen and Dornach Castles, of similar character, stand within a few miles of each other, each on an eminence, in the beautiful hilly country south of Bale. The keep, or donjon, at Pfeffengen occupies and encloses an irregular ovoid-shaped natural hillock,

Farnham Castle from the air

standing half without and half within the bailey. The shell is built against the vertical sides of the mound, which were probably scarped all round, and rises up as a mighty tower high above the mound. It probably dates from the twelfth century. The external face of this great donjon is studded all round, from base to parapet, with rough boss-like projections, consisting of stones tailed into the wall and standing well out beyond the face. This form of construction was employed by the Romans, and was recommended by Philo of Byzantium as a protection against attacks by stonethrowing engines.

The donjon of the chateau of Dornach, dating from the early years of the thirteenth century, is also built round a natural hillock, here of pear-shaped plan. It has no projecting stones on the outer face, but the hillock is so much higher than that at Pfeffengen that it occupies entirely the interior of the donjon up to the height of the parapet. The parapet (probably in its original state as shown on the drawing) was later adapted for artillery, and since destroyed. Approach to the battlements of the donjon from the outer gate was by way of a sinuous and steeply rising path, strongly defended at all points by towers and gates.

Farnham Castle, Surrey, has also a shell-keep of this type, dating from about 1140, its wall being built round a natural hillock, deeply scarped to form a vertical face. Here also the hillock rises to parapet level.

The great advantage of this kind of keep is that, while the battlements are easily accessible from other parts of the castle, the keep presents to the exterior a formidable wall of great height and strength, and its breach, leading only to solid rock, would be of no value to the enemy. At Pfeffengen there were residential quarters above the summit of the mound, but the keeps at Domach and Farnham were of purely military character.

NOTES

1. *V. H. C. Forfunati*, Frederick Leo, Berlin, 1881.
2. *Anglo-Saxon Chronicle*, anno 921.
3. *Florence of Worcester*, anno 887.
4. Jean de Colmieu, *Vie de Jean de Warneton, Eueque de Téroianne.*
5. Lambert d'Ardres, cap. CXXVIII.
6. *Duchesne Hist. Norman Script. Antiq.*, 1619, 180.
7. Surtees Society, Vol. LXX, 1878.
8. *The Antiquaries Journal*, Vol. XT, 1931, 240.
9. *Early Norman Castles*, by E. S. Armitage, p. 364.

Chapter 7
Rectangular Keeps, or Donjons

Meanwhile the more compact form of citadel, the rectangular keep, or donjon, was gradually supplanting that of shell shape. These keeps (of which the Roman and Byzantine examples noted above were prototypes) provided well-designed and powerful dwelling houses, which were at once convenient and formidable. During the eleventh century they were being built in many places in northern France, and were introduced into England soon after the Conquest. The White Tower of the Tower of London was begun about 1070, and each of the keeps at Canterbury and Colchester about 1080. They were followed in the twelfth century by numerous others, distributed all over England from Bamborough in Northumberland to Lydford on the borders of Devon and Cornwall.

Generally these keeps were built on the firm ground of the bailey and not on a mound; and stand either completely within the bailey, as at London and Canterbury, or at a strategic point in the curtain wall, as at Kenilworth and Corfe, and originally at Loches. At Clun, Shropshire, and Guildford, Surrey, the keep is built on the edge of a mound, the outer wall rising from the ditch; and at Lydford the keep stands completely on the summit of a mound.

The keeps were strongly built. They have thick walls, generally buttressed, and are from two to four storeys in height, each storey often being divided into two or more compartments by partition walls. The entrance doorway is normally on the second storey, and is reached by a stairway built against the side of the keep, the stairway often being contained in and protected by a forebuilding. At Arques, Newcastle and Dover the entrance is on the third storey, the stairway being carried up to that level. From the entrance floor access to the floors above and below was by means of mural stairways, either passing straight up within the walls or ascending spirally at one or more of the corners.

The principal, or great, hall was generally on the entrance floor, and sometimes had a mural gallfly running round the walls at a level high above the floor. Mural chambers and latrines opened off from the hall and from the other rooms. Fireplaces were formed either in the outer or in the partition walls, most often in the outer walls. There was generally within the keep a chapel, formed either in the main or the forebuilding, and also a well. At Dover there were two chapels, and at Middleham, Yorkshire, there were two wells. There was usually a postern, providing means of escape in the event of the main entrance being carried by the enemy.

On account of the combustible materials of which they were constructed, the roofs of keeps were vulnerable objects of attack by burning and other missiles. In the early period not only were the roofs constructed of timber, but they were often covered with shingles. As a protection against such attacks, the walls of the keeps, all round, were carried up so high above

Château de Loches, plan of the Donjon

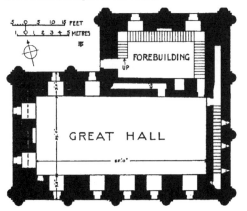

64

the gutters as to form a screen behind which the roofs were effectively masked. The well often descended to a great depth, and its pipe was carried up through two or three floors, with a drawing place at each floor. Latrines, with one or two turnings in their entrance passages for sanitary reasons, were formed in the outer walls, and opened off from the principal rooms.

Among the earliest rectangular keeps, now standing at sufficient height to indicate the original disposition, are those at Langeais and Lorhes, both in the Department of Indre-et-Loire, France, the first dating from the early part and the latter from the second half of the eleventh century.

The donjon at Langeais was of much greater length than width. It had a basement and two upper floors, the two lower storeys being apparently storerooms (for there are no windows in the existing walls) and the third storey the living rooms. The entrance is on the second storey. The living rooms are lit by round-headed windows with large internal

Château de Loches, section through Donjon

Colchester Castle: partition wall in Keep

Loches: The Donjon from the South

SECTION LOOKING WEST

Kenilworth Castle from the air

recesses: the voussoirs of the arches at the window heads are alternately of tile and stone. Only two of the walls of this donjon are now standing above the foundations, one of the long and one of the short sides. They are faced partly with squared rubble and partly with ashlar, are only 3 ft. 6 in. thick, but are strongly reinforced by buttresses at the corners and along the sides.

The donjon at Loches is one of the most imposing keeps in existence, and stands to-day almost complete externally. It consists of a main block and a large forebuilding, the latter being in all essentials of its design a part of the main building, and originally rising to the same height. The main block measures internally 65 ft. in length and averages 27 ft. in width. It is therefore more than double as long as it is wide. The walls are 9 ft. 2 in. thick at the base, are strengthened by huge semi-circular buttresses at the corners, and on the sides, and rise through four lofty storeys to the height of 122 ft. There are no internal cross walls above the basement. The entrance doorway is on the

second storey, and is approached by a stairway which rises up on three sides of the forebuilding. The rooms of the main block were dimly lit by small, narrow windows with large internal recesses. The third storey is reached by a straight mural stairway in the east end wall; and from here a spiral stairway of later date rises to the fourth storey and the battlements. The forebuilding, now only of three storeys, has a chapel in the third storey.

The White Tower of the Tower of London has a large apsidal projection for a chapel at the south end of the east wall and a round projection for a circular stairway at the north-east corner. The keep rises in four storeys – a basement and three upper floors – to the height of 90 ft. to the top of the parapet, and from each corner a turret projects high above the parapet. The walls are of great thickness, varying from 12 ft. to 15 ft. at the base. They are built of ragstone rubble with ashlar dressings, and are strengthened at the corners and sides by pilaster buttresses. Internally the

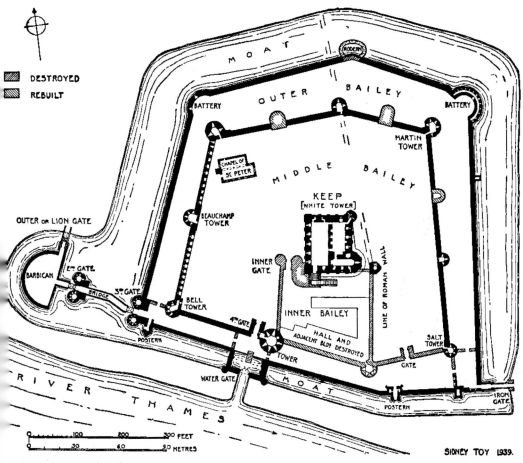

DESTROYED

REBUILT

Plan of the Tower of London

keep is divided in each storey into two large, halls and the chapel, its crypt and sub-crypt.

The entrance was at the second storey on the south, the approach to the doorway being through a forebuilding, long since destroyed. The doorway gave access to a large hall, 92 ft. long by 37 ft. wide, which was lit by windows, now considerably widened, and warmed by a single fireplace. Adjoining is another but smaller hall with a fireplace, and from the smaller hall a doorway leads to the crypt of the chapel. The spiral stairway at the north-east corner of the keep, which is 11 ft. in diameter, leads down to the basement, where there is a well, and up to the higher floors and the battlements. The third storey contains the great hall, the withdrawing room, or solar, and the beautiful vaulted chapel of St. John. Originally

the great hall and the solar rose to the full height of the keep from this level, as the chapel does, and the mural gallery, which runs round the walls from the south triforium of the chapel to the north triforium, overlooked these apartments. But at a later date the lofty storey was sub-divided by the insertion of floors at the level of the gallery. From the floor of the third storey two additional corner stairways led up to the gallery and the battlements.

The keep at Colchester also has an apsidal projection for a chapel at the south-east corner, and in other respects bears resemblance to the White Tower, though it covers a much larger area. It was probably designed to be of three storeys, but at present only the two lower storeys and fragments of a third remain. The walls are built of rubble, with lacing courses of

Tower of London from the Thames

Roman brick and dressings of freestone. They are strengthened at the corners by boldly projecting turrets and at the sides by pilaster buttresses. The main entrance, a slightly later insertion, is on the south side at ground floor level. It was defended by a portcullis and door, and was approached through a forebuilding, the remains of which were discovered recently. The original entrance was by a doorway at the west end of the north wall at second storey level. It was approached by a flight of steps built against the north wall, and defended by an arrow-loop looking down the steps.

The south side of the keep, where attack was to be expected, was built in an especially substantial manner, and contained small rooms, including the crypt and sub-crypt of the chapel. On the right of the present passage there is a well, and on the left a wide spiral stairway to the upper floors. The remaining portion of the floor space (about two-thirds of the whole) was divided by two cross walls, running parallel to each other, into one large and two smaller halls. One of the cross walls has been destroyed, though there are vestiges of it at each end. It was probably pierced by an arcade at the second storey. The other wall still remains, and is of exceptional interest. Throughout the full height of the first storey it is built of rubble, with lacing courses of Roman brick, in the same manner as the outer walls; but the upper portion is entirely of herringbone work.

The second storey was probably divided into two halls by the existing cross wall, as at present, the larger hall having an arcade running north and south in line with the wall which has been destroyed. Each of the halls was warmed by two large fireplaces. The remaining portion of this storey is occupied by what was intended to be the crypt, but what in the event became the actual chapel, and some smaller chambers. The chapel was to have been on the third storey, which seems never to have been completed, and of which only fragments of the lower walls remain.

There is no record of the existence of a third storey to tins keep, and there are strong indications that the original design was never fully carried out. It was probably found to have been conceived on too grandiose a scale. When little more than the existing height was attained the building appears to have been roofed over,

the present entrance opened out at ground floor level, and the internal apartments adapted to the limitations of a two-storey keep.

The keep at Canterbury was originally of three storeys, but the top storey has been destroyed. The walls are built of rubble with Caen stone dressings, are 9 ft. 2 in. thick, have a deep battered plinth, and have clasping buttresses at the angles and pilaster buttresses at the sides. Each storey was divided into five rooms by partition walls, now destroyed.

The entrance was in the middle of the west side of the keep at second-storey level. It was approached by a flight of steps built against the outside face of the wall, and admitted directly to the great hall in the middle of this storey. Both the entrance and the steps to it have been destroyed. The room at the south-west corner of the second storey (which was probably the kitchen) has in the corner a large fireplace of unusual construction. It is circular, 8 ft. 10 in. in diameter, and has a large circular flue which is carried up to a considerable height in the wall, to be finished with a domical head, the smoke escaping through loopholes between the flue and inner angles of the corner buttress outside. The lower part of the fireplace, where combustion occurred, is faced with herringbone masonry. A deep recess nearby opened on to the castle well, the pipe of which was carried up from the basement to the upper floors, and had a drawing place at each floor. A spiral stairway at one corner of the kitchen led down to the basement, where there were five cellars for stores. Three of the cellars had no windows of any kind, and the other two received such light and ventilation as were admitted through loopholes, the loopholes being set high up in the outer face of the wall, above the floor level of the second storey, and having their inner openings deflected rapidly downwards to the basement.

Another, and larger spiral stairway, at the north-east corner of the keep, led from the basement to the upper floors and the battlements. The rooms of the second storey were well lit by windows having internal jambs which are not splayed, but recessed back in three orders. The large apartment to the north of the great hall was probably the retiring room. It has a round-backed fireplace with flues to the outside face of the wall, and one of its windows has a large internal recess, 15 ft.

wide by about 19 ft. high. The small apartment to the west of this room, which was reached by a mural passage, was probably a sleeping chamber. There was a latrine, at second-storey level, at the south-east corner of the keep.

The keeps at Arques, Kenilworth, Corfe and Rochester were all built in the first half of the twelfth century, and those at Castle Rising, Newcastle, and Dover were built in the second half of that century.

The donjon at Arques, near Dieppe, was built by Henry the First of England about 1125. It has thick walls supported by heavy buttresses, and was originally of four storeys. Here the upper-most storey has been destroyed, and the whole structure is in a very ruinous condition; but the main points of its design are still discernible. The entrance was on the third storey, and was approached by a stairway built externally round two sides of the keep, and protected by an outer wall. The stairway was defended from two galleries, which ran along either side high above the steps, and could be occupied by defenders raining missiles on enemies advancing upwards.

The entrance doorway at the top of the stairs gave access to only one of the two halls of the third storey, for a partition wall, carried up through three storeys, divides each floor into two large halls, and there is no direct communication between the halls. To pass from one division to the other, or to either of the two floors below, it was necessary to negotiate a complicated system of wall passages and stairways, only known to the initiated. The top floor had no division; it was the key position to all parts and was evidently the head-quarters of the lord or chief officer. From this room the whole donjon could be commanded, and here was the only fireplace in the building, and an oven. A well, about 250 ft. deep, was carried up by a circular pipe to the third storey.

The keep at Kenilworth, called Caesar's Tower, is of exceptionally powerful construction. Its walls are 14 ft. thick, and are strengthened by massive turrets at the corners and strong buttresses at the sides. It is of two storeys, each storey being of great height. The walls are carried up so high above the level of the gutter

Dover Castle from the air

as not only to mask the roof, but to form two tiers of fighting lines: the battlements and, below them, rows of arrow-loops in deep arched recesses. The keep has no internal divisions, but one large hall in filch storey.

The original entrance, (altered about 1392) was on the second storey, and was approached by a flight of steps built against the west wall. From this level a large spiral stairway at the north-east corner of the keep led down to the ground floor and up to the battlements. At the south-east corner there is a well with a drawing place at each of the two floors. The north-west turret contains three tiers of latrines, but all the other turrets were formerly solid up to the lower tier of battlements and contained chambers above that level. The south-west turret was hollowed out in 1570. Most of the windows and doorways of the keep were greatly enlarged in the sixteenth century. When the castle was "slighted" in 1648 the north wall of the keep was blown down and the upper parts of the turrets destroyed.

At Corfe the keep (a large portion of which was blown down by gunpowder in 1646) consisted of a basement and two tall storeys above, each divided into one large and two smaller rooms. Here again the outer walls were carried up high above the roof, completely masking it, as the lines of the verges of the twin roof, still to be seen on the south wall, show. An external blind arcade was carried all round the walls just below the parapet, but there was only one tier of battlements. Shortly after the keep was built an addition was thrown out across the curtain wall, preserving the wall-walk by spanning it by a lofty barrel-vaulted tunnel.

One of the most remarkable points of this keep, and of the whole castle, is the excellence of the masonry. The walls are composed of a core of chalk and rubble faced with a very durable limestone, quarried locally; and the mortar used is so powerful that whole masses,

Rochester Castle: Great Hall of the Keep

having fallen from as much as 40 ft. when the castle was blown up by gunpowder in 1646, have held together so tenaciously as to remain on the ground unbroken to the present day.[1]

The keep at Rochester, built about 1130, is one of the most imposing and best preserved structures of its type. It is of four tall storeys with a turret at each corner and a forebuilding, containing the entrance porch, with chapel above, at the south-east corner. The walls are 12 ft. thick at the base, and rise, with a considerable batter, to the height of 113 ft., the turrets projecting up another 12 ft. A cross-wall, rising through the full height of the keep, divides each storey into two almost equal sections. The entrance is at second storey level, and is by way of flights of steps which begin at the outer face of the north wall, turn round the north-east corner and rise to the porch. The steps were commanded by the porch and by a gate, now destroyed, which was thrown across them at the corner; and there was a drawbridge immediately in front of the porch. Another doorway, defended by a portcullis, admitted to the main body of the keep.

The two large rooms of the second storey were lit by small windows. They have each a round-backed fireplace with flue passing to the outer face of the wall, and are provided with latrines. A well in the cross-wall has a drawing place in each of the first, second and third storeys. From the second storey two spiral stair ways, in opposite corners of the keep, rise to the upper floors and the battlements, and one of them also descends to the first storey. The great hall is on the third storey. Here, the cross-wall being pierced by an arcade, the lofty room extends across the whole floor space. There are two tiers of windows, the upper tier opening to a mural gallery, 14 ft. above the floor. There is a fireplace in each of the east and west walls, and there are four latrines. The arches of the arcade in the middle of the hall and those at the heads of the fireplaces and of the internal openings of the windows are all enriched with mouldings and chevron ornament. After the siege of 1215, when a breach was made in the keep, the south-west turret was rebuilt in its present round form.

In each of the keeps of Castle Rising, Newcastle and Dover the approach stairway is enclosed within and defended by the forebuilding. At Castle Rising, as at Rochester, the entrance is through a porch at second-storey level. Here, however, the keep is of two storeys only, except at one point. A noticeable feature of this keep is the extent of its external ornament, unusually great for a military building. But the ornament is so disposed, especially in respect of the long vertical mouldings of the buttresses, as rather to increase than detract from the impression of strength.

The keeps at Newcastle and Dover have many points of resemblance in design. Both have their entrance doorways at third-storey level; and in each case the long approach stairway is enclosed and strongly defended all the way up by the forebuilding. Both also have many mural chambers constructed in the thickness of their walls, and a mural gallery, high above the floor, running round the walls of their great halls.

Newcastle keep (which is much the smaller building) has no internal partition, each floor consisting of the central hall and the surrounding mural chambers. It was built 1172–1177. It consists of a vaulted ground floor and two upper storeys, the walls rising sufficiently high above the roof to mask it completely. The chapel (which is vaulted and richly decorated with chevron and other ornament) occupies the ground floor of the forebuilding, the stairway to the keep passing over its roof. It is entered at ground floor level from outside, and there was no doorway between the chapel and the other parts of the keep, indicating that the chapel was for the use of the garrison in general. The great hall, on the third storey, is very lofty; and its mural gallery, with openings to the hall in the end walls, is 30 ft. above the floor. The existing vault is modern. From the hall a spiral stairway at the south-east corner of the keep descends to the basement and rises to the battlements, while a straight flight of steps leading out of the stairway, at hall level, passes up through the east wall to the foot of a second spiral stairway, which rises to the battlements at the north-east corner. From the south-east stairway a postern opens out, high above the ground, on to the face of the forebuilding, where originally a gallery and bridge led to the wall-walk on the curtain of the castle, so that in the event of the keep being taken the defenders on the battlements could escape by either stairway, and gain the postern without passing through the great hall. There is another postern in the west wall at basement level.

A door on the north side of the great hall leads to a well-chamber which has a recess on either side of the well for a bucket. The well is 99 ft. deep, the shaft being lined with stone all the way down. There is no other drawing place directly from the well, but water was conveyed by means of pipes to drawing places in other parts of the keep. Two of these drawing places have been identified, one at the central pier in the basement and the other in the passage leading to the south-east postern.

The great square keep at Dover, built 1181–1187, consists of a basement and two upper storeys, and rises with two slight offsets to the height of 83 ft. to the top of the wall, square turrets at the corners rising 12 ft. above this level. The walls are well buttressed and of great strength, varying in thickness from 17 ft. to 21 ft., and contain many mural chambers at each storey. The forebuilding is strengthened by three towers, and contains three long flights of steps which begin at the south side of the keep and continue up the east side. At the head of the first flight there is a chapel, richly decorated with clustered shafts and arches with chevron mouldings; and at the head of the top flight there is a guardroom, facing down the steps and defending the entrance to the keep on its right.

Newcastle: plans of the castle

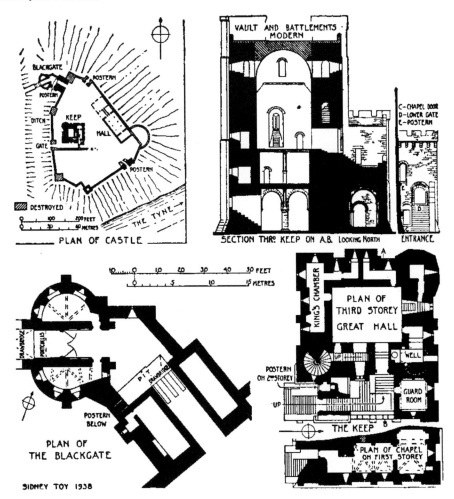

The main building is bisected by a cross-wall, which ascends through the full height of the keep dividing each floor into two long halls. The third storey, or entrance floor, contained the principal rooms, consisting of two large halls and the surrounding chambers; the upper gallery is carried all round the outer walls. From one of the mural chambers a narrow passage leads to a second chapel, which is constructed in the forebuilding above the lower chapel, and must have been for the especial use of the occupants of the keep.

The existing brick vaults covering this storey were built in 1800 for the support of artillery on the flat roof. A mural chamber on the left of the entrance doorway contains the well. Harold's well, as it is called, is about 350 ft. deep, and is lined with masonry to the depth of 172 ft. below the mouth. A recess beside the well contained a tank from which supplies of water were conveyed through lead pipes, buried in the thickness of the walls, to other parts of the keep. Two of these lines of pipes have been traced, and there are indications that there are others not yet completely followed. Another stone-lined shaft, formed in the central tower of the forebuilding, was probably another well, partly filled in, of which the passage in the second storey running in its direction and now blocked was a drawing place.

From the third storey two large circular stairways lead down to the lower floors and up to the gallery and the battlements. A postern opens on to the stairway in the forebuilding from a mural chamber at second storey level. It could be used either to attack from the rear an enemy advancing up the stairs or for escape.

On the Ile St. Honorat, in the south of France off Cannes, there is a keep which stands alone without any outer defences, and appears to have been in course of construction between 1073 and 1190. It was built by the monks of the Abbaye de Lérins as a retreat in time of trouble, and was restored in the fourteenth century and again in the fifteenth century, the machicolated parapet being added at the latter period. It is an irregular-shaped, tower-like structure of several storeys.

NOTE

1 Vide "Corfe Castle" by the Author, Archaeologia, Vol. LXXIX, 1929.

Chapter 8
Fortifications of the Twelfth Century in the Levant

Fortifications in the Levant during the eleventh and twelfth centuries continued to follow the traditions of the Byzantine empire. The towers were often circular, and the north, or Black, tower of the castle of Roumeli Hissar, built probably by Alexios Comnenus about 1100, may be taken as an example. Roumeli Hissar, the castle of Europe, and Anadoli Hissar, the castle of Asia stand facing each other across the Bosporus at the narrowest point of the Straits, about seven miles north of Constantinople. They were built to protect the city against raids from Russia and other countries bordering the Black Sea, but were remodelled and considerably enlarged after the Turkish Conquest.[1]

The Black Tower (so called on account of its grim associations) is 81 ft. in diameter, its walls are 24 ft. thick, and it rises in seven storeys to the height of 120 ft. The two uppermost storeys were added by the Turks about 1454; but originally (as at present) there was a broad fighting platform behind the battlements, and the roof was screened by a high encircling wall. The tower is faced throughout with coursed stonework, and has a deep battered plinth at the base.

The entrance doorway is on the ground floor, and from it a passage led straight through the wall to the central chamber on that floor. Opening from the right of the passage there is a spiral stairway which ascends to the level of the original battlements, and on the left is a circular mural chamber with a domed roof. Round the central chamber are three wide

Anadoli Kavak. Heiron Castle: The main gateway

75

Roumeli Hissar: The Black Tower from the Bailey

Anadoli Hissar from the Bosporus (Largely rebuilt in the Fourteenth Century)

recesses and two doors, each of the doors leading to a domed chamber similar to that from the passage. The second storey has neither recesses nor mural chambers, but on each of the third, fourth and fifth storeys there are two large recesses, one or two latrines, and a mural chamber near the stairway. The ancient timber flooring, repaired at various periods and added to when the upper storeys were built, still exists, though its condition is now decayed and treacherous. A dark passage near the head of the stairway leads to a point near the domed crown of a large circular chamber which descends in the thickness of the wall through two storeys. The purpose of this capacious mural chamber is probably for the storage of water, of which the tower would be in great need in time of siege. What were actually reservoirs, and sometimes even latrines, are often called oubliettes. It is interesting to record in this respect that M. Viollet-le-Duc, in the course of his extensive investigations, found only one pit which could definitely be called an oubliette, a prison below a secret pitfall; that is at Pierrefonds. He states that another existed at The Bastille, Paris.

During the Byzantine period, as well as subsequently under the Turks, the Black Tower was probably at once a fortress and a prison. The upper rooms, being for the soldiers, were amply provided with fireplaces, even the recesses (which were probably the sleeping places) having a fireplace each. The ground floor, with its recesses and mural chambers, where there were neither latrines nor fireplaces, was used as storerooms, and perhaps sometimes as prisons. Even in respect of the soldiers' quarters, it would be difficult to imagine any place more terrible than this tower. From ground floor to roof the building was in all but total darkness, and, with the exception of one mural chamber on the fourth floor, received only such light as filtered into it through narrow loopholes. At some period (probably after the Turkish conquest when the whole tower was used as a prison) even the loopholes were blocked, as they now are. The entrance doorway is protected by a machicolation, which passes 25 ft. up through the wall, and was operated from the fourth storey.

It is little wonder that, on account of its gloom, its strength and its painful associations, this tower was regarded with extreraversion, and that at the Byzantine period it was known as one the towers of Lethe or oblivion.

Among the finest military works of this period are the walls and towers at the north end of the land walls of Constantinople, between the towers of Anemas and the palace of

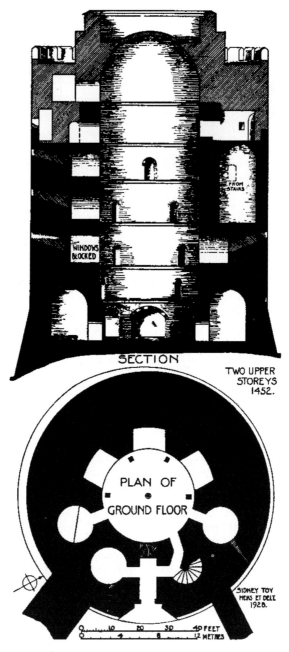

Roumeli Hissar: The Black Tower

Porphyrogenitus, built as a protection to the palace of Blachemae. A large portion of this wall, built by Manuel Comnenus, 1143–1180, is constructed with internal arcades of lofty arches and is 15 ft. thick. It is strengthened at frequent intervals by massive towers of varying shapes, round, octagonal and square, and all projecting boldly on the outside of the curtain

Anadoli Kavak: Heiron Castle from the south-east looking across the Bosporus

Kerak Castle from the South, with the Donjon in the foreground

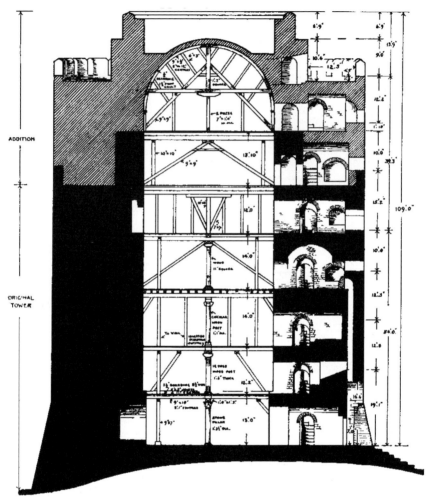

Roumeli Hissar: Section through the Black Tower (Sidney Toy mens. et delt. 1928)

wall. This work is built of large blocks of stone with brick lacing courses, several bricks thick, at intervals. A powerful tower of this period immediately north of this portion of land walls was designed to be at once a residence and a fort.

The castles at Roumeli Kavak and Anadoli Kavak, guarding the Bosporus, one on each side of the Straits, near the entrance to the Black Sea, were built about the middle of the twelfth century. They stand on high ground facing each other across the Straits, walls running down to the water's edge from them. The castle at Roumeli Kavak has been destroyed, but that at Anadoli Kavak, on the Asiatic side, called Heiron Castle, still retains its walls, wall-towers and gatehouse to a considerable height.

Heiron Castle consists of an upper bailey, on the crest of the hill, and an extensive irregular-shaped lower bailey which runs down the hill towards the Straits. It is built of large coursed stonework with brick lacing courses, seven bricks thick; and bears marked resemblance in its masonry to that portion of the walls of Constantinople built by Manuel Comnenus. The walls of the lower bailey are strengthened at long intervals by towers, circular on the outside and having a cruciform plan within, vaulted at great height. A portion of the south curtain wall is constructed with internal arcades.

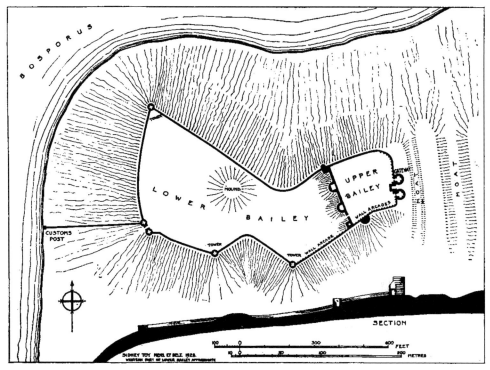

Anadoli Kavak: Heiron Castle, plan and section

The upper bailey is quadrangular. Its south and east walls, those most exposed to attack, are built with internal arcades. The wall between the two baileys, looking down the hill, is defended by four towers, and there is another tower near the west end of the south wall. On the east (the most vulnerable side of the castle where the ground rises slightly) there is a powerful gatehouse, and the curtain wall is defended by two lines of ditches. The gateway is flanked by two round towers, even now about 50 ft. high; and its passage, now blocked, was defended by a portcullis.

With the powerful Byzantine fortifications which fell into their possession as the result of conquest, the Saracens were able to defend themselves for long periods against the armies of the First Crusade, 1096–1099. Behind the walls of Nicaea, Antioch and Jerusalem they offered a stubborn resistance to the might and skill of Western Europe. Again and again the besiegers were repelled discomfited; and it is no small tribute to the skill, resource and intrepidity of the Crusaders that they were successful in that expedition.

The Saracens built their own military works largely on Byzantine models, but profited by the great experience they had gained in defence and attack. Their work attained a high degree of excellence under the powerful Sultan of Egypt Saladin, who, between 1170 and 1182, built the walls and the citadel of Cairo. These fortifications are among the finest works of military architecture built during the twelfth century. Scientific design and constructive skill are particularly marked in the gateways and towers.

The walls of the citadel of Cairo are 9 ft. 2 in. thick, are built of good masonry, and rise to a great height above the sand. They are protected at the corners and at frequent intervals along the sides by round towers, each containing two tiers of chambers with arrow-loops. Mural galleries, lit by windows on the inner face, run through the walls. Round the whole of this fortress there are three tiers of fighting lines; two from the towers and mural galleries and the third from the battlements.

Many additions and alterations were made to the citadel after the time of Saladin,

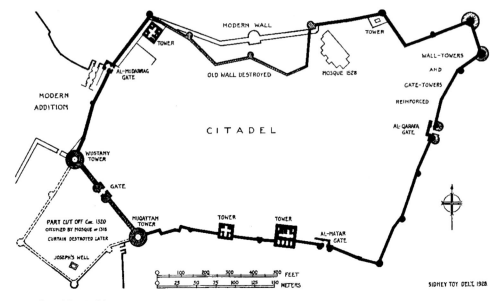

Cairo: plan of the citadel

particularly during the reign of his immediate successor. They include the building of large square towers near the middle of the south wall and at two corners of the north wall, and also the reinforcement of the towers of the north-east salient and of the Al-Qarafa gate by the addition of thick masonry round their outer faces. In the sixteenth century a projecting portion of the fortress was cut off by a cross-wall, having a large circular tower at each end and a gateway in the middle. But the main portion of the curtain and the wall towers are the work of Saladin, as are the three gates Al-Mudarrag, Al-Qarafa and Al-Matar. Each of these gates is built on an L-shaped plan, involving a right-angled turn in the passage through. "Joseph's Well," at the south-west of the citadel, has a large and deep rectangular shaft. Built round the sides of the shaft are wide flights of steps which descend to the water.

Meanwhile the building of fortresses was being pushed forward on an almost unparalleled scale in Palestine and Syria. Following the conquest of Jerusalem in 1099 by the Crusaders and the establishment of the Latin kingdom and principalities, powerful castles were raised in great numbers throughout the land from Antioch in the north to the Gulf of Akaba on the south. After the conquest the greater number of the crusaders

returned to Europe, and only about a quarter remained to consolidate the conquered territories and defend them from attack. The establishment of fortresses throughout the country was therefore essential. Castles were built along the coastline on the west, on the long vulnerable eastern flank facing the desert, in the mountain passes running axially north to south and at intervals east to west, and on the south defending the approaches from Egypt. A large number of these castles occupy commanding positions on hill tops, covering extensive areas. Some of them, as Tortosa and Giblet, stand at one end of a town which they defend, but of which they are independent. They are generally of very powerful construction, with thick walls rising from the summits of precipitous rocks, and faced with large stones, often with drafted edges.

In design and construction these castles represent much of the best of what was known of military architecture in their day. Their builders incorporated the latest developments from Western Europe together with such improvements as they had observed in Byzantine work; but, above all, took advantage of the experience they had so recently acquired in conducting their numerous sieges. They had been able to test the strength or weakness of the defences they had assailed. A large number of the castles date from the first half of the twelfth century, though many of them were refortined in the latter half of the twelfth and the beginning of the thirteenth century. Some of the castles stand on sites previously fortified, and incorporate some of the earlier defences.

In view of the isolated positions of very many of the castles, it was necessary to prepare for the contingency of long sieges. Lavish provision was made for the supply of water by the construction of large reservoirs, and for the storage of food by preparing ample cellar accommodation. A strong garrison must also be retained on the spot. At Margat there were sufficient supplies to last for five years, and there was a garrison of a thousand men. There is evidence of friendly relations between the occupants of crusader castles and the Moslem inhabitants of the neighbourhood. An Arab traveller of the period states that he visited many villages occupied entirely by Moslems who were living in the greatest amity with their Latin rulers, paying certain agricultural and other dues but otherwise masters of their own houses and affairs.

Many of the castles, as Subeiba, Beaufort and Belvoir, in the district between Galilee and the coast, are now in a very fragmentary and ruinous condition; others, as Kerak of Moab, Montreal and Sidon, retain considerable remains; while others again, as Margat, Scionc and Le Krak des Chevaliers, are almost intact as far as their principal defences are concerned, the last being the most complete. The castles dating from the early part of the twelfth century are characterized by thick walls, defended at intervals by square towers. Round towers are not generally introduced before the end of the century when they occur in repairs and additions, as at Margat and Le Krak des Chevaliers. In the early work there are two semi-circular turrets.

Kerak of Moab stands in a desolate country at the point of a land promontory at the south-east of the Dead Sea, a walled town, separated from the castle by a ditch, stretching northward from it. The castle (having the shape of a long isosceles triangle with the base towards the town on the north and the apex at the point of the promontory on the south) was built about

Saône Castle from the south-east: The outer ditch is on the right

Margat Castle from the east

1145, and remained in Latin occupation until 1188. The walls are defended at intervals by rectangular towers. The entrance was on the north, reached by a bridge across the ditch, and the donjon (a huge rectangular structure) on the point of the promontory at the other end. In 1188 Kerak was taken and refortified by the Moslems. They built the existing powerful donjon in front of the old one, and added an outer wall along the west flank of the castle. The donjon has a straight wall towards the bailey and a semi-octagonal face to the field.

Plan of Saône Castle

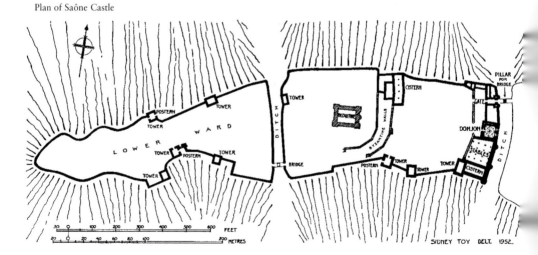

Sâone Castle, guarding the southern approach to Antioch, was built in the early years of the twelfth century. It stands on the summit of a land promontory, jutting westward and shaped like a long tongue, and is flanked on either side by a deep gorge, a rapid stream running through the north gorge. Two deep ditches are cut from side to side through the promontory, one to defend the entrance to the castle from the level ground on the east and the other, midway in its length, to divide the castle into two sections. The first, cut through the solid rock centuries before the invention of high explosives, is a remarkable feat of engineering skill. It is 426 ft. long, about 63 ft. wide and 92 ft. deep. Realizing that the width would be far too great for a drawbridge, the excavators left a square pillar of natural rock in the centre of the ditch opposite the gateway, and built upon it a square pier of masonry for the central support of the bridge.

The east end of the castle, being the point of approach, was strongly fortified. It has a very thick wall, defended by round turrets. The gate is placed at one end, a strong tower at the other and the donjon in the middle. The principal buildings are assembled behind this wall. The donjon is 82 ft. square externally, is of two vaulted storeys, and has a flat roof with a crenellated parapet. Its walls are 17 ft. 6 in. thick, and the battlements are reached by straight mural stairways. On the south of the donjon there is a spacious stable, and in the upper ward are two large reservoirs, one at the south-east corner and the other near the middle of the north wall. In addition to the gateway, there are three posterns, one on the south side of the upper ward and one on each of the north and south sides of the lower ward, all passing through the bases of towers, and two of them taking a right-angled turn within the tower. The south side of the castle, being more vulnerable than the north, is defended by a greater number of towers.

Sâone stands on the site of a castle built in the tenth century, of which the ruins of a donjon and three lines of curtain walls to the east of it still remain. The north end of the middle one of these walls no doubt forms the west wall of the large cistern on the north side of the upper ward, and the deflection of the plan of the cistern is occasioned by its following the contour of the wall.

Margat Castle stands on a hill overlooking the Mediterranean north of Tripoli. It occupied a most strategic position in the Latin defensive system, being on the borders between the principality of Antioch and the county of Tripoli, and lying adjacent to the territories of the Assassins. Doubtless it was on this account that it maintained the large garrison and laid in the extensive food supplies mentioned above. The site (which was previously fortified) was taken by the crusaders in 1117, and was held by the Mansoer family until 1186 when it was ceded to the Order of Hospitallers, in whose hands it remained until taken by the Egyptian Sultan Bybars some ninety years later.

Margat is a triangular-shaped castle with its apex on the south and its base towards the north, all the main buildings being concentrated in the inner ward about the apex. Except along the north side of the outer ward (where there is a sheer cliff face forming the base of the triangle, and where the inner wall only is continuous) the whole castle is surrounded by a double line of curtain walls, the outer being defended at frequent intervals by round towers. The terrace between the walls forms, a wide fighting space, with the outer parapet and towers in front and the inner wall rising to a higher level behind. The towers stand one storey above the terrace, and have each two tiers of battlements, one at terrace level and the other on the roof of the tower, reached by outside stairways. The circular tower at the north-west corner of the outer ward is of Moslem construction, and probably replaces one damaged in the siege conducted by Bybars.

The entrance is by a gatehouse of two storeys, which stands astride the terrace between the two walls in the middle of the west side of the castle, the approach road being defended by an outwork, or barbican, thrown across the path lower down the hill. The passage through the gatehouse is defended by a portcullis and heavy door, and by a machicolation operated from a mural gallery in the upper storey. The second gate, which pierces the inner wall some distance south of the first, is defended by a portcullis and door, and has on one side a large vaulted hall which was probably the guardroom.

The military and domestic buildings are arranged about the triangular court of the inner ward, the round donjon occupying the south

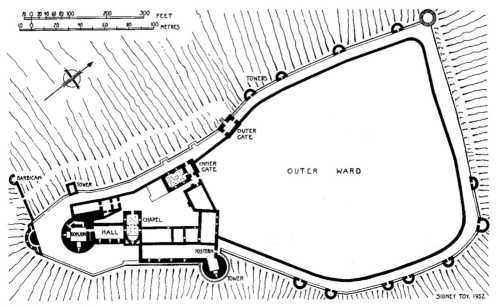

Plan of Margat Castle

end, the chapel a point on the east side, and the main halls formed in a two-storey building between the donjon and the chapel. The buildings on the north and north-east side of the court (now very ruinous) doubtless contained the kitchens, the service and storerooms and the official military quarters. The barracks for the men-at-arms were probably in the outer ward, now occupied by the houses of a village. A large round tower at the north-east corner of the inner ward formed a powerful defence on this more vulnerable side of the castle and for the postern behind it. The east side of the inner ward was further defended by a moat.

At the south angle of the outer wall, in front of the donjon, there is a powerful half-round structure which is solid but for a mural gallery with arrow-loops to the field. This bastion (which has a deep battered plinth) was mined during the siege by Bybars and partly destroyed, but was afterwards repaired. The chapel is of two vaulted bays. It has a semi-circular apse and a small vestry on either side of the apse. The donjon is an exceptionally powerful building of two vaulted storeys. There are straight mural stairways to the upper storey and the flat roof. The battlements at the summit are of two tiers, the arrow-loops of the lower

tier opening from a mural gallery, which runs all round the donjon, and those of the upper tier piercing the merlons of a crenellated parapet.

The chapel and probably some of the walls of other buildings of this castle are referable to the first part of the twelfth century; but the donjon, the large round tower at the north-east corner of the inner ward, both the first and second gateways, and the whole of the outer wall and wall-towers (indeed the whole of the defensive works as they stand, saving Moslem repairs) date from the period of occupation by the Hospitallers, and can be assigned to the end of the twelfth and first half of the thirteenth century.

Le Krak des Chevaliers, in the mountainous district of Syria, north of Horns, is the most powerful and imposing of all the crusader castles, and it is in the best state of preservation of them all. The site was fortified by the Latins in the early years of the twelfth century, and some buildings and walls of the upper ward are of that period. In 1142 the castle was given to the Knights Hospitallers, and was held by them until taken by Bybars in 1271. The whole of the outer line of the fortifications and most of the defences of the upper ward were built by the Hospitallers, and date principally from the end

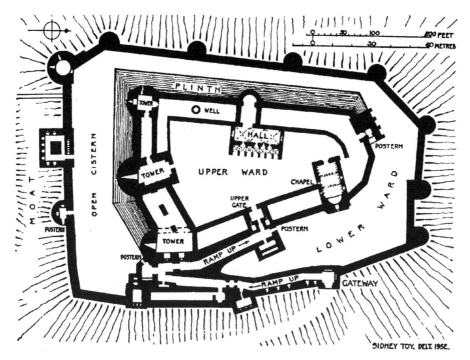

Plan of Le Krak des Chevaliers

of the twelfth and the first part of the thirteenth century. The large square tower in the middle part of the outer wall on the south side was built by the Moslems in 1285.

The castle stands on a hill, with precipitous falls on the east, west and north sides and a more gradual descent on the south, where it is defended by a moat. It is surrounded by two lines of powerful walls with wall-towers, enclosing two wards of which the innermost, following the steep rise of the hill, is on a much higher level than the other, its towers and battlements dominating the whole fortification. On the south and west sides, where the rise from the outer to the upper ward is greatest, the curtains of the latter are strengthened by massive battered plinths, which soar up to a great height, engulfing the lower parts of the towers and forming one of the distinctive features of the fortress.

The entrance to this stronghold is by a gateway on the east side of the outer curtain, placed at a point so far on the north of that side that an approaching enemy must defile up the path, in face of direct attack from the walls, along two-thirds of the whole length of the fortress before he reached it. From the outer gate the way to the upper ward was by way of a rising and sinuous vaulted passage, barred by four gates in succession and commanded from above by many machicolations. Finally the upper gate was defended by a guardroom in the rear, and the passage through by a machicolation, a portcullis and a heavy door, and further by a guardroom on either side from which men could issue directly on to the central hall of the passage. There are four posterns, one from the upper ward, two from points in the entrance passage and one in the outer curtain wall.

The buildings of the upper ward include the banqueting hall (a handsome structure of three bays with a vaulted portico occupying the full length of one side), the chapel and the formidable range of buildings, with three great towers, stretching across the full length of the south side. The chapel is a Romanesque building with a pointed barrel vault, divided into three bays by transverse ribs, and a semi-circular apse. At the sides the bays are divided by wallshafts, and have deep recesses with pointed arches. With the exception of the apse,

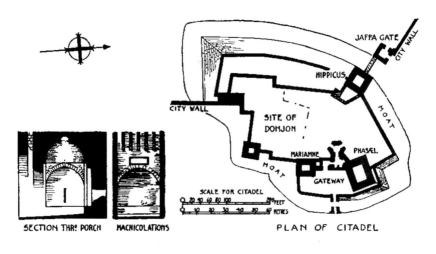

SECTION THRº PORCH   MACHICOLATIONS

PLAN OF CITADEL

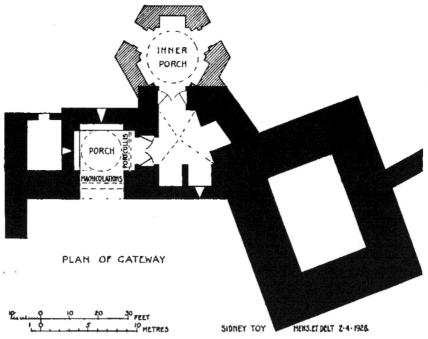

PLAN OF GATEWAY

SIDNEY TOY   MENS. ET DELT 2·4·1928.

Jerusalem: The Citadel

the chapel was rebuilt about 1170 after being severely damaged by earthquake in that year. The powerful range of buildings on the south side of the upper ward was a complete and independent unit forming the donjon of the castle and its last line of defence. It dominates the whole fortress and the field beyond in all directions. Here was the residence of the Grand Master and his principal knights, and its halls are richly decorated with delicate mouldings, rib vaulting and tracery. The provision for the supply and storage of water in this castle was on a very liberal scale. There was one large and deep well, nine capacious rain-water tanks, and a large open reservoir in the space between the two curtains on the south.

The immense strength of the upper ward of this castle was proved during the siege by

Bybars in 1271. After storming and mining the walls and towers for nearly a month, the sultan gained the outer ward, but there his forces were brought to a halt. Behind their powerful fortifications the knights resisted all the efforts of the enemy to proceed further, and it was only by resort to an ignoble artifice that entry was effected. A forged letter, purporting to be written by a friend to the Grand Master, and stating that Tripoli had fallen and that further resistance was therefore useless, was introduced within the walls. Probably all the more ready to be deceived on account of their exhausted condition, the garrison gave credence to the note and surrendered the castle.

Ghastei-Blanc (*Safita*), between Le Krak des Chevaliers and the sea, consists of a large donjon, of about 1200, defended by two lines of walls. The curtain walls are now very ruinous and obscured among the houses of a modern village, but the donjon is practically intact, and towers up above the surrounding houses like the cathedral above the city of Beauvais. It is of two vaulted storeys – the lower storey (built as a church and still used as such by the Orthodox Greeks) is a particularly lofty structure of three bays with a barrel vault and a semi-circular apse. The upper storey is fortified, and the flat roof has a battlemented parapet.

At Sidon, on the coast below Beyrout, there are two castles, one on the land and the other on an island a short distance out from the shore. The latter is connected to the mainland by a bridge, the passage on which could be severed at will. Both castles were built in the thirteenth century and are now very ruinous.

The citadel of Jerusalem, with its powerful towers and walls and its vast stores of grain and water, was unquestionably the stronghold of the city during the Latin occupation from 1099 to 1187. It incorporates what remains of the three towers, Hippicus, Phasael and Mariamne, built by Herod the Great and spared by Titus in AD70. Phasael, sometimes called the Tower of David (a name formerly applied to the whole citadel), still stands to the height of about 30 ft. above the ground, surmounted by later work. The ancient portion is built of megalithic masonry. In respect of the other two ancient towers, it is not so clear how much, if any, of the original masonry remains above the foundations. Generally the walls and towers of the citadel are built of mat embossed ashlar masonry which is so characteristic of crusader work; and in the recent clearance of debris and

Damascus: Wall and Tower of the Citadel from without

Aleppo: Gateway to the Citadel

accumulation carried out in the citadel evidence of crusader buildings has been brought to light; but, owing to the reconstruction by the Saracens of much of the upper parts of the walls and towers, it is now difficult to determine how much of the Latin work remains. The main gateway on the east side of the citadel was built in the latter part of the twelfth century and was probably the work of Saladin, bearing, as it does, strong resemblance to his work at Cairo. A deep ditch surrounded the whole fortress.

In addition to the three towers above mentioned there are two others, on the south side of the citadel, and all five are connected by a curtain wall enclosing a bailey. On the west, where the fortress is exposed beyond the city wall, the curtain is doubled. The donjon, which stood within the bailey, has been destroyed.

The main gateway is built on a Z plan, involving two turns in the passage through. The outer entrance is defended by a row of machicolations, concealed within the archway,

and the passage is further obstructed by a portcullis and two sets of heavy two-leaved doors. The hexagonal inner porch, rather of ornamental than of defensive character, was added in the sixteenth century. The main gateway is defended by a barbican, and there is an outer gate, built in the fifteenth century, and a drawbridge.

Damascus was by-passed by the armies of the first crusade, and was never long held by the Latins. Its citadel was built by the Saracens in the early part of the thirteenth century on the site of a much older fortress, some walls of which it incorporates. Standing on level ground within the city, it is entirely destitute of natural defences, and its walls and towers are therefore of a particularly powerful character. It has a trapezoidal plan, with exceptionally high and thick walls, defended at the corners and at short intervals along the sides by huge rectangular towers, strongly built and vaulted at each storey. Mural galleries with arrow-loops run through the walls and at the summits of the towers there are two tiers of battlements.

At Aleppo the citadel stands on a hill in the middle of the town, and is further defended by a wide and deep ditch which could be flooded at will. It occupies an ancient fortified site; but the existing buildings date principally from the thirteenth century and were built entirely by the Saracens. All are now in a very ruinous condition with the exception of the gatehouse.

The gatehouse, on the south side of the hill, is well preserved, and is one of the finest and most imposing of all the mediaeval gates. It was built in the thirteenth century, but refortified at a later period when the box machicolations were added. There is an advance gate, built on the counterscarp of the ditch; and from this a bridge of many arches across the ditch rises steeply to the main gateway – a huge and formidable structure, defended by machicolations across the whole front. The entrance arch is actually a tall and deep recess, with the doorway to the passage on the right flank. The passage follows a serpentine course through the building, involving four right-angled turns and the negotiation of three doorways. The inner portion of the gateway is divided into two sections, the first being a wide pillared hall and the second an open portico.

NOTE

1. *Vide* "The Castles of the Bosporus" by the Author, *Archaeologia*, Vol LXXX, 1930.

Chapter 9
Transitional Keeps of the Twelfth Century

During the whole of the twelfth century there was a constant stream of military forces passing to and fro between Europe and the Levant. The war between the Crusaders and Saracens, far from being confined to the main crusades, was incessant, and the expeditions to Palestine continuous. On their return from these expeditions the Crusaders proceeded to apply to their own fortification the knowledge and experience they had gained in their recent campaigns abroad.

The rectangular keeps and towers built at this time in Western Europe had the great disadvantage of presenting vulnerable corners to the sapper and the battering-ram, since the enemy could be attacked from one side only, and was sheltered by the corner itself against attacks from the other side. In the Levant the towers were often circular or multangular, and therefore presented no screen to the enemy at any point. On the other hand, a rectangular plan is much more convenient for the disposition of the rooms inside a building than a circular plan; and the development of the latter plan from the former was very gradual in Western Europe. It was not until the return from the third crusade at the end of the twelfth century that round keeps were built generally.

Meanwhile many keeps of a transitional character, containing some of the advantages of both forms, were built, and conspicuous among them are those at Houdan, Seine-et-Oise; Provins, Seine-et-Mame; Gisors, Eure; Fitampes, Seine-et-Oise; Orford, Suffolk; Conisborough, Yorkshire, and Longtown, Herefordshire.

The donjon at Houdan was built about 1130. On the inside the plan is square with splayed corners, but on the outside it is circular with four projecting turrets. There are two storeys, each of great height; the ground floor was the store room. On the upper floor was the

Houdan: Donjon from the south-west

Provins: Tour de César from the south-east

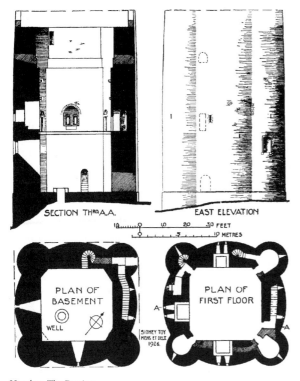

SECTION THRO A.A.   EAST ELEVATION

18......0   10   20   30 FEET
0   5   10 METRES

PLAN OF BASEMENT

WELL

PLAN OF FIRST FLOOR

A-   -A

SIDNEY TOY
MENS ET DELT
1926.

Houdan: The Donjon

carried up on all sides 16 ft. above the level of the gutter, to protect the roof.

The present entrance to the donjon, broken through the wall at ground level, is modern. The original entrance doorway is in the north turret, 50 ft. up from the ground, and was reached by a draw-bridge from the wall-walk on the curtain wall of the castle (now destroyed) which passed near the donjon at this point. From the doorway a straight mural stairway on the left leads up to the great hall. From here there are two spiral stairways: one (already referred to) leading up to the battlements, and the other (opening off from one of the chambers) descending to the basement. The wall between the entrance to the donjon and this last stairway has been broken through to allow ascent from the modern entrance. There is a well in the basement and a latrine in the second storey.

Keeps built in the middle and the latter part of the twelfth century often occupied strategic positions on a curtain wall of the castle, as at Conisborough and Gisors. When standing within and detached from the curtain, they were often surrounded by a narrow court and high wall, called a chemise. The approach to

great hall with chambers, formed in three of the turrets, opening off from the hall. The fourth turret contains a spiral stairway leading from the hall to the battlements. The walls are

Étampes: The Donjon from the south

Conisborough: The Keep from the west

the keep was then by a gateway in the chemise to the narrow court, and by a flight of steps built against the inside face up to the wall-walk on the chemise. At one point in this wall-walk a short wall with a drawbridge at the end was thrown across the court between the chemise and the entrance to the keep; and it was across this narrow path that the enemy must defile, exposed to attack from all directions, if he would gain his objective. The Tour de César, Provins, and the donjons at La Roche Guyon, Rtampes, and Chatillon-sur-lndre were all built on the design.

The Tour de Cesar at Provins was built about the middle of the twelfth century, and remains today one of the most interesting and best preserved of the transitional keeps. It stands upon a mound, and is surrounded by a battlemented wall, or chemise, which at one point extends down the mound to the bailey, enclosing a vaulted stairway of approach. Internally the plan of the tower is similar to that of the donjon at Houdan, but externally it is square at the base and octagonal above, with

four semi-circular turrets rising from the corners of the base.

The entrance was first by a vaulted stairway up the mound to the space between the chemise and the tower. From here a stairway led to the battlements of the chemise, and thence to a causeway and drawbridge across the interval between the chemise and the entrance doorway to the tower. From this doorway a short flight of steps, guarded on one side, led up to the great hall on the upper storey. In the upper part the chemise was taken down, and the causeway to the tower replaced by steps up from the court.

The donjon is of two storeys, both covered with stone vaults which are domed on the underside and flat on the upper surface. The lower storey, or basement, consists of a large room, lit by narrow windows placed high in the wall, and a mural chamber which was probably a prison. From one side of the large room a mural passage and steep flight of steps leads down to a well.

In addition to the great hall the upper storey has four chambers, which are formed in the turrets and do not open directly from the hall, but from mural passages opening from window recesses or stairways. A doorway in the middle of each of the north, east and west walls leads straight through to a small outside platform. M. Viollet-le-Duc suggested that from these platforms three other drawbridges and causeways radiated towards the chemise.[1] But while such an arrangement, presenting to the enemy on gaining the chemise, four points of attack on the tower instead of one, would be totally contrary to the principles of mediaeval defence, the shape of the platforms (incorrectly drawn in the Dictionnaire) and the remains of the enclosing walls indicate that these structures were fortified turrets. As seen from the toothing on either side, the small bracket-shaped platforms were each enclosed by a wall, probably with three arrow-loops to the field. Both the fireplaces in the hall and in the basement beneath are of later date.

From the hall one stairway leads down to the basement and another up to an external gallery, which runs

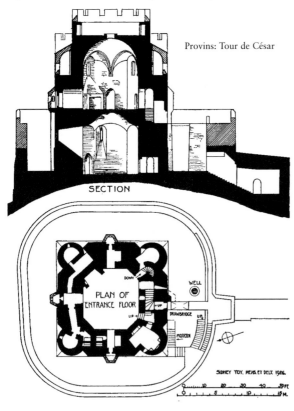

Provins: Tour de César

SECTION

PLAN OF ENTRANCE FLOOR

WELL

DRAWBRIDGE

MODERN

SIDNEY TOY. MENS. ET DELT 1926.

round the outer face of the upper part of the hall, and had loopholes (now destroyed) to the field. From this level, narrow mural stairways, constructed round the back of the dome, led first to the battlements on the turrets and then, higher up, to those on the summit of the tower, which were of two tiers. Since the external gallery occupies the usual position of windows, the hall is lit by a large circular eye in the crown of the dome, 35 ft. above the floor. The present battlements and pointed timber roof were built in the seventeenth century, and the original disposition of the summit is a question of conjecture. But it is most probable that the eye was open to the free passage of light, as in the Tour de Constance at Aigues Mortes, the screen walls which rose high above the vault being considered adequate defence against enemy missiles.

At Gisors the donjon built by Henry the Second of England replaced, and stands partly upon, the foundations of an older tower, built with the shell wall some fifty years before. It has an irregular octagonal plan,[2] is strengthened at the angles by massive buttresses, and is of four storeys. The original

Château d'Étampes: The Donjon

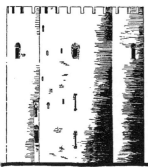

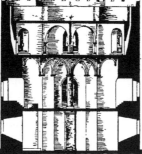

SOUTH EAST ELEVATION   SECTION

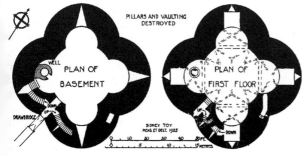

entrance stands only 8 ft. above the ground, and was reached by steps up from the court. Near this entrance there is a postern through the shell wall; and both the entrance to the donjon and the postern are screened behind one of the great buttresses of the donjon.

From the old entrance doorway a straight stair, built in the wall, led up to the second storey, and from here a spiral stairway rose to the upper storeys and the battlements. The ground floor (now broken into by a doorway) originally had neither window nor ventilation, and must have been reached through a trap-door in the second storey. Each of the upper storeys has one window, and at one of them there are two latrines, but there is no fireplace on any floor. Towards the end of the fourteenth century a separate spiral stairway, with the entrance at the head of a broad flight of steps and a doorway to each of the upper floors, was built in a turret against the east side of the donjon, the turret rising high above the battlements. The old entrance and mural stairs were then blocked.

The donjon at Étampes (another form of transition dating about 1160) is a large quatrefoil building of three storeys. Its floors and roof, originally supported by a central pier rising in stages from ground floor to roof, were all destroyed long since. The ground floor (where there is a well) had a timber ceiling; but the second storey (forming the great hall) was covered with a very fine interlacing ribbed vault, vestiges of which still remain. As a screen for the roof, the walls are carried high above the upper storey.

The entrance doorway is placed midway between the level of the ground and that of the floor of the second storey, and was probably reached by way of a wall and drawbridge, projected out from the chemise. The chemise has been destroyed. The doorway opens to a passage which has a mural stairway on the right and another on the left, that on the left leading down to the basement and that on the right to the upper floors. The entrance passage goes straight through the wall, so that an enemy who had

95

forced an entry and, unaware of the trap, had rushed straight ahead would fall on to the pavement of the basement 12 ft. below. The great hall was a handsome and lofty apartment. The well pipe was evidently carried up from the basement, with a drawing place here; and there is a latrine opening off one of the lobes, but there was no fireplace. From the great hall another mural stairway led to the third storey, and from there a spiral stair rose to the battlements. The third storey formed the living quarters. It has two fireplaces, a lavabo and a latrine.

Orford keep was begun in 1166 and finished in 1170. The plan is circular internally, but externally it has a multangular body from which project three large square turrets, spaced at equal intervals apart. A forebuilding, containing the entrance porch at second storey level, a basement below the porch and a chapel above it, is built in the angle between the south turret and the main body of the keep. The keep consists of a basement and two upper floors. The walls are carried up high above the level of the gutter, to defend the roof; and the turrets rise about 20 ft. above the battlements of the main body of the keep. In the basement there is a deep well, which is lined with dressed stonework and has handholds and footholds cut into the stonework for descent to the bottom.

The entrance into the keep is by a straight flight of steps into the porch, and from the porch a passage, barred by two doors, leads to the central hall of the second storey. Both this hall and that above in the third storey are well lit, and each of them has a fireplace. One of the turrets contains a spiral stairway running from the basement to the battlements. The others contain chambers; and since these chambers, if made the same height as the halls, would be disproportionately lofty, they are sub-divided into two storeys for one of each of the halls. The lower chambers in the turrets are entered by mural passages opening from the window jambs in the halls, and the upper chambers by mural passages leading round the walls from the stairway. One of the chambers of the second storey was the kitchen. It has two large fireplaces and a sink. The turrets have two tiers of chambers above the level of the roof gutter, one of the chambers containing a double oven.

Conisborough, one of the finest keeps in England, was built about 1180–1190. It is a tall cylindrical tower with very thick walls supported by six massive buttresses, the buttresses rising to the full height of the building. It consists of a vaulted ground storey, or basement, and three upper floors. Neither the first nor the second storey has any windows; and the only access to the former (which contains a well) is through a large hole in the centre of its vault. The entrance doorway is at the second storey, and is approached now by a modern flight of steps up from the courtyard. Originally there appears to have been a similar flight of steps leading up to a drawbridge before the doorway. From the second storey a mural stairway, rising concentrically with the wall, leads up to the third storey, and a similar stair rises to the fourth storey and the battlements. Each of the third and fourth storeys has a two-light window, a large fireplace and a stone lavabo basin; and there is a latrine opening from it by a sinuous passage. A vaulted chapel with a small sacristy, built partly in the wall and partly in a buttress, is entered from the east side of the fourth storey.

The battlements are now very ruinous, but it is clear from the parts which remain that the encircling wall and the buttresses were carried up to form a screen round the roof, and that there were two fighting lines: one from a gallery which runs round the roof at gutter level, and the other from the upper battlements, about 12 ft. above the gallery. Three small vaulted chambers and an oven, all formed in the buttresses, opened on to the gallery. The oven (like those at Orford in the same position) was probably for the use of the fighting forces, as well as for domestic purposes. It is 5 ft. 8 in. diameter, 3 ft. 7 in. high to the crown of its domical roof, and has a rectangular recess 6 in. deep in its floor. One of the three vaulted chambers was a dovecot, and is pierced by numerous holes about 6 in. square. It is probable that the gallery was covered by a vault or roof, for it had an inside wall 3 ft. 8 in. thick. Two stairways led from the gallery to the upper battlements.

The keep at Longtown, built about 1180, has also a cylindrical nucleus, but here the circular wall is supported by three half-round buttresses, one of which provides the necessary thickness for a spiral stairway and another for the flue of a fireplace. The keep stands on a high mound. It is of two storeys, and has a battered plinth 12 ft. high. The entrance doorway has been destroyed, but it appears to have been in the lower storey, the floor of which was about level with the top of the plinth. It was approached by a flight of steps up from the foot of the mound.

Differing from most of the oilier keeps of this period, the principal room at Longtown was on the ground floor. This room had three windows, each of two lights, and a wide fireplace. In one jamb of each of the windows there is a large cupboard recess. The upper room was relatively low, was lit by loopholes only, and has no fireplace; a doorway on one side opens to a latrine. The spiral stairway rises from the ground floor to the battlements. Here also the walls are carried up sufficiently high to mask the roof.

Reichenberg, Bohemia, has a keep of similar plan to that at Longtown.

Skenfrith Castle, Monmouthshire, built about 1190–1200, has a cylindrical keep with one semi-circular projection on its face. Here the projection is exclusively for the accommodation of a spiral stairway which was too large to be constructed within the wall itself. The upper part of the building has been destroyed. At present the keep consists of a

basement and two upper floors. The basement was lit by narrow loopholes placed high in the wall, and must have been entered through a trap-door in the floor above. The entrance doorway was at the second storey, and the spiral stairway ascended from this level. Excavations made in 1925 showed that the mound is artificial, composed of rubble and sand; but the foundations of the keep are carried down through this material to the natural soil beneath.

Trim Castle, Meath, Ireland, dating from the early years of the thirteenth century, has a keep of the same period, which is of transitional form though not so highly developed as the above examples. This keep consists of a square nucleus with a square turret projecting out from the middle of each side, the four turrets (one of which has been destroyed) thus commanding all the corners of the main body of the structure. The keep rises up from the top of the mound of an earlier fortification, but it is clear that its foundations are carried down to the natural soil beneath, for the walls of both the main body and the entrance tower on the east are built round and incorporate the material of which the mound is composed. Only the other projecting towers have basements. These basements are approached by

Plans of Trim Castle

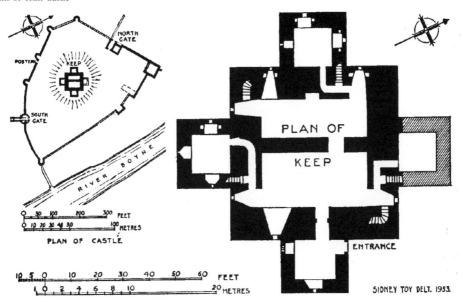

SIDNEY TOY DELT. 1953

97

Trim Castle: The Keep from the south-east

bridge, the drawbridge working between two high crenellated walls connecting the gate with the barbican. The passage through the gate is flanked by half-moon guardrooms, the walls of which are carried up to the full height of the gatehouse, giving the whole structure a similar form to that of the outer gate of the Blackgate at Newcastle.[3]

The keep of Castle Rushen, Isle of Man, has a similar plan to that of Trim, but here the wings have been added to an older square keep, dating from the latter part of the twelfth century. The south and west wing towers were built about 1200 and those on the north and east about 1340, the tower on the east being a tall gatehouse spread across nearly the whole of that face of the old keep.

stairs leading down from mural passages at the entrance floor, while stairways at two corners of the main body rise from the same level to the upper storeys.

The south gate of the castle is defended by a drawbridge and a small barbican beyond the

NOTES

1. *Dictionnaire Raisonne de l'Architecture*, Tome V, 64.
2. Enlart, *Manuel d'Archeologie Francaise*, Vol. II, 505, and Armitage, *op. cit.*, both incorrectly describe it as decagonal.
3. *Vide The Castles of Great Britain*, Sidney Toy, p. 150.

Trim Castle: The gatehouse from without

Chapter 10
Fortification and Buildings of the Bailey in the Eleventh and Twelfth Centuries

The curtain walls surrounding the baileys of the eleventh and twelfth century castles were sometimes perfectly plain, and had no other defence than their battlements, as at Eynsford in Kent and Trematon in Cornwall. But in many cases they are strengthened at strategic points by square towers, projecting on the outside. The wall-towers were spaced either widely apart, as at Ludlow, or concentrated on the more vulnerable side of the castle, as at Richmond, Yorks. Later in the twelfth century the towers were built closer together in order to command more effectively the panels of wall between them, as at Dover. At Gisors two of the wall-towers on the west side of the castle, dating about 1180, are built with prows, like the cutwaters of a bridge, the prows being carded to the full height of the tower.

When the castle stands upon high ground the curtain wall follows the irregular contours of the site, as at Ludlow and Richmond; but when upon level ground it is built with long straight sides, as at Skenfrith and Sherbome. The curtain wall at Skenfrith is composed of four perfectly straight sides, with a tower at each corner – the tower at one of the sides, built solid up to the wall-walk, is a later addition. Each of the corner towers consists of a basement and one upper storey; and it is worthy of note that the floors of the upper storey in all of the three remaining towers (one has been destroyed) were on exactly the same level, as though they had been set out by some delicate and precise instrument.

On level sites the curtain was surrounded by a moat, as at Sherbome, or defended partly by a river and partly by a moat, as at Skenfrith. But when standing on a hill the castle is generally defended on one or more sides by precipitous rocks or steep declivities. The moat was then confined to the side of the castle where the approach was more gradual, and the entrance gateway was usually placed on that side.

The defence of all fortifications in ancient and mediaeval times was principally from the battlements of the walls, gateways and lowers. But arrow-loops, or meurtrieres, made in the curtain at a level below the battlements, were introduced as early as 215BC, as already shown. They were described by Philo of Byzantium, about 120BC, and were built in the fortifications of Rome in the fourth and in those of Dara in the sixth century of our era. They do not, however, appear to have been in general use in Western Europe until the twelfth century, and not until the end of that century to have been built in the upper battlements.

Arrow-loops enabled the defenders to shoot at the enemy outside the fortress while they themselves remained unseen and safe from attack behind its walls. When built below the wall-walk each of them consists of the loophole (a narrow vertical slot on the outside face of the wall with deeply splayed inner jambs) and a recess in the wall behind the loophole for the accommodation of the archer. The splayed sides of the hole enabled the archer to direct his fire towards either flank as well as in front; and, since the sill was deflected steeply downwards from inside to outside, he commanded the ground below. The recess was often provided with one or two seats.

In the ancient form the outer hole was a simple vertical slot, those made at Syracuse in 215BC being 4 in. wide by 6 ft. high; and this

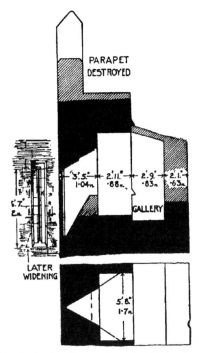

PARAPET
DESTROYED

GALLERY

3'.5.'
1·04m

2'.11."
·88m

2'.9.'
·83m

2'.1.'
·63m

5'.7.'
2m

LATER
WIDENING

5'. 8."
1·7m

Kenilworth Castle: Plan, and sectional elevation of battlements of keep

round three sides of the keep at this level. All the existing loopholes are in their original condition, except that in each case the lower third of the hole on the outer face is cut away so as to form a large triangular shaped foot, 2 ft. 6 in. wide at the base. The cutting was probably done during the civil wars of the thirteenth century in order to give the crossbows then in use greater lateral range. The cutting is roughly executed in the loopholes on the south side of the keep, but more skilfully done in those on the west. In each of those on the west a cross slot was also cut at the same time.

In their original condition the slots were from $\frac{1}{2}$ in. to 1 in. wide and from 5 ft. 6 in. to 6 ft. 7 in. high. The recesses for the archers are from 5 ft. to 5 ft. 3 in. wide by 7 ft. high to the crown of the heads, and contain stone seats built across the inner angles of the recesses.

Towards the end of the twelfth century the holes were generally constructed with small triangular feet, and were occasionally bisected by a short horizontal slot, giving the whole the form of a cross, as at Skenfrith and Trematon, both of about 1190, that at Trematon being inserted in older work. The horizontal slots, which were widely splayed at the back, gave the archer a wide lateral sweep for his arrows and bolts, and were introduced especially for the use of the crossbow. The loopholes in the battlements of the keep at Pembroke Castle, built about 1200, are cut square at the base. In all cases the enlargement of the base of the loophole was made to give the archer wider range when shooting low.

During the thirteenth century the loopholes were usually terminated both at the base and head by circular enlargements; and if there was

simple form was maintained in the earliest examples of the Middle Ages, though the width of the loop was reduced. Even after other forms were in constant use, and side by side with them, the simple slot was still employed, as about 1270 at Corfe, where are arrow-loops $1\frac{1}{2}$ in. wide by 12 ft. high. In the keep of Kenilworth Castle are arrow-loops, constructed about 1130, which pierce the walls immediately below the wall-walk in line with the roof gutter, and were entered from the gallery which passed

Arrowloops

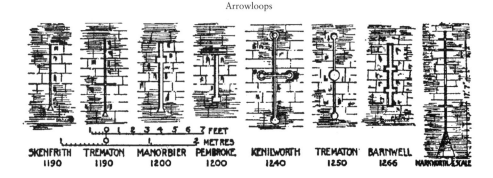

0 1 2 3 4 5 6 7 FEET
0   2 METRES

| SKENFRITH | TREMATON | MANORBIER | PEMBROKE | KENILWORTH | TREMATON | BARNWELL | WARKWORTH ½ SCALE |
| 1190 | 1190 | 1200 | 1200 | 1240 | 1250 | 1266 | |

a cross slot that also had a similar termination at either end, and in the water tower at Kenilworth. Sometimes the cross slot is omitted and its place taken by a circular hole, as at the gatehouse at Trematon, about 1250. At Bamwall there are two square-cut cross slots but none at the head or base. At the Grey Mare's Tail tower, Warkworth, are arrow-loops so long that they extend through two storeys of the interior. There are three cross slots to each loop and at the foot the loops are spread out to give lateral range for attacks on sappers.

WINDOWS

On the second storey of the gatehouse at Exeter are two windows, grouped together, which in design follow the Saxon tradition, and date about 1070. They go straight through the wall, have triangular heads and shallow recesses on the outer faces. But generally the windows of the upper, or living rooms of the eleventh century were from 12 in. to 18 in. wide by about 4 ft. high. They had round or flat external heads, flush with the external face of the wall; and their internal jambs and round rear arches were either splayed or opened out in order. The windows were set in wide and lofty internal recesses. Among the best preserved examples are those of the keeps of Loches and Colchester. At Canterbury the upper windows of the keep have each a series of three internal recesses or orders. The outer faces of these windows are so ruinous that it is

not possible to determine their original form. Generally light was considered to be of much less importance than safety.

The light admitted by the small windows and through the thick walls of the keeps at Loches and Colchester must have given but poor illumination to the great halls within. But on the other hand, while such windows could be quickly and effectively closed by shutters, even when open the danger from enemy missiles was relatively small. In the twelfth century, however, it was felt that more light to the living apartments was desirable; and the first effort in this direction (apart from increasing the width of the openings) was to make two openings in one recess, as in the donjon at Houdan, about 1130. Here the lights are each 1 ft. wide by 3 ft. 4 in. high and placed in the recess 2 ft. 9 in. apart. The recess is very wide, and is provided with seats on all three sides. There were similar windows in the keep at Longtown, about 1180, though here the wide mullions between the lights have been torn away.

At Conisborough, about 1190, the twin lights of the windows are much larger than those at Houdan or Longtown, each of the lights being 1 ft. 10 in. wide by 4 ft. 8 in. high; and, since the walls of the keep are very thick, the recess behind the lights is correspondingly deep. The lights at Conisborough are recessed inside for shutters, and the mullion has a projection in the middle, with a hole for the horizontal bar which secured the shutters when

Windows

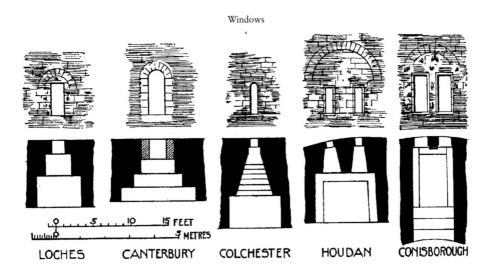

LOCHES   CANTERBURY   COLCHESTER   HOUDAN   CONISBOROUGH

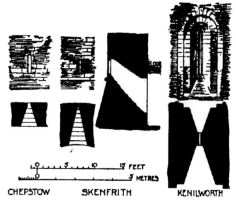

CHEPSTOW   SKENFRITH   KENILWORTH

Basement windows

Colchester Castle: fireplace in the keep

closed. When at a later period windows were constructed with much larger openings they were first defended by iron stanchions and saddle bars and subsequently by strong iron grilles.

The windows of ground floors (generally inserted for the purpose of ventilating the storerooms there) were narrow single openings. In the early examples the small openings were flush with the outside face of the wall, and the inner jambs and rear arches were widely splayed. Often their sills were deflected down rapidly from outside to inside. The lower windows of the north tower of the Chateau de Foix, those of the old hall in the middle bailey at Corfe and in the keep at Chepstow, all dating from the eleventh century, are perfect examples of their period.

In keeps these ground floor lights were generally mere loopholes, placed so high out of the reach of sappers that they were often above the level of the floor of the second storey, their inner lintels and sills being deflected rapidly downwards through the wall to the level of the rooms they ventilated, as at Canterbury, La Roche Guyon, and Skenfrith. In the twelfth century the openings were sometimes splayed on the outside as well as within, as in the keep at Kenilworth, about 1130, and that of Lydford, about 1150.

FIREPLACES

Fireplaces of the eleventh century were plain arched openings with semi-circular backs. Their flues, after rising up a short distance within the wall, passed through to the outside face, and terminated in one or two loopholes, the loopholes being generally concealed in the inner angles of buttresses. The lower courses of masonry at the backs of the fireplaces, where combustion occurred, were built of selected stones, often laid in herringbone work, as at Colchester and Canterbury.

Very little alteration was made in the design of fireplaces from the eleventh century until about 1180. From the early part of the twelfth century the jambs were enriched with small shafts and the arches with chevron mouldings, as at Hedingham and Rochester. But although the fireplace often projects out slightly from the wall and has a straight moulding at the head, as at Rochester, there is no real hood. Again, although in snell-keeps the flues were carried up through the wall to the wall-walk (a relatively short distance from the upper floors), the practice of carrying them through the wall to the outer face still persisted in rectangular keeps in the latter part of the twelfth century, as at Newcastle. At Newcastle, however, there is a change in the shape of the fireplace, the semi-circular plan giving place to straight backs and splayed sides.

The fireplaces in the keep at Conisborough, about 1190, show a marked development. The flues pass up to the top of the wall, where they terminate in a chimney, and the jambs carry a

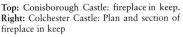

Top: Conisborough Castle: fireplace in keep.
Right: Colchester Castle: Plan and section of fireplace in keep

position they first took the form of hoards – or brattices – timber platforms projected out from the battlements in times of siege, which, in one form or another, had been in use from about 1500BC. By the end of the twelfth century AD temporary hoarding gave place in many new fortifications to machicolations in stone; but it was not until the end of the thirteenth century that this custom became general, and hoarding was employed at a much later date in older castles. As constructed in stone, the parapets were built out on corbels, the corbels being spaced sufficiently wide apart to allow for a large hole, or machicolation, between each pair of corbels.

The gateway into the bailey was generally a substantial building of two or three storeys, and was approached from across the moat by means of a causeway, often built upon arches, and a drawbridge. In addition to the main gateway there were usually one or more posterns, placed in such positions that escape could be effected or sally made from them unobserved by the enemy. At Dover there are two gateways in the curtain of the inner bailey, one at the east and the other at the west; and each of them was defended by a barbican.

The gateway at Exeter Castle, built about 1070, projects entirely outside the curtain of the bailey, while that at Ludlow, about 1090, with only a slight projection on the outside extends about 40 ft. within the bailey. In each case the gateway is surmounted by a tall strong tower which was virtually the keep of the castle.

The gateway at Exeter consists of a main body of three storeys and a lofty barbican which projects a short distance outside the entrance arch. The passage through is spanned at either end by a round arch of two orders, 10 ft. 3 in. wide. The outer arch is now blocked, and its details obscured; but it was probably defended by a two-leaved door, secured by a timber bolt. A moat passed along the curtain in front of the gateway, and was doubtless spanned at the entrance by a drawbridge. The barbican is formed by two deep buttresses, which project out in line with the lateral walls of the gateway, and an end wall built on a lofty arch spanning the space between the buttresses

flat arch, or lintel, built of voussoirs with joggled joints. Above the lintel there is a tall hood. Here the hood was a necessity of construction rather than an intentional development of design. For since the fireplace forms a chord across the circular chamber in which it is built, any wall upon the lintel to enclose the flue must naturally fall back against the sides of the chamber as it rises. But from this period hoods, projecting well out into the chamber and supported on either side on corbels or shafts, were built to fireplaces generally.

GATEWAYS

Gateways of ancient and Roman periods have been described in previous chapters. From, early times they were defended by portcullises and machicolations, as well as by stout doors. Machicolations were holes formed in the roofs of gateways and entrance passages through which boiling pitch, stones, darts and other missiles were thrown down on the heads of the enemy below. When over the entrance to the gateway, they also enabled the defenders to quench fires lit by besiegers to burn down the gates; and this appears to have been their original purpose. Flavius Vegetius, writing about AD390, says : "It is necessary also to have a projection above the gate with openings from which one can pour water on the fire which the enemy has lit."[1] Machicolations were also built on the crests of walls and towers to repel the operations of sappers at the base. In this

Exeter Castle: The gatehouse

at the height of the second storey. The battlements of the barbican were entered from the third storey of the main building, and formed a powerful fighting platform, commanding not only the field and both flanks, but also the entrance to the gate below. The upper storeys of the gatehouse must have been approached from the curtain wall, for there is no stairway from the entrance passage.

The gatehouse at Ludlow Castle, called the great tower, is one storey higher, and much more substantially built, than that at Exeter. About a hundred years after it was built a new entrance was made through the curtain near the tower, and this gateway passage was blocked at both ends, was covered by a stone vault and converted into a prison. The cross-arches of the gateway have been destroyed, and the north wall of the tower has been rebuilt; but as the result of investigations made in 1903–4 the original disposition and plan of the gateway passage have been recovered.[2]

The passage was divided by a cross-arch and

doorway into a short entrance porch, 8 ft. 6 in. long, and a passage 29 ft. 6 in. long; both the porch and the hall being enriched by wall arcades. Between the hall and the porch there is an unusual form of wicket-gate or sally port. A small doorway in the hall opens to a short mural passage, which leads round the side of the great doors and opens by another small doorway into the porch. The upper storeys of the tower were approached by a straight stairway constructed in the thickness of one of the side walls, and entered directly from the bailey. It is probable that the outer porch was commanded from above by a machicolation in the floor of the second storey, and was a kind of barbican; but alterations have removed all direct evidence of this arrangement.

The Bâb Al-Futuh, the Bâb An-Nasr and the Bab Zuwaylah in the city walls of Cairo were all built in 1085–1091. Each of these gates has a wide passage defended by two towers and a powerful two-leaved door. Between the door and the inner arch there is a large hall with vaulted recesses for the guard on either side. The towers of Bâb An-Nasr are square on the outer face: those of the other two gates are semi-circular.

The gateway of Sherbome Castle, built about 1120 by Roger, Bishop of Salisbury, is one of the most perfect of its period. It projects principally outside the curtain. Originally it consisted of the gateway passage and two upper

Cairo: Plan of Bâb Al-Futûh

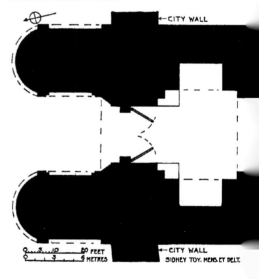

Cairo: Bâb An-Nasr from without

storeys : the present top storey was added at a later date. This gatehouse was exclusively for the use of the porter and the guard, for the rectangular keep and living quarters within the bailey are contemporary with it. The gateway passage has only one barrier, a two-leaved door, placed about a third of the way through from the outside, and there was no portcullis. The flanking walls of the passage are solid except at the end towards the bailey, where there is a small porter's lodge on one side and a spiral stairway to the upper floors on the other. The second and third storeys were for the use of the guard, and from the third storey doors open on either side to the wall-walk on the curtain. Recent excavations have brought to light remains of what appear to have been a succession of gates and connecting passage-

ways projecting out in line from the north wall of this castle.

The gateway of the castle of Newark-on-Trent, built 1123–1148, is of three storeys, and was defended simply by a two-leaved door placed midway in the passage : there was no portcullis. The upper storeys were reached by a spiral stairway which was entered from the bailey. This gatehouse appears to have been the keep of the castle.

The south gateway of Launceston Castle, built about 1160, is flanked by round towers, which project outside the curtain, and are built solid for their full height. The gatehouse (which must have extended some 20 ft. within the bailey) has been destroyed, with the exception of the outer wall and flanking towers. It appears to have been two storeys in height above the gateway. The towers projected so far beyond the outer doorway that they formed a narrow entrance, commanded from their battlements on either side. A portcullis passed down immediately in front of the doorway. This gateway was defended by a long and narrow barbican, which crossed the moat on low arches and was pierced by arrow-loops on either side.

The gateway to the inner bailey at Longtown, about 1180, is also flanked by solid round towers which project well out from the curtain wall. It probably did not extend into the bailey, consisting only of the existing portion and such rooms (now destroyed) as stood above it. The inner face of the curtain has been torn down at this point. At present the only barrier is a portcullis, set about two-thirds of the way through the narrow passage; but whether or not there were any doors beyond the portcullis there is not sufficient evidence to show.

Among the most scientifically designed gateways of the latter part of the twelfth century are those built by Saladin at Cairo,

1170–1182; and the finest of them is in that portion of the city walls on the north known as Burg Ez-Zefer. On the curtailment of the city on this side, the portion of the curtain, with its gateway and towers, which was cut off by the new wall was abandoned and allowed to fall into ruin.

The gateway at Burg Ez-Zefer projects entirely on the outside of the wall, and has its entrance on the flank and not on the front face, involving a right-angled turn in the passage. Close to the gateway there is a wall-tower and immediately on the other side of the tower a postern. The curtain at this point was defended by a wide moat and the gateway was approached by a bridge of two spans : the first from the outer bank to a stone pier in the moat and the second from the pier to a broad stone platform which fills the space between the gateway and the tower. The second part was probably a drawbridge which could be raised, but more probably drawn back on to the platform. The approach to the entrance was therefore strongly defended. For even if an

Château Gaillard from the south

Cairo: Burg Ez-Zefer: The east gateway

Cairo: Gateway of Burg Ez-Zefer

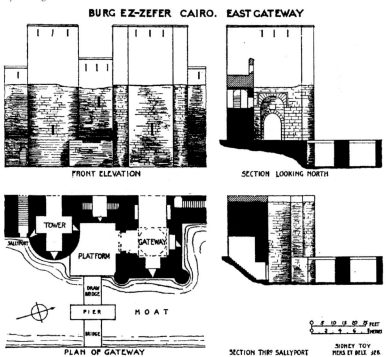

BURG EZ-ZEFER CAIRO. EAST GATEWAY

FRONT ELEVATION

SECTION LOOKING NORTH

PLAN OF GATEWAY

SECTION THR? SALLYPORT

SIDNEY TOY
MENS ET DELT. 928.

107

enemy had gained the platform, and had begun to assail the gateway, he would find himself, in a confined space, under deadly fire from the arrow-loops in the tower at his back, the curtain on his flank, and from the battlements on all sides. He was also open to attack from those issuing from the postern at his back.

The passage through was defended by a machicolation spanning the full width of the gate and by a two-leaved door secured by a long and stout timber bar. Piercing the arch above the door there are four holes about 4 in. square and 2 ft. apart. They are on the same plane as the door. Their purpose is somewhat obscure, but they were probably connected with some form of portcullis (for which there is ample room in the deep tympanum above the door) that could be dropped down in position in the event of the wood doors being broken through or destroyed by fire. The gateway and the curtain in which it stands are built of ashlar with a strong concrete core.

HALLS

Generally the buildings within the bailey include a large room, called the great hall, for the common life of the garrison. The hall sometimes stood near the middle of the bailey, but more often it was built against the curtain wall, the wall forming one of its sides. A kitchen generally stood near the hall, if not adjacent to it; and there was often a well near the kitchen. In some early examples the hall was virtually the keep of the castle; and such was the great oblong hall built by William Fitz Osbern at Chepstow about 1070.

The hall at Chepstow Castle, called the keep, stands on a narrow tongue of rock between the river Wye and a deep ravine. It is a powerfully built structure consisting of a basement and two upper storeys, and measuring internally 89 ft. long by an average of 30 ft. wide. It tapers slightly from one end to the other. The walls on the east and south, the most vulnerable sides, are much thicker than those on the other two sides. Though the upper storeys were re-modelled in the thirteenth century by the insertion of new windows and a transverse arch, the walling is original and retains the original windows in the basement and the internal wall arcading on the south and west sides of the second storey.

At Richmond Castle, Yorks., there is a long rectangular hall in one corner of the bailey which is contemporary with the earliest part of the curtain wall, about 1070–1080. Scotland's hall, as this building is called, with the living rooms and domestic offices adjoining, was the headquarters of the lord of the castle. The existing keep on the opposite side of the bailey was not built until the following century.

At the castles of Sherbome and Devizes, both built about 1120 by Roger, Bishop of Salisbury, the hall and its domestic offices were built within the bailey, near the keep and well away from the curtain walls. The hall at Sherbome is still standing though ruinous. It is part of a group which stands in the middle of the bailey, built round a square courtyard. The hall is in the north range, the domestic offices are in the east range and the other buildings, now destroyed, were on the south and west; the great rectangular keep occupies the south-west corner of the group. At Devizes the hall has been destroyed to the foundations. It was a large building with arcades on either side dividing it into a central nave and two aisles.

The hall of Leicester Castle, built about 1150, also has a nave and two aisles, though here, while the walls are of stone, the pillars and struts between the nave and aisles are of oak. It stands within the bailey with its axis running north and south, and, though considerably altered, its original disposition is dear. On the south of the hall were the kitchens, destroyed in 1715, and beyond the kitchens there is a vaulted undercroft measuring internally 50 ft. by 18 ft. The living quarters, now destroyed, were doubtless on the north side of the hall.

Constables hall at Durham, built against the north wall of the castle about 1170, is, despite later alterations, a well preserved and elegant structure of its period, of great length and height. It is of two tall storeys. The entrance is at the lower storey through a large and richly decorated doorway, which owes its almost perfect preservation to the fact that it was blocked for many years. It has a round head of five orders, alternately wide and narrow, and jamb shafts with cushion capitals. Two wide spiral stairways lead to the upper storey, the Old Constables hall now called the Norman Gallery. This is a very long room with arcades on both sides, and, though now divided, appears to have been originally open from one end to the other. The arcades have alternately

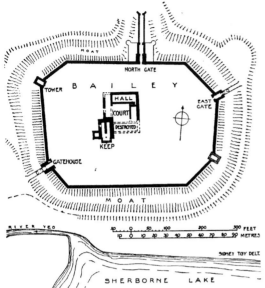

Plan of Sherborne Castle

large and small arches, the former opening to windows and the latter to recesses. All are richly decorated with chevron mouldings, and spring from detached shafts with scalloped abaci. The windows were originally twin lights with round heads.

CHAPELS

The chapel held an important place in the life of the castle. In many cases it was included within the keep, as described above. When not in the keep it generally stood in the bailey, as at Durham and Gisors. At Richmond, Yorks., the chapel, dating from the eleventh century, is in one of the wall-towers of the curtain; and in each of the castles at Bamborough, Castle Rising and Ludlow, all dating from the twelfth century, it stood isolated in the bailey. The circular nave of the chapel at Ludlow is embellished with wall arcades and elaborately moulded arches.

The old chapel of Durham Castle, built in 1072 against the north wall of the bailey, is a particularly beautiful little structure. It consists of a nave, with an arcade of four arches on either side, and two aisles. The round arches of the arcades are supported on tall circular pillars with capitals carved in grotesque figures, and moulded bases. The stone paving is original. It is laid in herringbone pattern, except for a path down the centre of the chapel, where the stones are set square.

The small chapel at Gisors was built about 1175 in the inner bailey, with its apse against the curtain wall and its nave standing out into the bailey. It was dedicated to St. Thomas a Becket. All but the apse has been destroyed, but that fragment indicates a very pleasing structure of dressed stone, the walls being of two tiers, separated by a string course, the lower tier with plain walls divided into bays by wall-shafts and the upper tier pierced by windows with moulded jambs and arches.

NOTES
1. Vegetius, Bk. IV, cap. 4.
2. *Archaeologia*, 1908, 257–328.

Chapter 11
Castles from about 1190 to 1280

The arduous campaigns of the Third Crusade resulted in a further development in military architecture, in Western Europe as in the Levant. Weak points in some of the existing fortifications had been clearly demonstrated. The crusaders had seen the great execution wrought by the powerful siege engines on both sides and the dire effects of sapping and mining, and realized that a more scientific plan than that hitherto adopted was essential.

The site now chosen for a new castle, where such choice was possible, was the summit of a precipitous hill, the citadel, or inner bailey, being backed against the cliff. The main defence was concentrated in the direction of approach; and here there were often two or even three hues of advance fortifications. Chateau Gaillard, Eure, built 1196–1198; Pembroke Castle, about 1200; and Beeston Castle, Cheshire, about 1225, are all of this order. In the case of castles already built, one or two outer baileys were added on the line of approach, as at Corfe and Chepstow. The living

Pembroke Castle from the air

quarters, with the hall, domestic offices and chapel, were now all built in the court of the inner bailey. The keep (often no longer the ordinary residence of the lord but essentially his last line of defence) is smaller than those built previously, but of more powerful and scientific design.

Among the first of these castles was the Chateau Gaillard, which stands on a precipitous cliff 300 ft. above the River Seine. It was built by Richard the First of England, and when complete in 1198 was one of the most powerful castles of the day. The statement that on the completion of the work Richard exclaimed: "*Ecce! quam pulchra filia unius anni*" (Behold! what a beautiful daughter of one year) rests solely on the authority of a chronicle of about 1436, accredited to John Brompton, a work which contains many fables, and about which Sir T. D. Hardy said: " There is no reason to believe that it was based on a previous compilation." The building accounts make it clear that the construction occupied three years.

There is no mention of the keep being used for defence, or of any resort to it, in the siege of 1203–4, and it is doubtful if it was complete at that time.

The castle consists of three baileys arranged in line, the inner bailey being on the edge of the cliff. The outer bailey (which had a triangular plan with the apex pointing towards the field) was completely surrounded by a moat, and there was a moat between the middle and inner baileys. The curtains of both the outer and middle baileys were strengthened by circular wall-towels. The curtain of the inner bailey has no wall-towers, properly so called, but on its outer face are a continuous series of corrugations, from the battlements of which the whole piece of the wall could be swept by flank shooting.

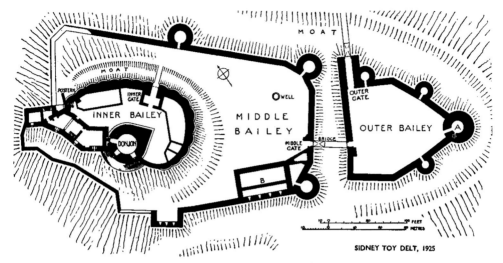

Plan of Château Gaillard

The donjon stands on the edge of the precipice, principally within, but partially projecting outside, the inner bailey, the portion outside rising up from a ledge of rock 40 ft. below the level of the courtyard. It is circular, except that the side towards the courtyard is thickened and shaped like the prow of a ship. The prow faces in the direction most vulnerable to attack from the sapper and the battering-ram. It formed a triangular wall, the full height of the tower, which might be attacked and its outer portion partially destroyed without serious effect to the inside of the donjon. Further, since it pointed directly towards the enemy, its oblique

Château Gaillard: The Donjon facing the Prow

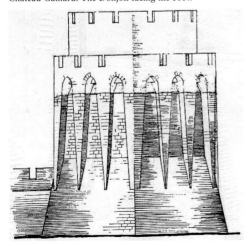

surfaces would deflect without receiving the full force of his projectiles. Additional protection against sapping was obtained by a deep battered plinth and by machicolations, now destroyed, which were supported on buttresses rising up the face of the donjon from the plinth to the battlements. If the summit was designed as these buttresses indicate, then this is one of the earliest examples in Western Europe of stone machicolations at the battlements. At present the donjon consists of two complete storeys, the lower storey being a store-room and the upper a guardroom. Above this level the walls have been destroyed, but apparently they were only carried up to a height sufficient to screen the roof, most of the corbels of which remain, and to form the battlements. Having regard to the position of the roof corbels on the inside and the inclination of the buttress like projections on the outside, there can be little doubt that the design proposed two tiers of battlements, one rising above and behind the other.

The entrance to the donjon was by means of flights of steps (now destroyed) up from the courtyard to a doorway in the upper storey. In this room are two windows, each of two lights; but there are no wall chambers, and there is no fireplace. From here descent to the lower floor and ascent to the floors above must have been by timber stairways, all long since destroyed, for there are no stairways in the walls.

In design and construction this donjon is of a purely military character, though no doubt

111

living rooms were designed for the floors above; but its main purpose was for observation and defence. The great hall, living rooms and domestic offices are built in the courtyard near the donjon; while other structures, now represented by foundations only, stood against the curtain in other parts of the bailey.

At La Roche Guyon, twenty miles further up the Seine, there is a donjon with a prow similar to that at Chateau Gaillard, but with plain instead of buttressed surfaces. It probably dates from the last half of the twelfth century, and a few years earlier than that at Chateau Gaillard. It stands on high ground, backed on to a precipitous escarpment, while the main buildings of the castle are on the river bank below the cliff. Ascent from the latter to the donjon was by way of a series of subterranean stairways and narrow ledges cut through and into the rock. All the existing buildings of the castle are of a period subsequent to the events recorded by Abbot Suger as having taken place at La Roche Guyon in 1109.[1] The château beside the river dates principally from the fifteenth century, though some parts of it are of the same period as the donjon.

The donjon consists of a central tower, a chemise and an outer wall, the outer enclosing the greater part of the chemise. All three are prow-shaped, and have their prows pointing in the same direction – away from the cliff and towards the line of approach. Though both of the outer walls were of considerable height, the central tower rises high above them. In the space between the tower and the chemise there is a well. A large portion of this space was roofed over, forming stores below and a wide fighting platform above, the platform running round the prow of the tower. There were therefore three tiers of battlements, one at the walk on the outer wall, the second from the chemise, and the third, high above the others, from the top of the central tower.

The entrance to the central tower is at second storey level, reached by steps up from the court. The basement, had neither light nor ventilation, and must have been entered through a trap-door from above. The second storey received its light through two loopholes, which externally are actually side by side with the windows of the third storey; but, their lintels and sills being deflected steeply down through the thick wall, they open out internally [o the second storey.

La Roche Guyon: Plan of the Château and section through Donjon

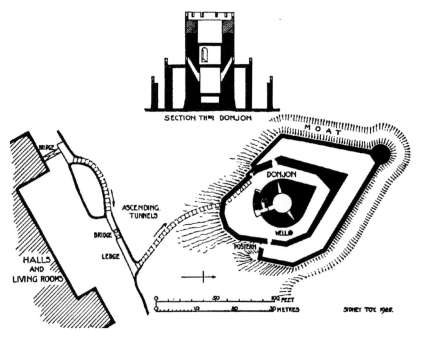

SECTION THRU DONJON

MOAT

DONJON

ASCENDING TUNNELS

BRIDGE

BRIDGE

LEDGE

WELL

POSTERN

HALLS AND LIVING ROOMS

50   100 FEET
10   20   30 METRES

SIDNEY TOY 1928.

Here also, though the tower is practically complete, there are neither wall chambers nor fireplaces; but a spiral stairway, formed in the thickness of the wall, rises from the second storey to the battlements, with a doorway to each floor.

At Pembroke the inner bailey of the castle, including the keep, was built about 1200 or in the early years of the twelfth century, and the outer bailey during the first half of the thirteenth century. The castle stands on a promontory at the junction of two rivers, the inner bailey being at the head of the promontory. Where the castle is protected by the rivers and their precipitous banks the curtain is relatively thin; but on the side towards the land it is 'thicker', and strengthened at intervals by strong circular towers. One long section of the outer wall was doubled at a later date. The halls and living rooms were in the inner bailey near the keep.

The keep, though by no means the largest, is one of the most impressive of these round towers. It is 54 ft diameter externally, its wall has an average thickness of 14 ft, and, rising through four storeys to the height of 80 ft., is crowned by a stone dome. The entrance was at the second storey, and was approached by flights of steps, constructed in a narrow forebuilding and ending in a drawbridge before the doorway. From the second storey a spiral stairway, constructed in the thickness of the wall, leads down to the basement and up to the upper floors and battlements. To compensate for the loss of strength occasioned by the stairway, the wall at this point is 19 in. thicker than elsewhere. At present the keep is entered at basement level by an opening which has been cut through the wall from outside into the stairway; and since a hole, made for a bar, occurs in the cutting, it has been suggested that the opening is original. But this is clearly not the case. The opening is driven roughly through an unusually massive plinth, 10 ft. high and 20 ft. thick at the base, and the hole for the bar was made for the door then inserted.

There are no windows in the basement, and the only light admitted to the second storey comes through two loopholes. Even the third and fourth storeys have only one window each in addition to loopholes. There is an original fireplace in each of the second and third storeys. At the battlements there are two

fighting platforms, one at the summit of the outer wall and the other above the crown of the dome. When put in state of defence, hoarding was built out in front of the lower parapet; and the holes for the brackets of the hoarding are still to be seen all round the keep. The dome is strongly built, is about 3 ft. 6 in. thick at the crown and powerfully backed at the haunches. A round tower of the outer bailey near the gateway also has a dome of similar construction at its summit.

A weak point in the design of many of the early round keeps was that there was only one doorway to the exterior. In the event of that doorway being carried by assault the position of those within was desperate; there was no escape. At Pembroke provision is made for such a contingency by a postern at the third storey which led out on to the battlements of buildings, now destroyed, near the living quarters.

The round donjuns built in France, in the early part of the thirteenth century were often vaulted in every storey, and had a postern in addition to the entrance doorway. The Tour du Prisonnier at Gisors, 1206, is of three storeys, and is vaulted in each storey. It stands at the corner of the curtain wall of the old castle, and is entered, at third storey level, from the wall-walk on the curtain on one side, and has a postern at the same level to the wall-walk on the other side. From the third storey stairways lead to the lower and upper floors.

At Rouen the Tour Jeanne d'Arc, built 1207, is also of three storeys; but here the interior has been extensively restored and the upper storey rebuilt. Apparently both the first and second storeys were vaulted originally. The base of the tower is solid, and the floor of the first storey is about 25 ft. up from the ground. At this storey there are two doorways, both reached originally by flights of steps up from the courtyard; and from here the upper floors are gained by a spiral stairway built in the thickness of the wall. Both this tower and the Tour du Prisonnier were residences as well as forts, each containing a large fireplace, a well and a latrine, that at Gisors having an oven behind the fireplace.

At the Tour du Coudray, Chinon, a round donjon of this period, mural stairways (here concentric with the wall) as well as the space inside the entrance doorway are commanded by machicolations which pass straight up through the wall to the wall-walk. The passage from the entrance doorway is not carried straight through to the interior, but, taking a sharp turn to the left immediately inside the doorway, rises by steps to a second doorway on the right; and at each turn there is a rectangular machicolation covering the whole space above. By this arrangement an enemy who had forced the doorway found himself checked in the passages and stairways by a deadly rain of missiles from above, while the defenders on the battlements could fight against the enemy within as well as those without the donjon.

The keeps now being built in Western Europe were generally cylindrical. But at Issoudun in France, about 1200, and Araberg, Austria, about 1230, they have prows, as at La Rochc Guyon, the prow at Araberg Castle being particularly long and sharply pointed. At Ortenberg, Bavaria, the keep, dating from the first half of the thirteenth century, is trapezoidal with a prow formed on the shortest side. Ortenberg Castle consists of three baileys. The inner and middle baileys are arranged in line north and south, the inner bailey being on the north. The outer bailey occupies a long and relatively narrow space, running north and south in front of the other baileys. Its gateway is at the north end, and therefore commanded by the defences of the inner bailey which rise high above it. There is a considerable rise from the outer to the middle and from the middle to

Chinon: Tour du Coudray

the inner bailey; and the approach is so formed that an enemy entering the gateway would be forced to pass through the whole length of the outer bailey in the teeth of attack from the inner and middle baileys in succession. Having arrived at the south end of the outer bailey, a turn northward, a long flight of steps, a barbican, and three other gateways had to be negotiated before the inner bailey was reached. The keep stands on the highest point in the middle of the inner bailey, the walls of which so closely surround it as to form a chemise. It commands all parts of the castle inside the walls, as well as the approaches from the outside.

The formation of approach ways in such a manner that they insured the greatest possible exposure to the enemy, as well within as without the castle, and the fullest defence to the garrison, was a prominent factor in mediaeval defence, and was often carried out with great address, as seen here at Ortenberg,

In Ireland there are several keeps, built during the first half and the middle of the thirteenth century, which have a rectangular plan with a round tower of bold projection and of three storeys at each corner, as at Carlow, Co. Carlow; Ferns, Co. Wexford; and Lea, Leix.

Some castles of the early part of the thirteenth century had a rectangular form with a tower at each corner, another in the middle of three of its sides and a gateway in the middle of the fourth side. One of the corner towers, built on a larger and more elaborate scale than the others, was the keep. The castle at Dourdan, Seine-et-Oise, built about 1220, is designed on this plan; and the inner bailey at Najac, Aveyron, built 1250–1260, is of similar character. In the latter, however, the buildings incorporate at one corner a square tower of about 1100. Here, the plan being oblong, there are lateral towers on the long sides only, and the gateway stands but a short distance from one of them and was under its command.

It was now realized that, if the defence was to be effective, the keep must be not only the place of last resort but the point from which all operations could be directed, and that as well after the enemy had penetrated into the bailey as while he was outside the walls. At Najac the curtains all round the inner bailey were provided with an elaborate system of stairways

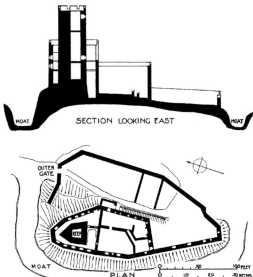

SECTION LOOKING EAST

PLAN

Ortenberg Castle

and passages, some apparent and others concealed, by means of which the defence forces could be rushed from one part of the fortification to another as the situation might dictate. All the operations could be directed from the great round donjon at the south-east corner of the bailey. Each section of the internal defensive system could be isolated from the others by means of barriers; so that if an enemy had penetrated into the courtyard, and had carried by assault one section of the curtain, that section could be cut off from the other defences.

Najac stands on the summit of a high hill, and is one of the most imposing, as it is one of

the most powerful, castles in the south of France. The donjon is of three storeys, vaulted and pierced by arrow-loops at each storey. By the provision of doorways at every storey the contact between the donjon and other parts of the castle was complete. There is an entrance at ground floor level, originally protected by a moat and drawbridge, and from this level a spiral stairway leads to the upper floors and the battlements. At the second storey, which forms the great hall, there are two outer doorways, one leading to a mural passage in the south curtain and the other to some building in the bailey now destroyed. At the third storey there are also two outer doorways, one to the battlements of the south curtain, and the other to those of the east curtain.

Some circular keeps were completely isolated outside the bailey by an encircling moat, spanned by a drawbridge. At Lillebonne, Seine Inferieure, the donjon, built about 1220, stood isolated at one corner of the castle and was entered by a doorway at ground floor level, the doorway being reached from the courtyard by a drawbridge across the moat. The donjon at Coucy, destroyed by the Germans on their retreat in 1917, was also isolated from the other buildings of the bailey

Château de Najac from the east

Château de Najac: Plan of the inner bailey

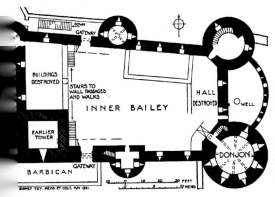

Aigues Mortes: Tour de Constance

Château de Coucy: The Donjon

by a moat, but here it interrupted one of the curtain walls, and was not completely outside the bailey.

The donjon at Coucy was at once the largest, strongest and the most magnificent of all mediaeval round towers. It occupied more than three times the area and was more than twice the height of the keep at Pembroke. It was built during the second quarter of the thirteenth century. It was of three storeys, all magnificently vaulted, and was a complete residence, having a well, fireplaces and latrines. Light was admitted to the interior through a large circular eye in the vault of each storey. The entrance was on the ground floor, and was defended by a drawbridge over the moat, a machicolation, a portcullis and two doors, and there was a postern on the second storey. The postern opened on to another drawbridge, thrown at great height across the moat between the donjon and a chemise, the chemise passing round on the outside of the moat in semicircular form to connect the curtain on one side of the donjon with that on the other. The whole of the active defence of this donjon was conducted from the battlements, where there were arrow-loops and corbels for hoarding.

The corner towers of the bailey at Goucy were designed with very great skill. Circular externally, all storeys above the basement were hexagonal internally with wide recesses opening off from each face, the recesses adding greatly to the size of the rooms. The plan of each of the upper storeys was so disposed that its sides, and therefore its recesses, passed across the angles of that below; so that the arrowloops in the recesses being set in alternate vertical planes provided the greatest possible range all round the tower. In addition, the even distribution of loads formed a great protection against the effects of sapping. The basements are circular both on the outer and inner faces, and their thick walls are strengthened by tall plinths.

At Aigues Mortes there is an enormous circular donjon, the Tour de Constance, which stands isolated by an encircling moat at one corner of the fortifications and was built about the middle of the thirteenth century. Here the donjon was originally a castle in itself, for the town walls, whether or not they entered into the original design, were not built until the last quarter of the thirteenth century.

The Tour de Constance consists of two storeys of large vaulted halls and a small basement. It is surmounted by a tall turret and beacon which were added about 1300. The walls of the tower are 19 ft. thick, and present a severe face to the exterior, being pierced only by arrow-loops and two small windows. Light is admitted to the interior halls and the basement through the large circular eyes, one in the centre of each vault, the uppermost piercing the flat roof. The entrance, reached from the town by a bridge over the moat, and the postern, on the opposite side opening directly over the moat, are both on the level of the floor of the lower hall. Each of them is defended by a portcullis and two doors. The entrance also has two machicolations and the postern one machicolation. Even if an enemy had passed these barriers and had entered the lower hall, he would still be under heavy fire on all sides from the openings of a mural gallery, which is carried round the hall 20 ft.

above the floor level, and from the hall above through the eye in the vault. The battlements of tills tower were adapted later for the use of artillery.

At Bothwell, Lanarkshire, the defences centred round a giant circular keep placed at one corner of a pentagonal bailey. Bothwell Castle stands on a promontory formed by a sharp loop turn in the Clyde, and was defended by precipitous banks on the sides towards the river and by a ditch on the land side. It was built in the third quarter of the thirteenth century, and the inner half of the keep is of that period. The outer half, from basement to parapet, was thrown down when the castle was laid in ruins. In 1336 Bothwell was again put in a state of defence and extensive works of building undertaken. A new wall was built from east to west across the middle of the bailey, and that portion of the castle south of the line only was retained and refurbished. The gap in the keep was closed by a straight wall built diametrically

Bothwell Castle: The keep from the Bailey

117

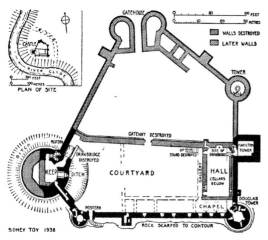

Plan of Bothwell Castle

across it. In a siege of 1337, though great damage was done to some other parts of the castle, the keep appears to have suffered little further injury.

Valence Tower, as the keep at Bothwell is called, stands on the extreme point of the promontory, commanding the river in both directions. It was 65 ft. in diameter externally, was octagonal internally, and the remaining half still rises to the full height of four storeys, the first storey being a basement below the level of the bailey. A deep moat on the bailey side isolated the keep from the other buildings of the castle. The entrance is at the second storey, and is skilfully placed near the curtain at the north end of the moat. Here a pointed projection stands out from the keep, and the doorway is set on that side of the projection next the curtain, so that the approach is in line with and close against the curtain, and is commanded by the wall-walk above. The doorway was defended by a drawbridge across the moat, a portcullis and a door, the drawbridge and portcullis being operated from a small vaulted chamber over the entrance passage. Above the chamber the projection out from the keep terminates in a semi-pyramidal spur.

The entrance passage, taking a turn to the right, leads into a fine hall, having a large window, enriched by jamb shafts, to the courtyard. Rising from corbels at the angles of the walls, and forming arches on the octagonal faces of the interior, are labels which at first appear to be wall ribs for vaulting, but which

are most probably only decorative arches. In any case the floors were of timber, that of the second storey, and probably also that of the third, being supported in the centre by an octagonal pier, the lower portion of which still remains in the basement. The floor of the second storey was also supported on stone arches thrown across the keep diagonally from the central pier to the walls on either side. A doorway on the south side of the hall opens to a passage leading to a latrine, and another on the north side to a spiral stairway leading down to the basement, where there is a well, and up to the upper floors and the battlements. The third storey (relatively plain in character) was probably the military quarters, and the fourth storey, with a large window of two trefoiled lights to the courtyard, the chief living room. The timber floor of the fourth storey and the roof of the tower were each supported on bulky wall posts, chases for which are to be seen in the walls, with wide spreading struts.

The parapet has been destroyed, but on the north side of the keep at the summit, high above the entrance doorway and the wall-walk on the curtain, are four boldly projecting corbels, spaced about 2 ft. 6 in. apart. They are the remains of a machicolation of three apertures, two of which commanded the entrance to the keep and the third the exit from the spiral stairway to the wall-walk on the curtain.

The wall-walks on the curtains leading north and south from the keep were protected by parapets both on the outer side and on the side towards the bailey, and were covered by high pitched roofs, the lines of the verges of which remain on the wall of the keep. The doorway leading out to the wall-walk on the north was closed against the keep and secured by a strong timber bar on the outer side, so that in the event of the entrance to the keep being forced its defenders could escape on to the wall-walk on the curtain and bar the door against the enemy. There are two posterns in the walls near the keep, one on the north side and another on the south.

Clifford's Tower, York, standing on the mound of an earlier castle, is a quatrefoil-shaped keep resembling the donjon at Etampes. There is no doubt but that it dates from the thirteenth century, though the "official guide" to the tower ascribes it (largely on account of its shouldered arches) to the fourteenth century. Shouldered arches occur both in England and France in the twelfth and in the early pan of the thirteenth century, as at Ludlow and Proving, in the twelfth, and Warkworth and Coucy in the thirteenth. The chapel (obviously of thirteenth century date) has suffered from violence and distortion, and two of its walls were rebuilt in the seventeenth century. The arcade against the keep was probably set in position after the wall behind it was built, and both it and the arch at the west have been altered. But the east arcade, now partly buried at the south end, is clearly contemporary with the wall in which it occurs, and there is no reason to suppose that the keep is of later date than the chapel.

This keep was built during the third quarter of the thirteenth century. The details, not only of the chapel but of the corbels at the base of the turrets and of the arrow-loops throughout, before mutilation, are unquestionably of that period. At the base of the turrets are large corbels, set at intervals, instead of a series of corbel courses forming a conical bracket, as in the later work at the outer gate at Harlech and the water gate at Beaumaris. Originally the arrow-loops were long slots 10 in. wide with a circular enlargement at the foot. The present square openings at the head, some roughly cut, were formed at a later period to give light to the interior which must have been very dark hitherto, the only original windows being two with pointed heads on the upper floor, now partly blocked.

The tower is of two storeys, and is entered at ground level through a forebuilding. The floor of the upper storey and the roof (both now destroyed) were supported in the centre by a pier, the foundations of which were found about seventy years ago. Both storeys are round by arrow-loops, placed so that those in the upper storey are in vertical plane midway between those of the ground floor. Two spiral stairways lead from the ground floor to the upper floor and the battlements, and two other stairways, formed in turrets at the re-entering angles of the lobes of the tower, rise from the upper floor to the battlements, the turrets rising from large corbels at upper floor level. The forebuilding is of three storeys, the first being the entrance porch, the second the chapel with richly moulded arcades, and the third a small chamber from which the portcullis was operated.

At the castle at Angers, Maine-et-Loire, the strength of the fortifications was concentrated largely on the curtain walls, built 1228–1238. The walls are constructed of slate bonded at

York: Cliffords Tower from the north-east

intervals by courses of dressed sandstone and granite, the alternate arrangement giving them a strong banded effect. They are of great height and strength, and are defended by powerful towers placed at short intervals in the wall. Both walls and towers have widely spreading battered plinths rising to about half their height, the plinths standing upon rock which is scarped to their contour. Not only are these walls powerful in themselves, but despite the fact that most of the towers have lost their upper parts, the general effect today is most imposing and awe-inspiring.

In many castles built in the early part of the thirteenth century the keep was omitted entirely, reliance being placed on the strength of the fortifications as a whole.

Beeston Castle, Cheshire, built about 1225 and now a shattered ruin, appears to have had no keep. It is perched on a high hill with sheer precipices on three sides and a steep slope on the fourth. The strength of Beeston lies largely in its inaccessibility. The castle consists of an inner bailey on the summit of the hill and a large outer bailey on the sloping ground which stretches away to the east. The curtain of the inner bailey was defended by three wall-towers, two of them, with the gatehouse, being set on the line of approach, away from the precipice and towards the outer bailey. Further protection on this side of the inner bailey is secured by a ditch about 30 ft. deep and 35 ft. wide, which has been cut through the natural rock from one precipitous side of the hill to the other – no small engineering feat for that period.

The Chateau de Boulogne, completed in 1231, has no keep. It is built on a polygonal plan, with towers at the corners and a gateway, flanked by towers, on one of the sides. The internal buildings are ranged against the curtain round a courtyard. The castle was

Angers: The Château from the south

surrounded by a moat, and was defended from arrow-loops, opening from tiers of mural passages in the curtain, as well as from the battlements.

Of the same order also are the castles of Maniace at Syracuse, and Ursino at Catania, built by the Emperor Frederick the Second in Sicily during the first half of the thirteenth century. Both these castles are designed on a square plan, with towers at the corners, and, in the case of Ursino, an intermediate tower in the middle of each side. The internal buildings stand against the curtain round a courtyard. At Ursino contact between the lower and upper floors is secured by spiral stairways constructed in two of the towers, the other six towers being occupied by chambers. At Maniace, where there are no intermediate towers, there are four stairways, one in each tower. This castle was defended on all sides by an outer wall.

The defence by double curtains, as adopted at Le Krak des Chevaliers and Maniace, was applied with great address in the thirteenth century to the fortifications of Carcassonne. Before that period the fortifications of Carcassonne consisted of a single line of

defences and a citadel or castle, the curtain wall and wall-towers dating from Roman and Visigothic times, repaired in the twelfth century. The weak points in these defences having been demonstrated during the Albigensian war, and in the siege of 1240, extensive additions and repairs were begun in 1247 and continued for about forty years.

The existing curtain was extended at one end, and many of the towers and gateways were rebuilt, six of the new towers, including those flanking the Narbonnais gate, having pointed beaks on the outer face. In addition, a second curtain with wall-towers was built all round the fortress outside the first, leaving a relatively narrow terrace, called the *lists*, between the two walls. At the north end of the town this terrace is commanded by a large and strong wall-tower which projects partly across it, and, at a point on the south where the two walls approach closely together, by a tower spanning the space from wall to wall and blocking the lists save for a passage which is defended by barriers and machicolations. So that in the event of the lists being carried by assault, its over running by the enemy was checked at these two points. On the

Carcassonke from the air

east side, where the fall of the ground is more gradual than on the west, a wide moat runs along in front of the outer wall from the north end of the town to the south end.

The citadel was also strengthened and a strong barbican added, the barbican extending down the hill beyond the walls and ending in a large circular outwork. In addition to the two gateways, one on the east and the other on the west side of the town, each of them piercing both curtains, there were six posterns in the inner wall and at least one in the outer wall. The posterns were placed in obscure positions and so high in the wall that they could only be reached by means of ladders.

In these works every known artifice and perfection of military architecture was employed, every contingency provided for. When complete, about 1285, Carcassonne was a formidable fortress, well deserving its widespread renown.

Castles such as those perched on the top of the hills overlooking the Rhine and those on isolated hills and rocks in the mountainous parts of Germany, Austria and Spain have strong natural defences in the sites they occupy.

The castle of Monte Agudo, near the city of Murcia in the south of Spain, is an example among many of such fortifications in that country. It dates from the latter part of the eleventh century, but was partly rebuilt and restored in the sixteenth century. Though very powerful in itself, being constructed with strong walls supported by massive buttresses, its defence depends largely on its inaccessibility, being perched on the summit of a precipitous hill.

Carcassonne from the south-west

Falkenberg from the west

In the Upper Palatinate of Bavaria, Germany, are some castles built on the top of a huge natural pile of boulders, as Falkenberg, dating about 1290. This castle stands on a massive pile of rocks at the end of a promontory overlooking the River Waldnaab, the promontory being cut through in two places on the line of approach. The entrance was by a bridge which crossed the last ditch between the counterscarp and a tall pillar of masonry, built up from the bed of the ditch near the castle wall. From here a drawbridge, placed at right-

Falkenberg: Entrance to castle showing pillar in ditch for the bridge

Plan of the Château de Chillon

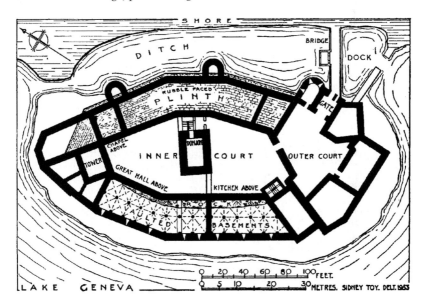

123

Raffenstein: The stronghold

angles to the bridge already crossed, spanned the gap between the pillar and the entrance doorway, which is in one of the lateral faces of a projecting tower. The curtain follows the

contour of the pile of rocks, and the buildings of the castle are formed between it and a small internal courtyard. A square tower, the donjon of the fortress, stands within the courtyard.

Some small strongholds in these mountainous, sparsely populated and insecure districts consist simply of a wall of masonry built across the mouth of a cave, as at Rappenstein, or on the overhanging narrow ledge of a cliff face, as at Kropfenstein, both dating from the early part of the thirteenth century, and both in the Eastern Province of Switzerland. At Loch in Bavaria, near the north bank of the Danube, a rectangular hall is built up inside the deep mouth of a cave, a tunnel running laterally from the mouth to an outwork and some smaller caves; further in from the cliff face is a spacious and lofty cavern. This retreat is defended by a tall and strong round tower, which stands out from the cliff before the mouth of the cave, a wall running down to the tower from the cliff face. Some castles are built on a rock within a lake, and are protected by the waters of the lake surrounding them. Such is the Chateau de Cnillon on Lake Geneva. Others, built on level ground on restricted sites within a city, are isolated within a wide moat, as the Chateau des Comtes at Ghent.

The Chateau de Chillon stands on an isolated rock off the east shore of the lake. It occupies a most beautiful site, the lake at this end having high mountains on either side. The castle is entered by a bridge spanning the ditch between the rock and the shore, and there is a small dock on the south side of the bridge. The earliest parts of the existing buildings, dating probably from the eleventh century, are the donjon and the greater portion of the wall surrounding the inner court. A remarkable feature of this early structure is the powerful plinth protecting the east, the more vulnerable, side of the fortress. It has a steep batter and extends from a level high in the inner wall down to a line beyond the outer face of the outer wall. Actually it covers the irregularities of the rock which, if left exposed, would facilitate attack. During the twelfth century the castle was considerably enlarged, a tower (called the

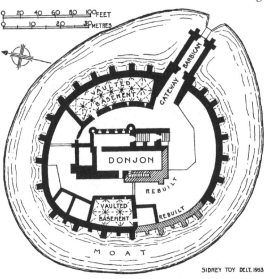

Ghent: Plan of the Château des Comtes

Château de Chilllon from the lake

Kropfenstein: The stronghold

Loch: Tower at entrance to cave

Tour du Due) added on the north, and an outer wall with ranges of buildings between that and the inner wall constructed all round the fortress. Extensive alterations were carried out about the middle of the thirteenth century when the wall-towers were built along the east wall. Below the buildings on the west side of the inner court, which include the great hall and the kitchen, is a magnificent range of tall vaulted basements, the vaults being supported by rows of round pillars in the middle, and rising from wall-shafts on the west and the natural rock on the east.

The Chateau des Comtes, Ghent, dates principally from about 1180. It has a relatively large rectangular donjon in the centre of an

Ghent: Château des Comtes from the south west

oval court, and is defended by a powerful curtain wall and a moat. Ranges of buildings with vaulted basements are built along the inside face of the curtain. During the fourteenth century the gateway was strengthened, bartizans were built on the buttresses of the curtain at the level of the wall-walk, and the whole castle was refortined. John of Gaunt was born here in 1340. In 1780 the castle was sold and converted into a factory, and was subsequently reduced to a state of ruin, floorless and roofless. The whole structure has been thoroughly restored in modern times, the destroyed parts rebuilt and new floors and roof inserted.

NOTE
1. Vita Ludouid Grossi Regis, cap. XVII.

Chapter 12
Weapons and Siege Operations of Later Roman and Mediaeval Times

The weapons, siege engines and siege operations of ancient and early Roman times have been described in previous chapters. During the later Roman periods and the whole of the Middle Ages until the introduction of artillery similar weapons, developed on more powerful lines, were still used and the same methods of sapping and mining employed. There is abundant evidence to show that as the barbarians came into contact with civilized nations the former studied and adopted the weapons and tactics of the latter, often improving upon them. Domitian found the Germanic tribes rather hasty in this respect, with the result that their first attempts were crude.[1] But at the siege of Rome AD537, the siege engines brought up by the Goths inspired wonder and terror in the hearts of the citizens as, standing behind the battlements, the Romans watched the advance towards the walls of great engines and tall siege towers from all sides.[2] Again, when in AD885 Rollo laid siege to Paris it was with the siege engines of his day.[3]

Among the hand weapons in use during the Middle Ages the bow and arrow still held a strong position, and that long after the introduction of the crossbow. The crossbow came into prominence in European warfare early in the twelfth century. It consisted of a wood stock, similar in form to the butt of a musket, and a bow fixed to one end of the stock. In the earlier forms the bow was made of wood or a composition of wood, horn, sinew and glue, but after about 1370 it was made of steel.[4] The bowstring was stretched by means of a lever or a small windlass, and the bolt, or quarrel, was released by a trigger. The wounds inflicted by this weapon were considered to be so barbarous that its use was proscribed by the

Lateran Council of 1139. But, despite this prohibition, the crossbow was in general use at the end of the twelfth century, and, except among the English, was the favourite weapon from that time to the latter part of the fifteenth century. In open warfare the English preferred the longbow, which was about 6 ft. long. The longbow was light, while the crossbow was heavy and cumbersome. With the longbow the archer could shoot about five arrows while the crossbowman was discharging one bolt; and he could keep his eye on the foe during the adjustment of a new missile, while the crossbowman's whole attention was required for this purpose.

In the defence of fortifications, however, where the crossbowman would have support for his bow and be himself secure from attack, the crossbow with its heavier missile, greater force and longer range was by far the superior weapon. The effective range of the longbow was about 220 yd.; that of a fifteenth century crossbow was from 370 to 380 yd., and with some bows even greater. In 1901 Sir Ralph Payne-Gallwey, using a crossbow of the fifteenth century with a steel bow, shot several bolts across the Menai Straits at a point where the distance was from 440 to 450 yd.[5] Much longer ranges have been claimed.

Scaling ladders were used at all periods, some of them being made of thongs, so that they could be thrown over the walls.[6] Battering rams were built within strong timber houses, which, as a protection from fire, were covered either with raw hides or iron plates[7] and mounted on wheels. They were brought up to the walls by teams of men working from the inside and propelling them along with poles. When in position, the wheels were removed and the machine fixed by wooden pegs.[8] The ram had an iron head, and was swung to and fro by picked men working on either side. Rams were cumbersome machines, and, working under constant exposure, were often destroyed. They were used in the early crusades, but were being gradually superseded by *trébuchets* and other projectile engines.

Siege towers, or *beffrois*, of many storeys were built of timber, covered with raw hides and mounted on wheels. Their great height enabled the besiegers to fight on a level with those on the walls, or even the towers, of the castle assaulted. When brought up close enough, a bridge was thrown across from the tower to the battlements of the castle, and those in the tower rushed across it on to the walls, while others passed up through the tower and on to the bridge in a continuous stream.

In addition to penthouses there were also cats, or mobile penthouses. The cat was a long one-storey structure built of stout timbers and covered with raw hides. It was brought up in position by means of rollers and levers, or by a system of pulleys and windlasses. Arrived before the walls, men working under its protection built a causeway across the moat; and when finally it was moved over the causeway it formed a secure shelter for those sapping the base of the wall. Mantlets, or wood screens protecting small bodies of archers, were placed in convenient positions for attack.

Projectile engines, worked by means of springs, thongs, twisted ropes or counterpoised weights, have been given various names, which may be grouped under three heads: *petrariae*, engines casting huge rocks; *ballistae*, or mangonels, for stones of about half cwt; and catapults, or scorpions, for casting smaller stones, darts and firebrands. By the end of the twelfth century projectile engines had become almost as powerful as early cannon. At the siege of Acre in 1189–1191 the King of France had a *petraria*, called Bad Neighbour, which by constant blows broke down part of the main wall of the city; and at the same siege one of the engines belonging to King Richard of England killed twelve men at one shot. This latter incident astonished the Saracens so much that they brought the stone ball to Saladin for inspection.[9] Even at the siege of Rhodes in 1480, when heavy artillery was used on both sides, a *trébuchet* throwing enormous stones

with great violence was brought up to the walls by the defenders and was successful in defeating the enemy at that point when fire-arms had failed.

As far as is known, none of these powerful engines has survived. Drawings from contemporary data have been made by M. Viollet-le-Duc and others. But with the exception of a sketch of one part of a *trébuchet* in the Album by Villard de Honnecourt, a thirteenth century architect, there are no reliable contemporary illustrations. A *trébuchet* is a powerful projectile engine, worked by springs and counterpoised weights; and the sketch illustrates its framed soleplate. If there were sketches of other parts of the engine in the collection they are among those which have been lost.

The missiles used included stones, darts, poles sharpened at the points, and firebrands. Fire was always one of the chief weapons used. Flaming torches, burning pitch and boiling oil were thrown from the walls on the besiegers; and burning and highly inflammable missiles were projected from the engines of both parties. Sometimes paving stones, or other similar materials which could be collected in haste, were used. In storming the castle of Thin, on the Scheldt in 1339 the French cast dead horses and other carrion from their engines into the fortress.[10] Greek fire, thrown from the engines, was used in the Levant.

When direct assault had failed, attempt was made to bring down the walls either by sapping at their bases, under the protection of penthouses, or by mining. Mining was often effective in reducing a fortress, and the only defence against it was countermining. During the Middle Ages both operations were conducted with great skill and address.

Siege operations are best understood, and the whole purpose of mediaeval defences appreciated, by a perusal of the very vivid descriptions of the sieges given by contemporary chroniclers.

SIEGE OF JERUSALEM, AD70[11]

After the Jewish revolt of AD66, in which the Roman armies had suffered serious defeat, it was decided to send a powerful expedition to Palestine to re-establish Roman authority and put an end to the frequent rebellions in that country. Owing to difficulties abroad elsewhere, and to changes of government and civil war at home, the expedition was delayed, and on arrival it was held up for five months in the siege and capture of Jotapha. It was not before the spring of AD70 that the Roman army, under Titus, appeared before the walls of Jerusalem. Despite the violent and deadly strife within the city between the factions into which the Jews were split up, Titus found himself faced by a valiant, brave and resourceful foe, ready to fight to the death behind its formidable walls.

At that time Jerusalem consisted of three main sections, arranged in line. The oldest portion, called the Upper City, was (as at present) at the south end. It was defended on all sides but the north by deep valleys, and was surrounded by a wall. The Temple protrudes from its north-east corner. The middle portion stretched northwards from the first, and was enclosed by the second wall. The third, while enclosing the second on three sides, extended still further north, and was enclosed by the third wall. All the walls were of powerful construction, of great width and height, and largely built of megalithic masonry. The defence of the city was apportioned between the two Jewish factions under their respective heads, John and Simon.

After a preliminary survey round the walls to select the weakest spot, Titus set up his siege engines, powerful battering-rams and slings, and began his attack, his men shielded behind timber mantlets. The slings were mighty weapons, capable of casting stones of one cwt. a quarter of a mile with terrific force. The Jews on their side set up their engines on the wall; and, while some of them rained stones on the enemy, others rushed out from the city, destroyed his mantlets and slew those behind them. Others again set fire to his siege works. Titus then ordered three lofty siege towers to be built, upon which his lighter slings were mounted, and from their high level commanded the defenders on the walls. These towers were too heavy to be overturned by any force issuing from the walls, and, being covered with iron, they could not be set on fire. They did great execution among the Jews. One of them (probably through faulty construction) fell down during the night, causing great consternation among the Roman troops, fearing treachery, before they knew the real cause of the loud crash. While the Jews were thus driven from the battlements, the largest and most powerful of all the Roman siege engines, called by the Jews the Conqueror, had been pounding ceaselessly at the wall, and eventually made a breach in it. The Jews then retired within the middle section of their defences, called the Lower City; and the Romans occupied the northern section, transferring their engines into it.

Titus now began the assault on the second wall, training his siege engines upon it, and setting up a particularly powerful battering ram against a tower in the middle of the north wall. In order to gain time,

Plan of Jerusalem AD70

129

the Jews staged a pretended dispute on the walls in sight of the enemy: one party representing themselves as prepared to submit to the Romans, in violent strife against others opposed to surrender; the first party calling on the Roman commander to send an envoy to arrange terms. Titus, thinking the move to be genuine, stopped the working of the ram during the parley, and sent an envoy to the walls. This man, on his approach, was shot at by the Jews, and Titus, realizing that he had been deceived, renewed the attack with increased violence. Soon the middle tower gave way, and the Jews, knowing they could no longer hold it, set it on fire and the enemy poured through the breach. The streets of the Lower City being too narrow for concerted action, and the breach in the wall not wide enough to admit large numbers at a time, the Romans were at first driven back; but, having widened the breach, they returned in great force, and now stood before the inner wall and the Temple. The outer wall was taken in fifteen days from the beginning of the attack and the second wall five days later.

Now the Jews were in great straits. Supplies were running out and famine raged among the dense population now confined within the walls of the Upper City – a population greatly increased by large numbers of persons who, before the siege, had come up to Jerusalem to keep the Passover and were unable to get away. Appalling conditions ensued, the gruesome and harrowing details of which are described at length by Josephus. Some persons, laying hold of such treasures as they could get access to and concealing them either upon or within their bodies, deserted to the enemy. Others, having risked their lives outside the walls to gather such wild herbs as they could find, were caught, tortured and crucified within sight of the city.

For his next assault Titus built at strategic points four tall platforms, on the top of which he placed his siege engines and trained them on the walls. The Jews now fought with a determination and courage born of desperation. They had 340 slinging engines, and had acquired great dexterity in their use. John, commanding the eastern flank of the defence, drove a mine out towards one of the Roman engines, and, having enlarged the cavity beneath the engine, strutting it with timber well daubed with pitch and other inflammable material, he set the timber on fire. When the

timber was consumed all above, roof of cavity, platform and engine, collapsed into the hole and were destroyed. Simon's forces defending the west flank, seizing torches, issued from the walls and, overcoming all resistance, restrained the operations of the battering-ram by physical force, drove away the attendants from the other engines, set the engines on fire and destroyed them also.

Following this serious check Titus decided to establish an absolute blockade; for there were still secret passages out of the city, known to some of the Jews, by which escape could be effected or supplies brought in; and to put a definite stop to all such means of communication he built a wall all round the city, with garrisons at proper intervals all along the line. Famine conditions within the city now reached extreme limits, sedition and murder were rife, disease rampant and the death rate enormous. On the completion of the wall (it took three days to build) Titus now concentrated the attack on the Temple and the tower of Antonio on the west side of it. Again he raised his engines on tall timber pedestals, and began the attack on the tower. While the battering rams and other engines were pounding at the tower, and sappers were working at its foundations, the ground beneath suddenly gave way, for they were working over the mine John had made in a previous attack, and a wall of the tower crashed into it. The Jews, however, having anticipated such an event, had built up another wall inside and the tower was still in their hands. Titus incited his men to mount the new wall over the ruins of the first, which now formed a kind of ramp up to it. This they essayed to do, and were at first repulsed, but on a second attempt at night they won the tower and established a garrison within it. And now the operations concentrated on an assault on the Temple.

A desperate hand-to-hand struggle with darts, spears and swords was the opening phase of the attack, the struggle lasting all night and well on to the next day, first at the entrance and then within the courts of the Temple. After a great slaughter on both sides, the Jews held their ground and drove the Romans back to the tower of Antonio.

The Jews now fortified the Temple itself, mounting their *petranae*, slings and other siege engines on the towers of the gates. Before renewing his attack, Titus, obviously anxious to save the Temple, made an earnest appeal to the Jews either to submit or change the venue of the fight. He reminded them of the respect with which the Romans had regarded the Temple, and of the partition wall which they had been allowed to erect, and proceeded: "Have not-we given you leave to kill such is go beyond it" [the wall], though he were a Roman? ... Why do you pollute this holy house with the blood of both foreigners and Jews themselves? ... I also appeal to my own army, and to those Jews who are now with me, and even to you yourselves, that I do not force you to defile this your sanctuary or offer any affront to it; nay I will endeavour to preserve you your holy house whether you will or no." This appeal fell on deaf ears: indeed it was attributed rather to fear than desire to save the Temple; and so the attack was renewed.

The assault began at night, and in the darkness a melee ensued in which it was difficult to distinguish friend from foe. The Romans set up their engines before the Court of the Gentiles. The outer approaches were first destroyed by fire, partly by the Jews themselves as a protective measure, and the Romans approached the inner walls. These walls proved to be so strong, the stones of such enormous size and the bond so good that, although they brought up most powerful engines and battered them without ceasing for six days and nights, they failed to make any appreciable impression. Sappers at the foundations at one point, though successful in removing the facing stones, were unable to effect a breach because the strongly built core still held firm. Efforts to scale the wall with ladders also failed, for the Jews repulsed the assailants and, making a sally, got possession of their engines.

Now the Romans set fire to the gates, which were of timber plated with silver. The fire spread within and raged for two days; then Titus ordered it to be extinguished, and held a council with his commanders regarding their further proceedings. Some of his officers favoured the entire destruction of the Temple, but Titus held strongly for its preservation, despite the fact that the Jews were using it as a fort. He decided to take it by storm, and a terrible struggle and slaughter occurred round the Altar of Burnt-offering. One soldier, indifferent to instructions, snatching a torch and mounting on the back of a companion, thrust it through a window of the inner court. The fire spread and, despite all efforts to quench it, raged violently throughout the whole building, and brought about its entire destruction.

After a further appeal to the Jews to submit had proved of no avail, Titus set up his engines against the Upper City. But now the contest had become too unequal; for, while the Romans were elated with victory, the Jews were utterly exhausted, and when one of the walls was broken down and the Romans came pouring through the breach those who could fled to the valley below and hid themselves in caverns, and the last line of defence was taken.

Then occurred the usual acts of violence, loot and carnage following such victories. Soldiers in parties, sword in hand, killed without mercy everyone they met and set on fire houses full of those who had fled into them, often finding houses containing the bodies of whole families who had perished in the famine. Titus gave orders that, with the exception of the three great towers in the citadel and a portion of the west wall, all the fortifications of the city were to be demolished. Eleven thousand persons perished in the siege and ninety-seven thousand were sent away captive – some to work in the Egyptian mines, some to be sold as slaves, and the rest to be reserved for slaughter in various ways in the amphitheatres.

SIEGE OF NICAEA, 1097[12]

On their march towards Jerusalem the armies of the First Crusade arrived before Nicaea in 1097 and laid siege to the city, surrounding those parts of the walls not washed by the shores of the lake. After they had scoured the neighbouring forests for timber for the construction of their siege engines, and had set the engines in position, they began their attack on the walls, hoping to accomplish the fall of the city by famine and assault. Finding that the citizens were receiving supplies by water through the lake, the Crusaders, with the help of Alexios, Emperor of Constantinople, transported during one night a fleet of ships seven miles overland on wagons and launched them in the lake, so cutting off that means of succour.

Meanwhile the engines, pounding away at the walls, met with vigorous resistance from the garrison, who pelted them with pitch, oil, lard, torches and other burning missiles, destroying the greater number. One large tower offered great resistance, and after incessant attack by two siege engines not a stone was moved. At length, when more engines were brought up against it and larger and harder stone missiles employed, some fissures were made in its wall. The base of the wall was attacked by a battering ram and by sappers with crowbars. But all these efforts were in vain, for the breaches made during the day were repaired by the garrison during the night. Eventually a very strong penthouse was built and brought up to the tower. Under the protection of this covering, on which flaming material and huge rocks were thrown without effect, sappers worked away at the base of the wall.

As the sappers dug out the masonry they supplied its place by props and stays, and when a cavity of sufficient size for their purpose was made, combustible materials were thrown among the timber work. The men then set fire to the props and escaped back to the camp, leaving the penthouse where it was. At midnight, when the props were consumed, the tower fell with such a deafening crash that the sound could be heard from a great distance. After that event the citizens, realizing that their case was hopeless, surrendered themselves to the Emperor Alexios and the city was taken.

SIEGE OF ANTIOCH, 1097–1098[13]
Antioch at this period was a city of great extent, about three miles long by two miles wide, and was bounded on the north by the River Orontes. It stands partly on the plain and partly on the slopes of a high hill, the citadel standing on the highest point on the southern boundary. On their arrival at Antioch from Nicaea the Crusaders proceeded to attack the city. Investment of such extensive lines and difficult ground was probably deemed impracticable and the armies disposed themselves before the principal gates and built four forts.

Here the Crusaders met with strong and effective resistance. The garrison was under the command of a skilful leader, who had powerful engines mounted on the walls, and was thus able to repel the enemy's attacks. Destructive sallies were also made from one of the gates, and to counter this manoeuvre the Crusaders blocked the gate by rolling great rocks and heavy logs of oak against it. It was only by the

treachery of one of its Emirs that the city was eventually taken. This man, having killed his own brother, introduced some of the Crusaders on to the battlements by means of a rope ladder. They, walking round to a postern, let in others, and the whole band proceeding to the main gate let in the rest of the army.

As evidence of the host of thieves and cutthroats who, in the hope of full licence for their deeds, had attached themselves to the Crusaders in their long march through Europe and Asia Minor, once within the city this rabble ran amuck. A dreadful massacre ensued in which neither sex nor age was spared. Demanding the names of the most important houses, they entered them, slew the domestics and, penetrating into the private apartments, transfixed alike nobles, mothers of families and infants. Pillaging everywhere, they carried away rich vestments and vessels of gold and silver.

An incident during this siege might well be recorded. The report had spread that there were enemy spies among the army of the Crusaders and at a council of leaders Bohemund undertook to deal with the matter. One night, when the usual preparations for supper were being made, Bohemund brought some Turks out of prison, sent them to the slaughter-house, ordering that their throats were to be cut and their bodies roasted, prepared, and carefully laid out as for eating. He also gave instructions that if any inquiries were made as to the meaning of these proceedings, the answer to be given was that the princes had issued orders that henceforth all prisoners and spies were to be treated in the same manner and eaten by them and their people. The report which thereupon spread abroad that the invaders were people of abnormal cruelty, who not only imprisoned and tortured their enemies but also ate their flesh and drank their blood, sent a thrill of horror throughout the Levant.

SIEGE OF JERUSALEM, 1099[13]
In the following summer the Crusaders appeared before Jerusalem and, having disposed their forces round the city, set up their engines in convenient positions and began the assault. The Turks also set up engines on the walls, noted the construction of their enemy's machines that they might copy the designs, and returned the fire with great vigour. Flaming

torches, rope dipped in sulphur, oil, pitch, fragile pots filled with inflammable materials and breaking easily on impact, and all sorts of similar missiles were thrown from the Turks' machines on the engines and siege towers of the Crusaders to destroy them by fire.

The Crusaders built three particularly strong siege towers and moved them up to the walls at three different points, one of them being brought up piece by piece during the night and assembled in position. Each of the towers had a drawbridge on one side, which, when close enough to the wall, could be let down to the battlements and so form a way for the troops into the city. From the summits of these towers men with *ballistae*, bows and other weapons poured a rain of missiles on the battlements opposite them. The towers themselves were met with showers of missiles from the walls; and so effective was the Turkish response that those occupying the upper parts were rendered dizzy by the constant rocking to and fro, and the towers began to spread at the base.

Among the engines of the Crusaders was one which threw enormous stones with great force. It did great execution among those on the battlements, and the enemy's attacks on it had no effect. The Turks then brought up two witches and set them on the wall in order that they might curse the engine; but a missile from this machine struck and killed both witches as well as three other women who were with them. However, the defence of the city was so well conducted, and the fire on the engines and towers of the besiegers so effective, that the Crusaders became despondent and considered drawing off the attack, but eventually decided to renew their efforts.

In order to deaden the impact and shock of missiles, the Turks had suspended outside the walls sacks of straw and tow, cushions, carpets and timber beams. The Crusaders on the north side of the city, having filled the ditch and brought up one of their towers close to the wall, cut down two of the suspended beams. They then set fire to the sacks of straw, mattresses and other combustible materials suspended before the walls, and the wind, blowing from the north, drove such dense volumes of smoke into the city that those on the walls could neither open their mouths nor their eyes, and had perforce to beat a retreat. The Crusaders then let down their drawbridge on the wall-walk, using the timbers they had cut down as beams for the additional support of the bridge. The defenders having been driven away by the smoke, the troops then entered the city with little opposition, using ladders in addition to their tower and bridge. On entering they opened the gates, and the rest of the forces poured into the streets. Meanwhile the forces on the south side, hearing that the city had been taken, applied ladders to the wall and entered without opposition.

Now again a scene of most awful massacre and butchery ensued. The troops rushed through the city killing everywhere, sparing none, man, woman or infant, dragging out into public places those who had hidden themselves and slaying them like beasts. In this scene of carnage the forces from the north and those from the south met in the centre of the city.

SIEGE OF ACRE, 1189–1192[1]

Acre was defended on one side by the sea and on the other by three lines of fortifications and a citadel within the third line. On the south there was a harbour protected by a mole with a strong tower at the end of it, called the Tower of Flies, on account of the swarms of flies collected on the offal thrown out here. On the arrival at Acre in 1189 the armies of the Third Crusade began their attack on the city both by sea and land.

The fleet having erected on their galleys a tall siege tower and other engines, all covered with raw hides, made a vigorous attack on the Tower of Flies. Those in the tower, assisted by the citizens who came to their aid, responded with equal energy. They threw Greek fire at the siege tower and on the other machines of their foes, and destroyed them, so the attack from this side failed. On the land side the Crusaders were more successful. They first fortified their own camp, and then threw up a barrier in front of the walls running round the city from shore to shore. All supplies being now cut off, the Turks, stricken with famine, offered to surrender on condition that they should be allowed to depart with their property unmolested. This condition was refused, and the siege was protracted for two years.

The Crusaders now constructed three siege towers, which were built up in storeys and reached to a greater height than the walls of the city. Twisted ropes were hung in front of the

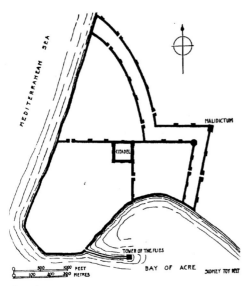

Plan of Acre in 1189

towers to deaden the force of missiles. There were also battering-rams, one of which was covered with iron plates, and a large number of powerful projectile engines, the latter not only attacking the walls, but covering the advance of the towers. But the Turks possessed no less powerful engines, and made valiant resistance. Their machines cast stones of immense weight at great distances, destroying everything they struck. They broke in pieces some of the besiegers' petrariae and rendered other machines useless. Speaking of the defenders, the chronicler says: "Never were there braver warriors of any creed on earth; and the memory of their actions excites at once our respect and astonishment."

Recourse was then to mining. At one point the French made an attack on a strong corner tower called the Cursed, and by diligent digging made a cavity, supporting its roof with logs of wood. But the Turks by countermining reached the same spot, and frustrated their designs. At another point Richard, King of England, made an attack on a tower, both by mining and projectile engines, with the result that the tower, or its outer wall, was brought down. But when the men tried to rush through the breach they were repelled. Then a company of Pisans ran forward, and they also were driven out, the Turks fighting with their swords and with Greek fire.

Eventually, their fortifications partly destroyed and themselves greatly reduced in numbers, the Turks submitted to severe conditions of surrender, many of which were beyond their power to perform. Even so, as they departed penniless from the city, their spirit and courageous bearing struck admiration in the hearts of all who saw them.

SIEGE OF CHÂTEAU GAILLARD, 1203–1204[16]

The strength of Chateau Gaillard was put to a severe test four years after it was built, when it was attacked by Philip the Second, King of France, and held for King John of England by Roger de Lacy. In 1203 Philip advanced towards the castle, and, after desperate struggles on both sides, took the town of Les Petit Andeleys, which King Richard had built on the Seine at its foot. Having regard to the strength of the castle, Philip decided to starve the garrison into submission; and, with this end in view, he dug two lines of trenches, running from the water at the base of the hill on which the castle stands to the top of the hill and from there down to the river on the other side. At intervals in the space between the trenches he built timber towers, and placed guards, not only in the towers, but also all along the intervals between them. The area enclosed between these lines of fortification and the river included not only the castle, but also the little valleys surrounding it. Philip's troops then sat down for about three months to await events; and thereupon ensued one of the most terrible episodes in the history of the Middle Ages.

On the hillside between the town and the castle there was a thickly populated street of houses,whose inhabitants,when the town was taken, retired up to the castle and were received within its walls. But as the siege was prolonged one thousand of them were sent out and were allowed to pass the French lines. Later, as the reserves of supplies were being consumed, de Lacy, selecting those most useful to him, sent forth all others to the number of four hundred, including infirm men, women and children. They went out with joy; but when the gate was closed behind them they were met with a volley of missiles from the French, who had been ordered to allow no others to pass. Then, repulsed on both sides and under continuous attack, they found themselves confined to the valleys between the castle and the French trenches. There they remained during a severe winter suffering intensely from want, hunger and exposure, endeavouring to sustain their existence on such winter herbs as they could find. Dogs which had been driven out of the castle were seized and eaten, the skins as well as the flesh. A newborn infant was immediately devoured. Their condition was so deplorable that at length, after three months of intense suffering, those of them who survived were allowed to pass through the French lines; but nearly all of this remnant died on taking food.

In the spring of 1204, following these events, Philip set up his siege engines on the high ground to the south-east and began his assault on the castle. His engines included petrariae, mangonels and a very high siege tower. He also built a long penthouse for the protection of those engaged in filling the castle ditches. To his attack the garrison replied vigorously with stones from their own engines, causing considerable loss to the besiegers. The French then began sapping operations, under the protection of their shields, on the salient tower of the outer bailey, and were successful in excavating a cavity, strutting, firing the timber and in bringing down the tower. The outer bailey was then taken, and the French proceeded to attack the remaining works.

Against the curtain on the south side of the middle bailey there was a building which had latrines on the lower storey, and contained a chapel in the upper storey, the chapel having a window in the outer wall. A French soldier, observing this window, with some companions made efforts to reach it. They searched along the river bank for the outlet of the drain from the latrines, found it, crawled up through the drain and gained a point just below the window of the chapel. Here, mounting on the shoulders of one of his companions, the soldier sprang up to the window, and with a cord brought up the others also. Having got within, they began to make a great noise, and the garrison, believing that a great number of the enemy had entered, set fire to the building and retired within the inner bailey. Those who had entered, however, were able to protect themselves in the vaults; and before the fire had died down they rushed out, lowered the drawbridge between the outer and middle

baileys so that the French troops could enter, and the middle bailey was taken.

Then the French, under the protection of one of their machines, proceeded to undermine the wall of the inner bailey; but by countermining on the other side the garrison broke into the French tunnel and drove them out. But now the wall, weakened by being undermined on both sides and battered by a powerful petraria, throwing enormous blocks of stone, was fractured, and the French, rushing through the breach, entered the inner bailey. Even then, none of the garrison surrendered, but all fought as long as it was possible to do so.

SIEGE OF ROCHESTER CASTLE, 1215[17]

Rochester Castle, having fallen into the hands of the disaffected barons, was laid siege to by King John in 1215. John brought up his siege engines against the castle, and pounded relentlessly at the walls, his troops working in relays. But the besieged replied with such effect, and caused such execution in the ranks of the royal forces, that other methods of attack had to be adopted. The king then employed miners to break through the curtain; and, when a breach was made and the troops had entered the bailey, the garrison, after a valiant fight, retired within the keep. The miners then applied themselves to the keep, and broke into that also. Even then those within fought desperately, and the troops, suffering great loss, were compelled to retreat again and again. At length, having sustained a siege of nearly three months, and been brought to the verge of starvation, the garrison surrendered. The south-east angle of the keep of Rochester Castle was rebuilt about this period, and is very probably the point where the breach was made.

SIEGE OF DOVER CASTLE, 1216[18]

In the following year, on the invitation of the insurgent barons, Louis, Dauphin of France, crossed the Channel with a strong force and laid siege to Dover Castle. With his powerful petrariae and other siege engines Louis made a violent and incessant attack on the walls. The garrison under the command of its constable, Hubert de Burgh, replied with such devastating effect that the French, feeling their loss, moved both their camp and their engines further back. Meanwhile King John died and Louis and the barons, thinking that England was now in their power, called upon Hubert de Burgh to surrender, offering him great honours and high position. But Hubert and his knights refused to surrender, and the siege was raised.

Among the examples of siege works still existing are those of St. Andrews Castle, Fife, made during a siege in 1546–1547. Here the besiegers drove an underground tunnel towards the castle from a point about 130 ft. from the walls. Countermining was then undertaken by the garrison, and, after some tentative efforts to locate the advancing mine, they eventually broke into it at a point about midway between the walls and the starting point of the mine. The countermining was so exact that, although the mine had deviated from a straight course, the countermine broke into it at its end, and at the convenient level immediately above the heads of the enemy. Both mine and countermine are still preserved.

NOTES

1. Tacitus, *The Histories*, Bk. IV, 23.
2. Procopius, *History of the Wars*, Bk. V, cap.
3. Guillaume de Jumiège, Bk. II, cap. XII.
4. Steel was known to the Ancients in 1000 B.C., and Bows of Steel are mentioned in II Sam. XXII, 35, and Psalms XVIII, 34.
5. *The Crossbow*, Sir Ralph Payne-Gallwey, p. 14.
6. Acts of Stephen, Bk. I.
7. Geoffrey de Vinsauf, Bk. I, cap. LX.
8. *Anna Comnena*, Alexias, Ek. XIII.
9. Geoffrey de Vinsauf, Bk. Ill, cap. VII.
10. Froissart.
11. Josephui, *The Jewish War*. Bk-;. V and VI.
12. *Anna Comnena*, *op. cit.*, Bk. XI, and William of Tyre.
13. William of Tyre.
14. William of Tyre.
15. Geoffrey de Vinsauf.
16. Guillaume-le-Breton. Prose and verse descriptions.
17. Roger of Wendover.
18. Ibid.

Chapter 13
Castles from about 1280 to 1320

The course of this history has now reached a period when some of the most powerful castles of any age or country were built in Great Britain. Extensive experience in sieges, both at home and abroad, had shown the King of England, Edward the First, and his barons the weak points of existing fortifications, and in the new castles they built these defects were rectified. Though considerable attention was still paid to outworks the general tendency was to concentrate the central defence on a square castle, enclosed by two lines of walls with a strong tower at each corner of the inner line. Powerful gateways now take the place of keeps, and there is a more liberal provision of gateways and posterns.

A serious defect in the earlier castles lay in the fact that there was generally only one gateway and one postern. The last word in war, whether carried out on a large or on a small scale, must always be starvation. A king might be secure behind the walls of an impregnable castle; but unless he had adequate means of bringing in supplies, of making sorties or of effecting escape, he was doomed eventually to capture when surrounded, without relief, by a force superior to his own. In the new castles more gateways were provided, and, in many cases, the difficulties of investment were increased by extensive outworks as well. The design of the inner bailey also secured greater mobility to the defence forces and greater facility of command.

One of the earliest of these castles was that of Caerphilly, Glamorgan, built about 1267–1277. Caerphilly Castle stands on what was an island in a lake, the lake being fed by a stream and held in by a great screen wall, or dam, forming the barbican. The main portion of the castle is rectangular, and is surrounded by two lines of walls, the inner wall having a tower at each corner and a large gatehouse in

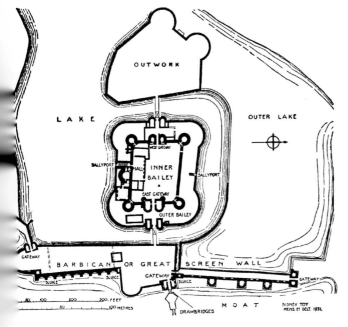

Plan of Caerphilly Castle

the middle of each of the east and west walls, and the outer wall a gateway east and west in line with those of the inner wall. The towers of the inner wall have such bold projection beyond the corners that the outer faces of the panel of wall between them were completely commanded by, and could be swept from end to end by, missiles from the arrow-loops and battlements. The outer wall is lower and thinner than the inner, and in place of towers the curtain takes a circular sweep round the corners. The east gateways look towards the barbican, from which they were approached by a drawbridge. The west gateways look towards an outwork, which stood in the same lake as the main buildings, and was reached by a drawbridge on this side. The hall and living rooms are built against the curtain on the south side of the inner bailey, and the kitchen, bakehouse and other domestic offices in the space between the two walls, behind the hall (above).

In addition to the main gateways, there are three posterns in the inner bailey: one on the south and two on the north; and two in the outer bailey, one on the north and one on the south. The postern on the south side of the inner bailey is in line with that in the outer bailey on this side, and opens directly out of the hall to a vaulted stairway down to a doorway in the outer wall. The inner and outer doorways are each protected by a portcullis. From the posterns in the outer wall supplies could be brought in, sorties made, or escape effected by boat across the lake. The circulation of the inner bailey was greatly facilitated by a mural passage, which was carried all round the walls about 15 ft. above ground level, and checked by portcullises on either side of both gatehouses.

The massive screen wall, sustained on one wing by a series of huge buttresses and on the other by three strong towers, is a most powerful and imposing work of military engineering. Through it run three sluices, by which the level of the water in the lake was regulated, and behind it is the long and spacious barbican. The citadel of Caerphilly was the east gateway of the inner bailey, which could be held as well against an enemy within the bailey as against one without.

Though the underlying principles may be maintained, the design of a castle must always depend largely on the character of the site it occupies and the purpose it has to fulfil. Again, the defensive factors of surprise and secrecy themselves demand endless varieties of plan and disposition of parts. Flint Castle, built 1277–1280, Conway, 1283–1287, and Caernarvon, 1285–1322, each formed part of a general scheme which included a fortified town.

At Flint the ultimate stronghold is a cylindrical keep, which stands isolated at one corner of a rectangular fortress, like the donjon at Lillebonne and the Tour de Constance at Aigues Mortes. The keep at Flint (only the lower portion of which remains) was a powerful structure, 71 ft. in diameter and probably of three storeys. It was approached from the inner bailey by a drawbridge over the moat, and entered at a level midway between the basement and the second storey. From the entrance passage steps in front led down to the basement and a wide spiral stairway on the left to the upper floors. In design this keep resembles the huge round towers at Old Cairo. It is built of two concentric shells, which in the basement are separated by a circular vaulted passage, but in the upper storeys were connected by thick radial ribs, dividing the inter-space into halls and chambers. The second storey (only the lower portion of the walls of which remain) has a large central hall surrounded by five rooms of varying size. One of them, containing the well shaft, built up from the basement, was probably the kitchen. The partition walls dividing the five rooms, radiating toward the centre, diminish in thickness as they pass from the outer to the inner shell, and latrines are formed in the wide outer ends of three of them.

Gonway Castle stands on a high rock on the shore of the estuary, and, following the contour of the rock, is long and relatively narrow. It is defended by eight towers and has a gateway at either end, each gateway being flanked by two of the towers and covered by a barbican. A cross-wall divides the castle into two baileys of unequal size, the outer bailey containing the great hall and the domestic offices of the garrison, and the inner bailey the royal apartments and private offices. The gateways are constructed through the curtain wall, and are defended by the adjoining wall-towers. There are no gatehouses. The security of the

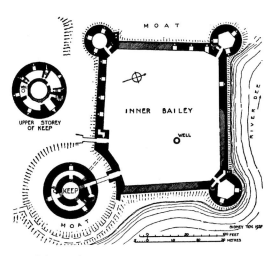

Plan of Flint Castle

castle depends largely on the difficulty of access to it. On the west, the town side, entrance was effected only after climbing a steep stairway, passing over a drawbridge and through three fortified gateways, all in face of direct fire from the towers and walls on every side. The approach from the estuary was commanded for the whole of its course by the east barbican, which towered high above it, and by a tower in the estuary.

In the inner bailey there are two posterns in addition to the east gateway. One of them is in the south wall, and stands high above the rocks on the edge of the river. It would be of service in an emergency by the use of a rope ladder, like those at Carcassonne. The other is in the north-east tower. This tower contains a beautiful little chapel, and has, in addition to the postern, means of exit by stairways and passages in all directions. It probably contained the royal chambers. The circulation of the wall-walk is uninterrupted all round the curtain and on the cross-wall, thus enabling the defence forces to be rushed speedily to any desired point. All the towers, on the sides facing towards the field, have beam-holes for hoarding; and four of them have high turrets from which the approach or distant operations of an enemy could be observed.[1]

Caernarvon Castle stands on relatively level ground, though there is a fall from the east (where there was a mound) to the west. The plan resembles an hour-glass, narrow in the

middle and bulbous at both ends. It is a very powerful structure, surrounded by strong and lofty walls, and defended by two gatehouses and nine wall-towers, many of the towers having turrets, as at Conway. The north side of the castle faces towards the town and the south side towards the river. One gatehouse, called the King's Gate, stands in the middle of the north wall, and provided direct entrance from the town to the inner bailey in the west portion of the castle, and probably (perhaps by less direct passage) to the outer bailey. As originally designed, this gatehouse was to extend across the castle to the south wall and form the division between the inner and outer baileys; but only a portion of this extension now exists, and the whole was probably never completed. Queen's Gate at the east end of the castle is the entrance to the outer bailey, and stands clear of the town walls.

In the inner bailey there are three posterns: one from a tower in the north wall, opening to the moat between the castle and the town; one in the south curtain, giving access to the river; and a third, called the Water Gate, giving access to the river from the Eagle Tower at the extreme

Caernarvon castle from the air: Eagle tower in foreground

west of the castle. The Eagle Tower is an especially strong and well defended building, and preserves in its design practically all the elements of a keep. From it the whole fortress is commanded. It contains a private chapel and has a gate by which entry could be made or escape effected.

Attached to the north side of the Eagle Tower are the remains of a wall 13 ft. 6 in. thick, which jutted north-west out into the river. This fragment contains one jamb of a low gateway with the groove for the portcullis by which the gate was closed and, at a higher level, an entrance passage that led to the chamber over the gateway from which the portcullis was operated. It has been suggested that the space north of the tower and west of the town wall to which this gateway admitted was occupied by a gatehouse; but since the gateway is at water level, and there was no through way except by water, it is much more probable that the space was occupied by a dock and that the fragment is the remains of the fortified entrance into it. The town wall here is not diminished in thickness on approaching the tower, as it was on the east side of the castle, and was on both sides at Conway.[2]

The curtain and towers on the south side of the castle have two tiers of mural passages with arrow-loops to the field. On the north front, towards the town, some of the arrow-loops are so constructed that from one recess archers could be shooting in two or even three different directions; in others openings from three recesses converge towards one loophole. When put in a state of defence, the castle was bristling with archers standing at different levels behind the defences. On the south side, including those on the battlements, there would be three tiers of armed men.

A continuous wall-walk, like that at Conway, though it facilitates the operations of the garrison while it is held, is a serious menace when one part of it is carried by assault, since the whole could then be overrun. At Caernarvon all the towers stand astride of the wallwalk, so that if any section of the curtain was carried it could be isolated by closing the passage through the towers.

The internal buildings are now represented principally by foundations, but the towers and curtain walls are practically intact. Caernarvon Castle, with its powerful fortifications almost complete, ranks among the finest examples of military architecture of the Middle Ages.

Harlech Castle, Merioneth, built 1285–1290, and Beaumaris Castle, 1295–1320, both show the development of the principles of defence suitable to the sites they occupy.

Harlech Castle stands on a hill. It consists of a rectangular fortress, enclosed by two lines of walls and forming the inner and middle baileys, and an outer bailey which extends down the precipitous slopes of the hill and covers only the north and west sides of the main fortress. The east and south sides are defended by a wide moat The inner bailey has a tower at each corner and a large gatehouse in the middle of the east front, the towers having the same bold projection as those at Caerphilly. There is a postern in the north wall and another, leading out of the great hall, on the west. The middle bailey (actually a narrow terrace between the two walls) is obstructed at one point by a cross-wall with a doorway. It has two gateways, one in front of the gatehouse and the other on the north, opening to the outer bailey. There are also two posterns, both opening to the outer bailey.

The outer bailey presents to the field a rising series of precipitous rocks, and the approach through it from the water gate at the foot

Harlech castle from the air

of the hill to the upper fortress was by way of a steep path cut into the cliff face along the inside of the west curtain. Any other line of approach would involve a perilous climb over the rocks to the north gateway. The road up by the path was intercepted by a drawbridge and gate, and ended in another gate, below and commanded by the south-west tower. A long wall, jutting out from the main fortress, intercepted the passage from one part of the outer bailey to the other. From the north and west, therefore, the castle was strongly defended, both by nature and military art.

But the vulnerable side of the castle is the east front, which faces towards higher ground; and it is here that the military strength of the fortress is concentrated. The east front of the inner bailey is powerfully built. It has a gatehouse in the middle and a strong tower at either flank: one panel of the wall is 12 ft. 4 in. thick and the other 9 ft. 8 in. As at first designed, the other three walls were to be only about 6 ft. thick, like those at Criccieth Castle, but after they had been carried up to about one-third of their present height it was decided to make them stronger, and as finished they are about 9 ft. thick. The approach from the east was by a bridge with a drawbridge at either end, the passage across the bridge being under attack, not only from the gateways, walls and towers in front, but also from the wide wall-walk of the outer bailey on the right flank. Beyond the bridge the inner bailey was obstructed by the outer and inner gateways.

The outer gate was closed by a two-leaved door only; but the long passage through the inner gate was closed by a stout timber bar, three portcullises and two doors, while it was commanded from above by eight wide machicolations.

At Harlech, the gatehouse was the stronghold of the castle, and, before the erection of the later stairway in the courtyard, could be held against the inner bailey as well as against the exterior, the inner system of door, portcullis and machicolation being reversed against the bailey. The gatehouse stands astride of the wall-walk on the curtain, and commands the circulation by doorways on both sides; but otherwise the walk is continuous all round the walls.

Beaumaris Castle stands on level ground on the seashore, and the disposition of its defences is much more regular than those at Harlech. It consists of two lines of fortifications, forming the inner and outer baileys; and, except at one point on the south where the sea enters to form a small dock, is surrounded by a moat. The inner bailey is almost square; its walls are about 15 ft. 6 in. thick, and are defended by six towers and two large gatehouses, the gatehouses being in opposite walls like those at Caerphilly. Each of the gateways was defended by three portcullises and two doors, and (as far as the remains indicate) by series of machicolations, all arranged in a manner similar to the defences of the inner gateway at Hariech. Both gateways could be held against either the inner or the outer bailey. The south gateway was further protected by a small barbican. Both the gatehouses were substantial structures containing large halls and rooms. In the intermediate tower on the east there is a beautiful vaulted chapel.

The wall-walk is continuous except at the gatehouses, where it is barred by doorways on both sides. The doorway on either side of the north gatehouse is placed slightly clear of the inner face of the wall, leaving an open space across the angle between the walk and the doorway. This space was spanned by a bridge, which was probably of timber and could be removed as desired, thereby completely isolating the gatehouse from the walk. Vestiges of the stone supports of the

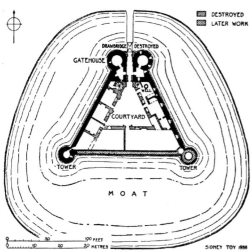

Plan of Carrlaverock castle

bridges remain. This gatehouse was the stronghold of the castle. Circulation round the walls was greatly facilitated by munil passages, at a level about halfway in their height, which, except for a portion at the north-west, ran all round the castle and into the gatehouse.

Where suitable stone slabs were difficult to obtain, the surfaces of wall-walks were frequently covered with lead; and the grooves for the lead flashing are still to be seen in the parapets of many castles, as at Conway. At Beaumaris a considerable portion of the lead flashing itself remains in the parapets at the north-east corner of the walk.

As originally finished, about 1290, the castle consisted of the inner bailey only : the outer wall was added about 1316–1320. The outer curtain is constructed in nine panels, is strengthened by many walltowers, and has gateways on the north and south. Its gateways are placed considerably out of line with the inner gateways, thus involving the exposure of the flank of an enemy entering the outer and proceeding to the inner gates. The north gateway is in a fragmentary condition, and was probably never completed. Near the south gateway there is a small dock which runs in from the sea between the town walls and a tall pier, called the Gunners Walk, the pier jutting out from the outer curtain of the castle. The Gunners Walk defended the dock on all sides, and not only from the battlements on the top, but from a mural passage and chamber below them. A door at the head of the dock opened to the outer bailey.

At Villandraut, thirty miles south of Bordeaux, there is a rectangular castle, built 1306–1307, which is of similar character to those in Wales; but there is only one curtain wall and one gatehouse. This castle has a tower of bold projection at each corner, a gatehouse in the middle of the south wall and a postern in the north wall. Here the towers are vaulted in each storey, and, in order to facilitate the construction of the vaults, they are hexagonal internally, though round externally. The castle is surrounded by a moat.

TRIANGULAR AND CIRCULAR CASTLES
Caerlaverock Castle, Dumfries, following the contour of the rock on which it stands, is constructed on a triangular plan. The first castle probably dated from the latter years of

the thirteenth century. This building was destroyed in 1312, was afterwards rebuilt and again destroyed in 1356. It was rebuilt a second time at the end of the fourteenth or the beginning of the fifteenth century. But at each reconstruction the original plan of the castle as described in a poem of about 1300[3] has been preserved, and, as can be seen on close inspection, much of the old walling incorporated. What is called the the old castle, a short distance away, has a different contour, and can in no way be the castle referred to in the poem. Caerlaverock has a powerful gatehouse, with flanking towers, at one of its angles and a circular tower at each of the other two. It is surrounded by a moat. The internal buildings, ranged round a triangular court, are all of various later periods.

Castello di Sarzanello, forty miles north of Pisa, built about 1325, is also designed on a triangular plan. Here there is a round bastion, open at the back, at each corner, the bastions being continuous with, and of the same height as, the walls. The walls are high, are strongly built and, with wide spread plinths rising halfway up their sides, present a very

Plan of Castello di Sarzanello

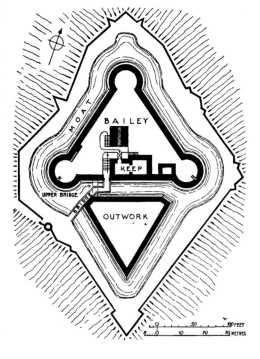

142

San Gimionano: Town from the North-West

formidable appearance. They are defended all round by machicolations at the level of the battlements. The gateway enters through the south wall under the protection of a rectangular keep, which is built up against the inside face of the wall, and overlooks the approaches as well as the bailey. The castle is defended on this side by an outwork, which is also triangular, and stands base to base with the other, a moat passing between them.

The outwork has no bastions, but its walls are of the same height as those of the main building, and their battlements are connected by a high bridge across the moat. An encircling moat is carried round outside all the walls, and there is a wall beyond the moat. Entrance to the castle is by a long bridge which passes over the moat near the outwork, takes two turns in the cross-moat and ends at the entrance gateway, being under direct attack from the battlements of the outwork, as well as those of the main building and the keep, during its whole course.

Castello de Bellver, Majorca, and the Chateau de Montaner, Hautes-Pyrenees (the first dating from the early part of the fourteenth century and the second from the latter part) are both circular in plan; and Queenborough Castle, Sheppey, Kent, built 1361 and destroyed in

Plan of Castello de Bellver, Majorca

143

Castello di Sarzanello: entrance to Castle between Bailey and outwork

the seventeenth century, was also circular. In all three the halls and living rooms were built round inside between the curtain and an inner wall concentric with it, in much the same manner as the shell-keeps of an earlier period.

At Bellver there is a round wall-tower on each of the east, west and south sides of the curtain. On the north there is a strong circular tower, which stands clear of the castle but for a high singlespan bridge thrown across between the tower and the battlements of the curtain. The gateway and its elbow-shaped barbican are placed near this tower, and are completely commanded by it.

Château de Montaner is built of brickwork. Here the curtain is supported at intervals by buttresses, and has at one point a square tower, the donjon of the castle, which commanded the entrance gateway. The château is surrounded by a moat.

Queenborough differed from the other two castles in being enclosed all round by an outer bailey and a particularly strong outer wall. This outer wall was concentric with the inner curtain, was surrounded by a moat, and had a gateway on the west and a postern on the east. Each of the passages across the bailey from the outer gates to the inner curtain had a screen wall on either side to prevent the bailey being overrun in the event of the outer defences being carried by assault. The main building, which was much higher than the outer wall, was defended by six round wall-towers, two of them being placed close together in order to defend the gateway which passed between them.

NOTES

1. "The Town and Castle of Conway," by the Author, *Archaeologia*, Vol. LXXXVI. 1937.
2. The King's Boat in North Wales is referred to in *Close Roll*, 18 Edw. II, 1325, ro. I.
3. *The Siege of Caerlaverock*, ed. Nicholas, 61–63.

Chapter 14
Towns, Fortified Bridges, Fortified Churches, and Towers

From the earliest times cities grew up below, and were associated with, a citadel, or acropolis, which occupied a dominant position on one side of their defences. Athens, Mycenae and Thessalonica (Salonica) in Greece, and Priene in Asia Minor, are among numerous ancient examples of this design; and, although the plan was not much pursued by the Romans, except as at Rome where the Castra Praetoria was added to, and outside, the older Servian walls, it was extensively followed in succession by the Byzantines, the Saracens and the nations of Western Europe, the citadel being sometimes at or near the centre of the town, as at Aleppo and Damascus. A Norman town frequently stretched away from the foot of the castle of the lord to whom it belonged, the keep having the bailey on one side (that toward the field) and the town on the other, the mound on which the keep stood often jutting well into the town. The castle therefore occupied a commanding position, from which it could either protect the town or, in the event of the town being taken by the enemy or the disaffection of the townsmen, defend itself against it. Totnes, Launceston, Pleshey and Gisors are examples of this plan.

In the latter part of the thirteenth century many new towns were built in the south of France and in England and Wales, those in Britain as well as a large number of those in France being founded by Edward the First, who was also Duke of Aquitaine. Where the site permitted, these towns were rectangular, as Monpazier in France and Flint in Wales, but many are irregular in shape, as Liboume, near Bordeaux, and Winchelsea, near Hastings. There were always parallel streets running through the town from end to end, and others cutting them at right angles and dividing the town into rectangular spaces. One of the spaces was the market place, which had therefore continuous streets passing along on all four sides, but none crossing the centre. The church stood in a square, generally near the market place. Many fortified towns in France, Spain, Italy and elsewhere in Europe are built on the top of high hills surrounded by flat uninhabited country. In Italy (where until modern times there was perpetual strife between the principal factions, Guelphs and Ghibellines, and between the many states into which that country was split up) private security was not only menaced by attack from without the town, but also from within its walls. In some towns, therefore, in addition to the communal fortifications every important house had its own tower, built both for observation and defence. San Gimignano is an outstanding example.

Standing on the top of a high hill twenty miles north-west of Siena, San Gimignano, though a relatively small town, possessed twenty such tall private towers, thirteen of which still rise to a considerable height, while others exist to the roof line of the house to which they belong, their upper parts having been destroyed. Seven of these tall towers, including the campanile of the collegiate church, are ranged round the main square of the town, now called the Piazza Vittorio Emanuele. The houses, which are mainly of mediaeval or Renaissance date, themselves rise to a considerable height. The streets of the town are narrow, and are paved with large stone slabs with falls toward the centre to drain off rain-water. They have no footways.

The palaces and large houses built in many European towns in mediaeval and Renaissance times, particularly in Italy and Spain, present to the street tall, severely plain walls of forbidding aspect, pierced only by openings which are defended by strong iron grilles. The main windows look out on to a large open court within the building, around which the rooms of the house are ranged, and on which decorative features are lavished. The court is surrounded by two tiers of galleries with richly sculptured arcades, and there is a sculptured fountain playing in the centre. Siena, Bologna, Toledo and Leon are among numerous towns possessing fine, unimpaired houses of this design.

In laying out the plan of the defences of a town some especial conditions had to be taken into consideration. Unlike a castle, the space within the walls was occupied by blocks of houses, which if not properly planned would greatly impede the circulation of troops. The open market place, forming a rallying point in time of siege, was generally placed near the centre of the town, and from it streets led towards the gateways and the walls. As in Roman camps and towns, there was a road, called the pomerium, all round the defences behind the walls. This road gave direct access to the curtain, and its towers at all points, and enabled the rapid, movement of troops and engines from one part of the fortifications to another.

The towers of town walls were often built with no wall at the back and show an open gorge towards the town, either crossed by a stone arch at the level of the wall-walk on the curtain, or quite open for its full height save for a timber floor at that level. They project principally on the outside, and on the inside their lateral walls, passing across the wall-walk, end abruptly, either flush with the inside face of the curtain or slightly beyond it.

Towers of this character are seen in the fortifications of Visby, Conway, Caernarvon and Avignon, the first three dating from the thirteenth century and the last built between 1350 and 1374. They are, however, by no means characteristic of the defences of towns, but occur frequently in the curtains of castles, as at Framlingham, about 1200, and Corfe, about 1270, in England; at Ferrara, Villafranca and Verona, in Italy, all three dating from the fourteenth century; at Smederevo, on the

Danube, built 1432; and at Roumeli Hissar, on the Bosporus, in the walls built in 1453.

Often the tower was entered from the wall-walk by a doorway on one side only; and to pass from that side of the tower to the other it was necessary to ascend to its battlements, so that if one section of the curtain was taken by the enemy that section could be isolated by removing the timber stairways in the tower at either end. This arrangement can be seen clearly in the town walls of Conway, though the work is in places broken away. On one side of the tower there was a doorway from the wall-walk to the timber floor in the interior of the tower, but there was no doorway on the other side. To reach the walk on that side it was necessary to ascend to the battlements by a timber stairway within the tower, and descend by a flight of stone steps built against the tower on the outside.

But these open-backed towers were relatively weak, and the reason for their employment was probably a saving of material and labour in construction. Once an enemy had penetrated within the town or castle they could no longer be held, and not all of them could be used as a check to the circulation of the wall-walk, like those at Conway. At Avignon there are doorways to the wall-walk on either side of the towers and a stone bridge across the gorge from one doorway to the other. At strategic points in the curtain, such as sharp angles and places particularly liable to attack, the towers were usually built without a gap at the back. At Conway the tower at the west angle of the town is closed at the back to the height of the wall-walk of the curtain, though open above that level, while that at the north angle is complete for its full height.

In order to protect the panels of curtain between the main wall-towers there were often smaller towers at mid-distance, the latter either rising from the ground or corbelled out from the wall. At Visby, Gotland, midway between each pair of large wall-towers there is a smaller tower, which is corbelled out from the wall on both faces and sits upon the wall like a saddle. Both main and intermediate towers are open at the back. At Avignon there are, in places, two turrets between each pair of wall-towers. Here the turrets are flush with the inside face of the wall, but on the outside stand upon buttresses which rise from the ground. Their battlements

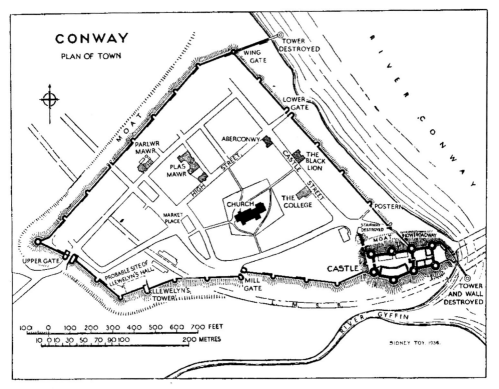

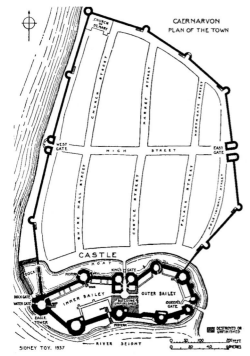

Caernarvon Castle: Plan of town and castle

are reached by flights of steps up from the wall-walk on the curtain on either side.

The wall-walks on the curtains of towns are reached by means of flights of stone steps, built against the inside face of the walls at many points along the fortifications. Once gained, they were continued all round except where interrupted by the wall-towers or by a castle at one end of the town. If the town was taken by an enemy, or its inhabitants had become hostile to the lord of the castle, it was desirable that some isolation between town and castle was secured. For this reason, the curtain walls of the town on approach to the castle on either side were reduced considerably in thickness, and the wall-walk came to an end at a point many metres from the walls of the castle, as at Conway and Caernarvon. This mediaeval defensive measure was not appreciated by those who some years ago tore down the thin portion of the town wall on the north side of Conway Castle, presumably thinking it modern, because thin, though the old thin portion is still to be seen on the south-west side of the castle.

Visby: Walls and towers

Many of the towns of Central Asia, of India and of China are enclosed by fortified walls dating from mediaeval and later periods.

In China the capital city and the principal towns are surrounded to the present day by walls so substantial, lofty and formidable that the mediaeval fortifications of Europe are puny in comparison. These walls are said to date principally from the Ming, 1368–1644, and the following Manchu dynasties; but it is obvious that many of them relate to much earlier periods, for, while extensive architectural works were carried out by the Ming and later emperors, the restoration and strengthening of existing defences took as important a part as the building of entirely new ones. The walls are built of brick, many courses thick, on a composite core and have low plinths of stone; they have either plain surfaces or are strengthened at frequent intervals by large square bastions. At the base they are from about 50 ft. to 70 ft. thick and, battered on both sides, rise to great heights, round-headed openings with crenellated parapets. The gateways are large, plain, round-headed openings, closed by large and heavily built timber doors. In comparison with the immensely strong walls, the gates appear to be vulnerable points of attack, but they were surmounted by towers occupied by companies of guards. Marco Polo states that at the time of his residence in China, in the last quarter of the thirteenth century, each of the gates of Peking had a garrison of a thousand men.

Peking: Gateway from the Chinese city to the Tartar city

Nanking, in the province of An-Hwei; Sian, in Shensi; and Tsinan, in Shantung, may be taken as examples of these fortified towns. Nanking is surrounded by a great wall thirty miles in circumference, and reaching in places to the height of 70 ft. Sian is surrounded by powerful walls, many miles in circuit, with square bastiony and with towers above the gates. The fortifications of Tsinan are also formidable and extensive. Here there is a decorative band, consisting of three rows of pointed dentils, immediately below the parapet. An estimate of the powerful character of these walls of the Chinese cities can be formed by comparison with the men and objects in the accompanying illustrations.

The city of Peking consists of four distinct parts, three of them, on the north, enclosed one within the other, all four surrounded by walls;, and together they cover an area of twenty-six square miles. The outer enclosure on the north (the Tartar city) is exposed to the field on three sides, and is covered by the Chinese city on the fourth, the latter being an oblong area extending slightly east and west beyond the lines of the other. There are six gates in the outer walls of the Tartar city, seven in those of the Chinese city and three others in the wall between the two; all the gates have barbicans. There are bastions at the angles of the walls, and the whole area is surrounded by a moat.

The barbicans are powerfully built and are of the same thickness and height as the walls they adjoin; large towers rise high above both the inner gates and the middle part of the outer walls. In the barbicans of the Chinese city and in those between the Chinese and Tartar cities the passage is straight through from the outer to the inner gates while in those of the exposed walls of the Tartar city the outer gate is at the side involving a right angle turn to the inner gate.

The central portion of the Tartar city is surrounded by a second wall, enclosing the Imperial city, with its palaces, gardens and lake; and the central portion of that again is surrounded by a third wall, enclosing the Forbidden City, into which, during the Manchu regime, no Chinese might enter. The walls of this last, which enclose the particular palace, halls and service buildings of the emperor, are defended all round by a moat. All these defences are massive and of great strength. The walls of the Tartar city vary in thickness from

Walls of the city of Thenan, Shantung

Peking: North wall of the Tartan city

Peking: Barbican of the central gate in the west wall of the Tartan city

50 ft. to 74 ft. at the base and rise, with battered sides, to the height of from 36 ft. to 40 ft. at the wall-walk, where they are still from 42 ft. to 62 ft. thick. The walls of the Chinese city, though slightly lower, are very formidable structures.

Despite the powerful character of their walls, these Chinese towns would appear to be almost defenceless against missiles rained down upon them from above. For, in addition to the highly combustible materials of which many of the houses in the streets are built, the gates and bastions are surmounted by tall and widely spread timber belvederes, most vulnerable to attack by fire and bombs.

It would seem that until the end of the thirteenth century the Chinese were unacquainted with the powerful siege engines already in use some fifteen hundred years before in Europe and the Levant. On the occasion of Marco Polo's visit to Siang, province of Hupch, about 1280, he found the city under siege by the troops of Kublai Khan. The city had held out for three years, and the investing army, seeing no hopes of reducing it, were about to raise the siege when the Europeans counselled delay whilst they showed them how the place could be taken. Under the direction of the visitors,

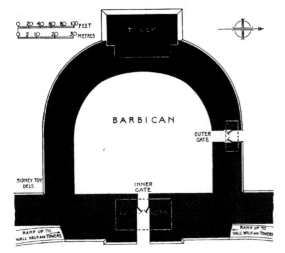

Peking: Plan of the middle barbican in the west wall of the Tartar city

powerful petrariae were constructed and set up, which cast stones of 300lb. weight. The missiles were directed, not at, but over the walls; and the inhabitants, under this (to them) novel method of attack, showers of heavy stones raining down upon them incessantly and spreading destruction in all parts of the city, became demoralized and surrendered.

FORTIFIED BRIDGES

The gateways of a town were more numerous than those of a castle, and their positions in the curtain were largely governed by the situation of the highways on which they opened. If one of the approaches to the town was by way of a bridge across a river it was important that the bridge should be fortified and protected on the far side by a barbican or tete-du-pont.

Many fortified bridges of the Middle Ages still exist throughout Europe, and among them that at Tournai, built in the thirteenth century, the Puente de Alcantara at Toledo, mainly of the same period, and the bridges at Verona, Orthez and Cahors, all dating from the fourteenth century, are particularly fine and well preserved examples.

At Tournai the Scheldt runs through the middle of the town; and at two points, where it passes through the defences, the curtain walls on either side were connected by fortified bridges. That on the north side of the town, the Pont des Trous, still exists. It is a covered bridge of three spans, pierced by arrow-loops on both sides and defended by a square tower at either end. The Ponte Castel Vecchio, Verona, was built by Can Grande the Second as part of the

Tournai: Post des Trous

fortifications of his castle, and was defended by the great square tower of the castle on the town side of the bridge, and originally by a tower and two drawbridges on the far side. This bridge was very seriously damaged during the late war, but was restored in 1951.

The Font Vieux at Orthez, Basses-Pyrenees, crosses the River Gave in three unequal spans. It is defended by a tall tower, which rises in the middle of the bridge over a fortified gateway. Pont Valentre at Cahors, Lot, one of the most imposing bridges of mediaeval times, is of six spans, and is defended by three towers, one in the middle and one at either end. All the towers stand across the road above fortified gateways, and have crenellated parapets, the parapets of the end towers being machicolated. This bridge was defended on the far side of the river from the town by a tete-du-pont.

Verona: Ponte Castel Vecchio

Orthez: the fortified bridge

Monmouth: The bridge from the south

The bridge over the Monnow at Monmouth is the finest among the few examples in Britain. The bridge was built about 1272, and the gateway, standing upon it and defending the passage, about 1290. The passage through the gateway was defended by a row of machicolations, a portcullis, and a heavy two-leaved door. The bridge stood in advance of the

Cahors: Pont Valentré

walls of the town, and a second gateway had to be carried before the town was gained.

FORTIFIED CHURCHES

Some churches situated in isolated places or in border countries subject to raids from both sides were fortified against surprise attack. Les Saintes Maries, near Aries, and the churches at Royat, Puy de Dome, and Luz, Hautes-Pyrenees, are examples in France; and Ewenny Priory, Glamorgan, many church towers on the borders between England and Scotland, and St. Michael's Mount, off the coast of Cornwall, are examples in Britain.

The fortifications of Les Saintes Maries and of the church at Royat consist of continuous machicolated parapets carried round the walls, the walls being pierced by small windows and very strongly buttressed. At Royat the upper parts of the parapets have been rebuilt, and the central tower is modern. The church at Les Saintes Maries was built in the twelfth century, but the present fortifications date from about the middle of the fifteenth century, and the parapets at Royat appear to be of about 1400.

At Luz the fortifications defend a twelfth century church, and were built in the fourteenth century. They consist of a high crenellated wall, with a deep battered plinth, which surrounds the church, and a square keep built on the north side between the church and the wall.

Ewenny Priory stands in the debatable country between England and Wales. The church is a severe and strongly built structure of the twelfth century, but the existing fortifications all date from the first half of the fourteenth century, when the precinct wall was rebuilt, a tower added to the south gate and the north gate rebuilt. The battlements on the church tower were also added at this time, though they have been repaired at a later period. Thee precinct wall and wall-towers are embattled and pierced by arrow-loops. The passage through the north gateway was defended by a portcullis, a two-leaved door, and by machicolations in its vault. The defences are all directed against attack from without.

Many churches in the border county of Cumberland have fortified towers where the priest and others could find relative security in time of a surprise raid. The tower at the west end of Great Salkeld, dating principally from 1390, is an example. It is of five storeys, and is surmounted by an embattled parapet. Both the first and second storey are vaulted. The entrance is from the west end of the nave. It is defended by a yett (a door consisting of an iron grille with oak panels), and opens on to the second storey. From here a stairway descends to the basement and ascends to the third storey (where there is a fireplace) and the battlements.

St. Michael's Mount is a steep rocky hill standing a mile out from the shore in Mount's Bay. Except at low tide, when a narrow causeway of rock connects it with the mainland, it is completely surrounded by the sea. The castle, a most imposing group of buildings, stands on the top of the hill. It was in ecclesiastical hands at the time of Edward the Confessor and became an appendage of the

St. Michaels Mount from the west, entrance near the middle of the west front. Tower of church beyond

Les Saintes: Maries from the south-east

Royat: the fortified church

Abbey of Mont St. Michel, in Normandy, about 1100. In 1190, it was fortified against Richard the First and in 1473, with a small garrison, held out for six months against a siege by Edward the Fourth, who had with him a force of 6,000 men. The castle passed into the possession of Syon Abbey, Middlesex, about 1421 and at the Dissolution was given into lay hands. In 1569, Col, John St. Aubyn lived on the Mount and was the last to maintain a garrison there.

The original entrance, defended by a portcullis, is at the head of a steep flight of steps on the west side of the castle. The central and highest point of the Mount is occupied by the church, with the lodgings of the friars and military on the west, the cloister and refectory on the south and the Lady chapel, long since devoted to domestic uses, at the north-east. The church was rebuilt in the fourteenth century. Considerable additions and works of repair have been carried out in modern times.

Luz: fortified church from the north-east with the keep on the right

TOWERS

During the fourteenth century some of the existing castles were strengthened by the addition of powerful towers, built either within the bailey, as at Foix, Arege, or in the curtain walls, as at Warwick.

The Château de Foix stands on the summit of a precipitous hill, and consists of two baileys, one within the other, defended by a barbican on the east and an outwork on the west. In the inner bailey there are three towers. The nucleus of the castle is the rectangular tower, which stands

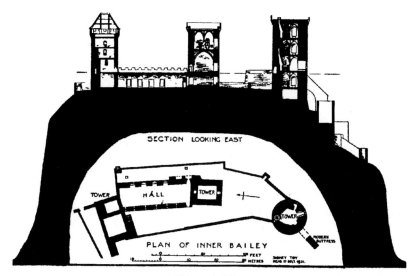

SECTION LOOKING EAST

PLAN OF INNER BAILEY

Château de Foix

at the north end on the inner bailey. It dates principally from the eleventh century, but incorporates masonry of a still earlier period, built of coursed rubble with lacing courses of Roman brick. The machicolated parapet was built probably in the fifteenth century. To this a long hall of one storey and a second rectangular tower at the other end of the hall were added at a period now difficult to determine, owing to later and modern alterations. The hall and both towers are shown on a seal of 1215, and it is probable that the additions were made in the twelfth century.

About the middle of the fourteenth century the second tower was either remodelled or completely rebuilt, and as then finished was the donjon of the castle, being much larger and stronger than the north tower and containing the principal living rooms. It is of three storeys, is vaulted in each storey and has a flat roof with a machicolated parapet. The second storey is a lofty room with one window and a small mural cell, probably a latrine now blocked. The third storey (which is vaulted in two bays) has two large windows, a fireplace; and a cell similar to that below. At the south end of the west side of the room there is a small window and nearby a postern through the wall, the latter being reached by a descending flight of steps. The postern provided a way of escape by rope ladder on to the roof of a building, now in ruins, on this side of the tower.

The entrance doorway is at second storey level, and opens off from the roof of the long hall between the towers; and from the entrance passage a spiral stairway leads to the upper floor and the battlements. Owing to the fact

Château de Foix from the west

that some of the early work has been destroyed and many alterations and repairs carried out, it is not clear how the roof of the long hall was reached from the ground. The existing flight of steps built against the hall, blocking one of its windows, and the doorway cut into the tower at the head of the flight are modern. But whatever may have been the way up, once gained and the approach cut off, the flat roof of the long hall formed a magnificent fighting platform, defended by battlements on either side and a strong tower at either end. The round tower at the south of the bailey was added in the fifteenth century.

Warwick Castle consists of an oblong bailey, running east and west, and a high mound at the west end of the bailey. It is defended on the south by the River Avon and on all other sides by a wide and deep moat. On the summit of the mound are the fragmentary remains of a polygonal shell-keep, dating probably from the twelfth century. The keep stood partly within, but mainly outside, the bailey. The existing fragment consists of three sides that were (and are) within the bailey, and is joined to the curtain wall at either end. To this fragment battlements (built flush with the inside face of the keep, instead of the outside) and two turrets have been added. The entrance doorway was

also rebuilt. These efforts in "landscape gardening" were made apparently in the seventeenth century. But the three sides, clearly considered to be in too good a condition to be pulled down, were preserved and strengthened by the addition of five buttresses.

The castle suffered considerably during the Civil Wars of the thirteenth century; but it was raised to a fortress of great strength in the fourteenth century, when a strong wall, with a gatehouse in the centre and a tower at either end, was built on the east side of the bailey, and extensive living and service quarters were erected against the curtain overlooking the river. In the fifteenth century a large tower with corner turrets was added near the middle of the north curtain, and in the sixteenth century a water gate to the river was built between the living quarters and the keep.

Caesar's Tower, at the south end of the cast wall, is of trefoil plan, and rises to the height of 133 ft. from the foot of the missive plinth, 49 ft. below the level of the bailey, to the top of the upper parapet. It is of six storeys, all vaulted except a small rectangular chamber at the fifth storey, the vaults being exceptionally thick and

Warwick castle: Caesar's tower from the river

Warwick castle from the air

strong. The lowest storey is below the level of the bailey, from which it is entered by a doorway and flight of steps down. It was a prison. The next three storeys are alike in design. In each there is a large rectangular room with a fireplace, a sleeping chamber and a latrine. There are two tiers of battlements, and the two uppermost storeys of the tower rise behind a narrow gallery at the level of the first tier. The sixth storey is a large hexagonal guardroom. Both the upper and lower parapets are pierced with cross-shaped arrow-loops, and the lower one is machicolated all round.

The approach to the tower was from the wall-walk on the south curtain, leading from the domestic buildings, and the entrance doorway stands at the head of a flight of steps up from the walk. This door admits directly to the spiral stairway at a level about 3 ft. below the floor of the fourth storey. The stairway has doorways to each of the floors except the fifth, which is entered from the gallery. The doorway into the foot of the stairs from the bailey is modern. On the north side of the tower a second stairway descends from the gallery to the wall-walk on the east curtain. This second stairway has now been broken into on the inside to form a passage through from the fourth storey; but originally, to pass from one section of the curtain to the other, it was necessary to mount the stairway on one side of the tower, traverse the gallery, and descend the stairway on the other side.

Guy's Tower, at the other end of the east wall, is of five storeys, and is surmounted by a single line of machicolated battlements. All the storeys are vaulted, and the design of the interior is similar to that of Caesar's Tower.

In Scotland and in the Border counties in the north of England fortified towers, with no other defences than the wall enclosing the courtyard (called the barmkyn) in which it stood, were now being built in large numbers. There are early examples of such towers, as at Pendragon in Westmorland, built in the twelfth century, but they were principally of the fourteenth century and later periods. These towers, though varying in size and internal arrangements according to the status and means of their builders, aree generally of rectangular plan, are, of three or four storeys, and have thick walls crowned by embattled parapets. The upper storeys are reached by

spiral stairways, formed at the corners of the towers and terminating in turrets, or cap-houses. Either the first or the second storey is covered with a barrel vault. Often one or two of the upper storeys are vaulted, and, when the top storey is so covered, the roof is formed by having flat stone slabs on the upper face of the vault.

The entrance is usually either at the first or the second storey. When on the second, it is reached by a movable stairway; often an outer doorway at the first storey, as at Closeburn, Dumfries. The first storey was the storeroom, and often contained a small prison. The upper storeys contained the hall, the great chamber and the living rooms. Mural chambers were formed at the corners of the tower; and in some cases, as at Craigmillar and Chipchase, greater space was obtained at one corner by a projecting wing, which was carried up to the full height of the tower, and contained the entrance lobby at ground level and mural chambers in the upper storeys. Clearly the privacy and social amenities of such confined quarters were restricted, and additional accommodation was often obtained by sub-dividing the storeys. Chipchase, Northumberland (dating from about 1350), Craigmillar, Midlothian and Treave, Kirkcudbright (both built in the latter part of the fourteenth century) are all good examples. Many of the towers were subsequently incorporated in other defences, as Craigmillar, where the present inner bailey, with its buildings, was added in the fifteenth century and the outer bailey in the sixteenth century.

Chipchase Tower stands on the left bank of the North Tyne, ten miles north of Hexham. It is built of stone in regular courses, and measures externally 51 ft. 6 in. by 34 ft. On the south-east corner is a projection, 3 ft. deep by 20 ft. wide, running the full height of the tower, containing the entrance lobby, at ground floor level, and tiers of chambers above. A spiral stairway rises from the entrance lobby to the upper floors and battlements. The tower is of four storeys, the first storey being covered with a barrel vault.

The entrance doorway was defended by a portcullis and a door secured by two timber bars, the portcullis being operated from a small chamber over the doorway. The first storey was the storeroom. It has neither windows nor ventilating shaft. At one end there is a well, the water from which appears to have been drawn at the second storey through a trap-door in the vault. The second storey, containing a fireplace and a double locker, received but dim light through two loopholes. The third and fourth storeys were well lit halls, with fireplaces, latrines and mural chambers. An oratory, with stone altar and piscina, is formed at the north-east corner of the third storey, and there is a kitchen at the south-east corner of the fourth storey. On the summit there are two tiers of battlements, the lower tier being machicolated; and there is a round turret corbelled out at each corner with machicolations in line with those of the tower.

Craigmillar Castle is built on an eminence, and its tower, among the finest and best preserved of its type, stands on the edge of a low cliff, the baileys stretching out on either side of it and at the back. The tower consists of an oblong body with a wing on the side towards the cliff. The main body is of four storeys. The second and fourth storeys are vaulted, and each of these storeys is divided from that below by a timber floor, built in line with the springing of its vault. In the wing the second, third and fourth storeys are vaulted. A fifth storey was added in the sixteenth century.

The entrance was most skilfully defended. It is placed at the re-entering angle of the wing, and was reached only after passing round at least two sides of the tower and along the face of the cliff. Immediately in front of the doorway was a deep chasm, spanned by a drawbridge. The floor of the entrance lobby was 3 ft. below the sill of the doorway, and was commanded from above by a small guard-room, so that an enemy who had broken through the door would stumble and have his attention diverted by the sudden drop and be at the mercy of those in the guard-room above. The chasm is now filled in, and the floor of the lobby has been raised. From the lobby a doorway on the left leads, by a lofty passage through the wall, to two doors, one above the other, the lower door giving entrance to the first storey and the upper door to the second storey. The upper door (which must have been reached by a ladder) was therefore so placed that it could be used to defend the passage. It is now blocked. Both the lower storeys were dimly lit by loopholes.

To gain the upper rooms it was necessary to ascend in succession three spiral stairways, marked C, D and E on the plans: the first from the lobby to the guard-room, the second from this level to that of the great hall, and the third from the great hall to the top floor and battlements, the short passage from one stairway to the other at each level being barred by a door. The great hall is on the third storey. It is lit by three windows, and has a wide fireplace at the west end. On the north side of the fireplace a passage and flight of steps lead down through the wall to a doorway on the outside face of the tower. This doorway (later adjusted to rooms built here and now destroyed) was probably a postern by which escape could be effected. The passage goes straight through the wall, and is not likely to have led to a latrine, as has been suggested. A doorway on the north-east corner of the hall opens to a mural chamber, and a doorway at the south-east leads into a kitchen formed in the wing.

The roof of the tower is of low pitch, and consists of stone slabs laid directly upon the crown of the upper vault. The parapet rises flush with the wall-faces, without either corbels or string course.

Threave Castle stands on the edge of an island on the River Dee, and was defended on those sides not washed by the river by a ditch. It consists of a great tower, built by Archibald, Earl of Douglas, known as Archibald the Grim, in the fourteenth century, and an enclosing courtyard, the wall of which, now in fragments, was built probably towards the end of the fifteenth century. The tower measures 62 ft. by 40 ft. externally. It is of five storeys, and its walls are 8ft. thick at the base; the second storey is vaulted. The second storey was the kitchen. It has a wide fireplace at one end, three lockers, or cupboards, and a latrine. The entrance doorway is at this level, and from one corner of the room a spiral stairway rises to the upper floors and battlements. The only means of access down to the first storey was through a trap-door in the kitchen floor. This storey has in one corner a large well, and in the opposite corner a small vaulted prison or pit. Near the well there is a stone sink, with a drain to the outside. The pit is screened off by walls 4 ft. thick. It has a ventilating shaft and a latrine; but there are no windows, and the only entry was

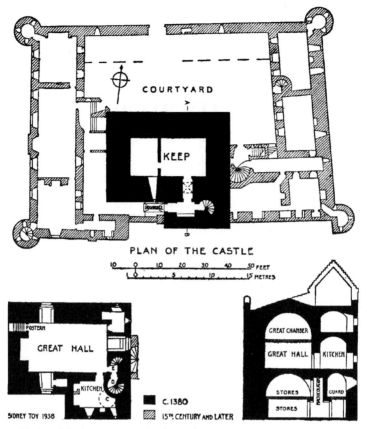

PLAN OF THE CASTLE

GREAT HALL

POSTERN

KITCHEN

SIDNEY TOY 1938

■ C.1380

▨ 15ᵀᴴ CENTURY AND LATER

GREAT CHAMBER

GREAT HALL   KITCHEN

STORES

STORES   GUARD

Craigmillar castle with plan of third storey and section through keep

through a trap-door in its vault. The third and fourth storeys are well lit rooms with fireplaces and latrines. There is also a latrine in the battlements. From the third storey a postern led straight through the wall to a point immediately above the entrance to the tower. When the outer wall was built this postern apparently gave access, by a timber bridge, to the room over the gateway. Two corbels which may have helped to support such a bridge have been cut flush with the wall below the doorway. A corbel projecting out from the battlements high above this is probably all that remains of a machicolation, defending both the postern and the entrance below it. At fifth floor level there is a large hole carried through the thickness of the wall all round the tower. It was probably for bonding timbers, originally buried in the walls and long since decayed. The clear span from side to side at this height is 27 ft.; and without such powerful ties the lateral thrusts of the roof and upper floors would seriously menace the stability of the walls.

On the faces of three sides of the tower, in line with the square openings of the low fifth storey, there are triple rows of holes. It has been suggested that these holes were made for hoarding, but they cannot have been for such a purpose. They are not very deep, conform to no known method of construction of hoarding, and do not occur on the entrance side of the tower where such defence would be mostly needed. The holes are arranged alternately in the same manner as those of a dovecot, and were doubtless made for a colony of pigeons, like those at the summit of the keep at Conisborough.

Chapter 15
Curtains, Gates, and other Defences to about 1400

Curtains and wall-towers were now usually built with deep battered plinths, for greater stability and additional protection against sapping operations. Sometimes the plinths were of great thickness at the base, ascended high up the walls, and were continuous round the curtain and towers, as at Angers and Sarzanello. At Le Krak des Chevaliers the south and west walls of the inner bailey (which are more exposed than those on the other sides) have massive plinths so thick at the base that they project much beyond the outer faces of the wall-towers, and in rising absorb the lower parts of these towers. They die into the wall at a level over three quarters of the height of the curtain.

Towers with prows were described in Chapter Eleven. The towers were often now built square at the base and round or semi-octagonal above, thus having the double advantage of a widespread solid base, difficult to sap, and an upper surface with no sharp corners to hide the sappers. In earlier work the corners at the base were adjusted to the upper surfaces by deep triangular splays, as at the south-west tower at Chinon, built in the twelfth century. At later periods the angles were occupied by pyramidal spurs, as at Marten's Tower, Chepstow, built about 1250. The wall-towers of Visby, Gothland (also of this period) are square for about half their height and octagonal above that level, the corners terminating in pyramidal spurs. Later in the thirteenth century the spurs often rise to within

Chepstow: Marten's tower with spurs at base

Goodrich: south-east tower with tall spurs, keep within the castle on left

a few feet of the parapet, as in the towers in the screen wall at Caerphilly, about 1275, and the south-east tower of Goodrich, Hereford about 1300. During the fourteenth century wall-towers were often square throughout their full height, though at corners and strategic points they were octagonal or round.

Watch towers, commanding the field in all directions through loopholes, were often built out on corbels at the angles of curtain walls, or towers, at the level of the wall-walk.

BATTLEMENTS

The wall-walks on the curtain between the towers, and on the towers themselves, were defended on the outside by crenellated parapets, and often had low walls on the inside. The merlons, or projecting portions of the parapet, behind which the defenders were secure from attack, were normally from 6 ft. 6 in. to 9 ft. high and 5 ft. to 6 ft. wide. The embrasures were from 2 ft. 3 in. to 3 ft. wide, and had a breast wall about 3 ft. high. Through these apertures arrows were shot and missiles hurled at the assailants. From about the end of the twelfth century the merlons were often pierced in the middle by arrow-loops. In some examples the coping of the merlons was finished with a roll moulding to prevent arrows which had struck the lower pan of the slope from glancing over the parapet. The projecting water drips at the base of the coping also served the same purpose. At the Eagle Tower, Caernarvon (where the parapet is 9 ft. 4 in. high and there is a roll on the top of it), the projection at the base of the coping is carried down the sides of the merlons, thus protecting the embrasures from arrows glancing along the sides of the merlons.

The walks were often paved with stone slabs; but, where such material was difficult to obtain, they were sometimes covered with lead, and the grooves for the lead flashing are still to be seen in the parapets of many castles. Rain-water falling on the walks was drained off through gargoyles projecting on the outside face of the walls.

In times of siege the circulation of the wall-walk behind a parapet, with frequent embrasures, must always have been attended with considerable danger; and from the thirteenth century the embrasures were often covered by wooden shutters, placed on the outside. The shutters were hung from the top, worked in sockets on either side, and opened out from the bottom. Even when opened sufficiently wide to permit attack on the enemy operating below, they still formed adequate protection to the defence forces. The sockets were so made that the shutters could be lifted up and removed on occasions when the embrasures would be required for access to hoarding built outside. At the barbican, Ainwick Castle, Northumberland, the sockets were cut in the stonework, the trunnions fitting into a hole on one side and into a slot on the other. When the wall-walk was roofed, the shutters were often in two parts, the upper part kept slightly open for light and ventilation. At the upper gate in the town walls of Conway two embrasures of the parapet, facing each other above the entrance passage to the gateway, are each shielded on the side towards the field by a large and thin slab of stone, which projects out at right angles from the adjoining merlon.

Sketch of hoarding

Single shutter   Double shutter

As already noted, hoards were employed from the remotest times. They were in general use during the Middle Ages, and some of them still exist, as at Laval, where the circular donjon is surmounted by hoarding, probably erected in the thirteenth century. In the curtains and towers of large numbers of fortifications, of various mediaeval dates, holes for the brackets supporting the hoards are to be seen at the level of the wall-walks.

Hoards, or brattices as they were often called, were temporary wooden galleries erected on the outside of parapets in time of siege to protect the bases of walls and towers against sapping operations. These galleries are built upon rows of beams, each beam being about 10 in. square and long enough to pierce through the parapet, to which they were

Taffauges: Tour de Vidame

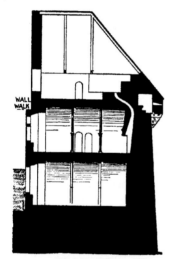

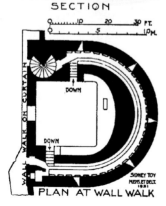

Tiffauges: Battlements of the Tour de Vidame

wedged, and project as a bracket about 5 ft beyond the outer face. Boards were laid across the brackets to form a foot-pace, wide apertures being left at intervals for machicolations; and the gallery was protected on the outside by a screen and covered with a pent roof.

Tiffauges: Tour de Vidame from without the castle

Extensive buildings of timber on the walls being a constant source of danger and disaster from burning missiles, hoards were being gradually replaced by stone machicolations. The first step in this direction was to build immediately below the parapet rows of stone corbels on which the hoarding could be built when required, as was done about 1240 in the donjon and towers at Coucy.

Towards the end of the thirteenth century machicolated parapets of stone were built at the most vulnerable points, as above the gateways, while provision was still made for hoards in other parts of the castle. At Conway Castle, 1283–1287, the walls containing the east and west gateways were surmounted by stone machicolated parapets from end to end, while the towers and the lateral walls contain beam holes for timber hoards. But it was not until the fourteenth century that machicolated parapets were in general use. The walls built at Carcassonne about 1285 have plain parapets with holes for hoards. In some cases, as at Caernarvon and Harlech, there does not appear to have been any provision even for hoarding, reliance being placed on the design of the defences and the ability of the garrison to keep the enemy from the walls.

At Sarzanello, about 1325, the walls and bastions all round the castle, including the outwork, are defended by machicolated parapets, arranged in groups of seven or eight with short intervals between each group; and at Avignon, some forty years later, they were carried continuously all along the curtain and wall-towers of the city.

At the Chateau de Tiffauges, Vendee, there is a powerful wall-tower, Tour de Vidame, of about 1500, which has a machicolated parapet and, rising directly from the crest of the parapet, a stone covering, which is the lower, and only remaining, portion of the highpitched stone roof. Here the wall-walk is actually a mural gallery, roofed with flat stones, and having on one side the parapet, pierced by loopholes 6 in. square on the outside and spaced at wide intervals apart, and on the other side, against the wall, a continuous stone seat, with footstep, for the guard. The machicolations, with 2 ft. openings, are continuous all round the gallery on the outer edge of the foot-pace. At one end of the gallery there is a spiral stairway to the lower floors of the tower, at the other end a latrine and door to the wall-walk on the curtain, and two flights of steps lead out of the gallery into the interior. The acoustic properties of the gallery are noteworthy. Two persons, seated one at either end of the stone bench and speaking in an undertone, can hear each other distinctly. The present gable and the timber roof are modern.

In some fortifications the base of the curtain wall was defended on the outside by a vaulted passage, or casemate, which ran along from tower to tower above the inner edge of the moat and was pierced with arrow-loops to the field. At Gisors the foot of the curtain was originally protected by breastworks, but in the fourteenth century the breastworks were replaced by casemates, a section of which still remains on the west side of the castle. At the Chateau de Domfront, Omc, the wall opposite the town was actually a revetment, built against the face of the steep rock of the ditch; and casemates were formed in it by cutting a gallery along the face of the rock behind the revetment with arrow-loops through the revetment.

GATEHOUSES

Considerable advance was made during the thirteenth century in the design and construction of the principal gates. The gateways were flanked by towers which formed part of a gatehouse of three or four storeys, and the approaches were defended from the battlements of the gatehouse and from the arrow-loops in its towers. The entrance was defended by one or more drawbridges and the passage through by machicolations, portcullises, two-leaved doors and from arrow-loops.

Drawbridges were operated in several different ways. Some of them, as at the Burg Ez-Zefer, Cairo, appear to have been simply drawn back upon a platform in front of the gate. Others, as at Conway, were hinged on the inner side and, by means of chains attached to the outer side and by pulleys, were raised up until they stood vertically against the face of the gate and formed an additional barrier to the passage. This was a very common method. Many drawbridges, as at Caerphilly and Caernarvon, moved on a pivot fixed a short distance from the centre of their length. When raised the inner portion dropped down into a pit, and the outer and longest portion rose up

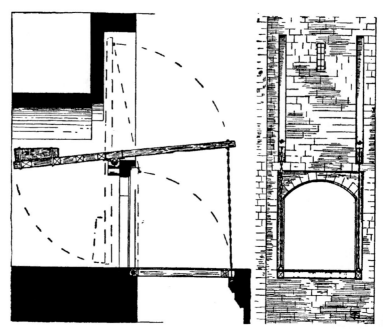

Method of raising drawbridge with counterbalance beams

to block the gateway. The counterbalance of the inner portion greatly facilitated the raising operation, while the pit formed an additional obstruction.

Another method, introduced about 1300 and much employed in France and Italy in the fourteenth and fifteenth centuries, was by means of long beams mounted over the entrance arch, one on either side, at the base of tall vertical recesses. The beams worked on a pivot at their centres, and projected half outside and half inside the gateway. Chains connected their outer ends with the outer side of the bridge, and the latter, being hinged on the inner side, was raised by means of counterbalances on the inner ends of the beams, and no pit was required. When the bridge reached a vertical position it fitted into a square-headed recess, and the outer ends of the beams fell back into the vertical slots above them. When, as was frequently the case, there was a small doorway for foot passengers on one side of the main archway it had a separate bridge and beam.

In a further method (of which there are three examples in England) the pivot was placed near the middle of the bridge, and, when raised, the outer end of the bridge dipped down into the moat and the inner end swung up to block the passage. Since there was neither moat nor pit at the inner end, three long horizontal grooves, into which the stout beams of the bridge fitted when down, were formed in the gateway passage.

The portcullises were generally made of oak, plated and shod with iron, and moved up and down in stone grooves. They were usually operated from a chamber over the gateway by means of ropes or chains and pulleys, and sometimes also by a winding drum. Machicolations opened out at the entrance to and in the vault, or roof, of the gateway passage. The doors were sometimes armoured with iron plates.

The order in which these defences were arranged varied slightly, but generally the portcullis was placed in front of the door which it defended, and the machicolations either between the portcullis and the door, as at Gorfe and Pembroke, or in front of the portcullis, as at Parthenay and Porte Narbonnaise, Carcassonne. Often there were two or three systems of these defences arranged at intervals through the gateway, as well as an additional machicolation at the entrance.

The town gateways at Parthenay, Deux Sevres, dating from the latter part of the

Parthesay: Porte St. Jacques

At Pembroke the gatehouse of the outer bailey, built about 1250, was defended by a barbican, and in the gateway passage are two systems of barriers, each consisting of a portcullis, a machicolation and a door, while beyond the inner door there is a third machicolation. All the machicolations are wide openings in the vault, spanning the passage from side to side. The passage was further under attack from arrow-loops in the walls on either side. Projecting from the inner wall of the gatehouse, immediately above the passage, there was a fighting platform or gallery. The gallery was built between two stair turrets, and was entered by a doorway through the inner wall of the gatehouse. On the side overlooking the bailey there was a crenellated wall, built on an arch thrown across the space between the two turrets. The gallery provided for the contingency of the gateway being carried by assault. From its commanding position an enemy emerging from the passage, and rushing into the bailey, could be attacked vigorously from the rear.

Mediaeval gateways reached their fullest and highest development in the latter part of the thirteenth and the early years of the fourteenth century. The main gateway is often defended by an outwork, or barbican, with its own gate or gates.

Porte Narbonnaise at Carcassonne, about 1285, a powerful structure of four storeys, was defended by a semi-circular barbican with an entrance on the flank. The main gateway has on either side a large half-round tower with a

thirteenth century, are flanked by towers built in prow-shaped form. Porte de L'Horloge, leading from the town to the castle, has lost its battlements, but Porte St. Jacques, at one of the entrances into the town, is complete, and is one of the most imposing structures of its kind in France. The drawbridge over the town moat has been replaced by a stone bridge. The entrance is defended by machicolations at the battlements, and the passage in succession by a machicolation, a portcullis and a door.

The gateway into the middle bailey at Corfe Castle was defended at the entrance by a portcullis, a machicolation spanning the full width of the passage, but divided into four sections, and a two-leaved door. It was built about 1240. On the inner end of the passage, now much destroyed, are vestiges of other defences.

Pembroke casle

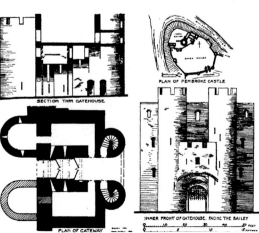

165

prow pointing outwards and rising to the full height of the gatehouse. The passage through was very strongly defended: first by a chain, stretched across from tower to tower, and then in succession by a machicolation, a portcullis, an armoured door, a large square machicolation in the vault of the passage, arrow-loops in the walls on either side, a machicolation and a portcullis, the last two being at the inner end of the passage. In addition there is provision for hoarding at the battlements.

One of the finest barbicans is that formed by the screen wall at Caerphilly. It has a gateway in the middle and one at either end. The middle gateway is further protected by a causeway and two bridges. When the castle was put in state of defence the outer bridge was probably drawn back over the causeway; but the inner bridge worked on a pivot, one end descending into a pit and the other rising up blocking the passage, as described above. The passage was defended by a portcullis, a heavy door, and a series of machicolations stretching across its full width.

The east gatehouse of the inner bailey of Caerphilly Castle was, as noted above, the stronghold of the fortress. The outer portion of this very fine structure has been destroyed, but the inner portion remains to practically its full height. The defences of this inner part of the passage were evidently designed against possible

Leybourne castle, Kent: Gateway

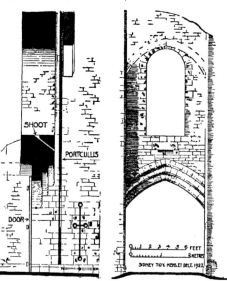

attack from the bailey. The doors closed against the bailey, and the portcullis is on the bailey side of the doors. In the vault are six holes, three in front of the portcullis and three between the portcullis and the door. These holes were perhaps for throwing lethal substances, which would spread in falling, on the heads of assailants, or they may have been additional water shoots. There is not sufficient height in the recess for the use of obstructive poles. A common method of attack on a gate was to pile up faggots or other combustible material against it and set fire to the pile, with the object of burning down the doors. In this gateway at Caerphilly provision is made to quench such a fire by pouring water upon it from a shoot just above the head of the archway. Here the outer dressings have been mutilated, but in the gateway of Leyboum Castle, Kent, dating about 1300, the shoot is, or was in 1927, intact. At Leybourn the slot for the outlet of water, resembling the hole in a post-box, measured 1 ft. 7 ft in. long by 2 in. and opened out funnel-shaped in the sill of the window above. There are indications that it was lined with lead.

The gatehouse of Denbigh Castle, built in the latter years of the thirteenth century and now in ruins, was a powerful and skilfully designed structure. It consisted of three towers arranged in triangular form round a central hall, two of the towers flanking the gateway on the north and the third standing within the bailey on the south. There was a moat in front of the castle on this side, and the gate was defended by a drawbridge working on the pivot and pit principle. The gateway passage is in two sections, the first leading to the central hall, a large octagonal apartment originally vaulted, and the second from the west side of the hall to the inner bailey, thus involving a right-angled turn within the hall. The outer section was defended by two portcullises and two doors. The assailants who had passed the first barriers, below the machicolations which the destroyed vaults doubtless contained, and had penetrated into the hall, found themselves under attack from five arrow-loops in the surrounding walls as well as from machicolations above. The hall passed, the inner section of the gateway (probably defended in a similar manner to the outer) had still to be carried.

The defensive principles of mediaeval gateways reached their culminating point in the

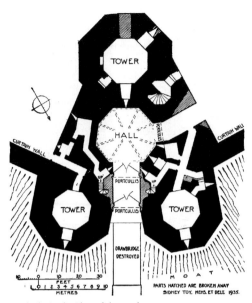

Denbigh Castle: Plan of the gatehouse

King's Gate at Caernarvon, built to its existing extent 1316–1320, but probably never completed. In essence the design of this gate is similar to that at Denbigh, with two passages at right-angles to each other and a large hall at the junction; but the defences are more numerous and the passages longer than at Denbigh. This gate also was approached by a drawbridge working on the pivot and pit principle.

The first passage was defended by four portcullises and two doors, and was commanded from above by seven lines of machicolations. The outermost machicolation covers the head of the first portcullis so that, when required, the portcullis could be drenched with water. From a point about a third of the way through, the passage gradually opens out, both in width and height, to another point about two-thirds of the way through, when it becomes parallel again. The passage was under attack from numerous arrow-loops on either side and its middle portion, from a level 12 ft. above the ground, was commanded by six doorways, three on either side, through which heavy missiles could be thrown down both to attack the enemy and to obstruct his entrance. The chambers behind these doorways are approached by steps down from the floor above the gateway. Only one side of what was to have been apparently an

octagonal hall, and only one side of the passage leading from the hall to the inner bailey, now exist. But these fragments indicate the design, and show that the inner passage was to be closed by a portcullis and door at either end, those at the inner end set to operate against the bailey. So that throughout the whole gateway there were to be six portcullises, four doors, numerous machicolations and a great number of arrow-loops in the side walls.

The gatehouse at Warwick Castle, built during the latter part of the fourteenth century, is defended by a barbican which forms an extension of the gateway. The barbican consists of a forebuilding of three storeys and two lofty walls which flank an open court between the forebuilding and the gatehouse. The passage, with a rapid rise of the footway from exterior to interior, goes straight through from end to end, and is defended by one portcullis at the entrance to the barbican and by one portcullis and one door at the entrance to the gatehouse. There are also three lines of machicolations, one at the barbican, behind the portcullis, and two at the gatehouse, behind its portcullis. The entrance to the barbican is commanded by its flanking turrets, and the entrance to the gatehouse by the battlements round the court. Passage through the court was not only strongly defended from the battlements of the side walls, but also from those of the forebuilding, on the same level, and, in particular, from a gallery in the forebuilding, at second storey level, facing towards the court. There was no connection between the gateway of the barbican and its upper storeys. The latter are entered from the gatehouse by a door opening on to the battlements of the south wall of the court and from the bailey by a rising mural passage in the same wall.

The gatehouse rises three storeys above its passage, and has four turrets, one at each corner. The turrets are carried high above the roof, and are connected by single arched bridges with parapets. There are therefore three tiers of battlements : the lowest on the roof and lateral walls of the barbican; the middle tier on the roof of the gatehouse ; and the third, made continuous by the bridges, on the summit of the turrets; and all three are in direct contact with each other by spiral stairways. There is a door to the wall-walk on the curtain on either side of the gatehouse, but, as at Caesar's Tower, the

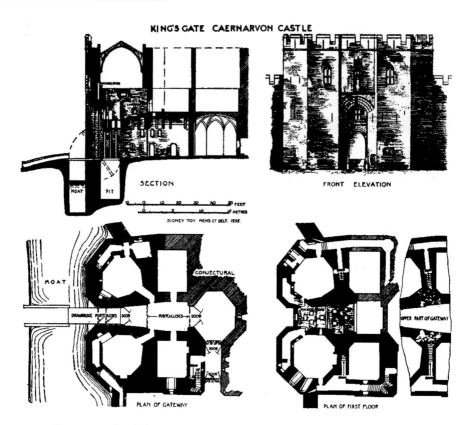

KING'S GATE CAERNARVON CASTLE

SECTION

FRONT ELEVATION

MOAT PIT

SIDNEY TOY MENS ET DELT. 1935.

PLAN OF GATEWAY

PLAN OF FIRST FLOOR

way across from one side of the curtain to the other was over the roof, and not through the gatehouse.

At Nevers, France, there is an interesting and well preserved city gate, the Porte du Croux,

Nevers: plan of the Porte du Croux

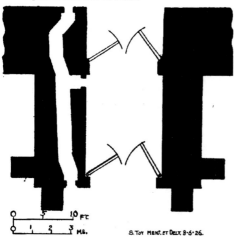

S. TOY MENS. ET DELT 8·6·26.

dating from the end of the fourteenth century. It is a lofty structure defended at the summit by barbicans and a machicolated parapet. The carriageway was protected by two double-leaf doors and the footway, with a door at either end, passed so sinuously through the wall that from one end it was impossible to see what was occurring at the other. The moat, which has been filled in, was crossed by two drawbridges, one for the carriageway and the other for the footway; the beams of both when raised falling back into long vertical slots. The upper stages of the gate, which have been much restored, were readied from the wall-walk or the curtain.

In Scotland and the Border counties the entrances to castles were usually defended by iron gates, called yetts. Yetts are powerfully forged iron grilles, hung on hinges and secured either by iron bars, drawn across the passage from out of a socket in the wall on one side and fitted into another on the other side, or by bolts attached to the yett. There are two methods of construction. In Scotland the bars

Nevers: Porte du Croux

Doune Castle: Leaf of Iron Yett

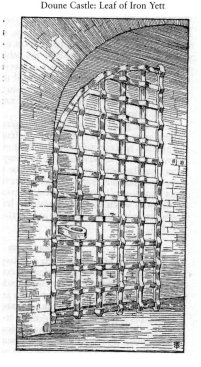

composing the gate are forged that the vertical and horizontal pieces penetrated or formed sockets for the others in alternate series. Also the grille work was left open. In England all the vertical bars passed in front of the horizontals and the joins were riveted and clasped alternately. The spaces between the verticals were then filled in with oak boards, and so the yett was solid. At Doune Castle, Perthshire, dating from the latter years of the fourteenth century, the gateway was defended at the entrance by a machicolation and a yett, and apparently at the inner end by another yett, now missing. The remaining yett is of two leaves, hung on hinges 51 in. diameter, one of the leaves containing a small wicker gate (below). It is made of $1^{3}/_{4}$in. by 11 in. bars, crossing each other in meshes $7^{3}/_{4}$ in. square, and was secured when closed by an iron bolt 2 in. square. This heavy bar was drawn out from a socket in the wall by a handle forming part of it, across the passage behind the yett, and fitted into a socket on the other side.

STAIRWAYS

In the earliest periods contact between the various storeys of a donjon or tower was by straight stairways formed in steep passages in the thickness of the walls. At later periods straight mural stairways were often used for some storeys, and in particular in the first storey, white spiral stairways were employed elsewhere. In the Levant the straight mural stairway was the general form and the spiral stairway the exception. In round towers the stairways were often concentric with the walls. In Western Europe the spiral stairway was the normal form, though the straight stairway was employed at all periods.

Spiral stairways during the eleventh and the greater part of the twelfth century were built upon spiral vaults, winding round a central newel. The vaults were constructed on timber centering, which was probably moved upwards as the work progressed, and the steps, composed of flat stones or bricks, were laid upon the upper surfaces of the vaults. By this method of construction, while relatively small material could be used for the steps, the width of the stairway was unrestricted. But the method absorbed a considerable amount of time, and the urgent demands of military building required a more expeditious process.

169

From about the end of the twelfth century spiral stairways were composed entirely of a series of steps, each step being cut out of one stone and sufficiently long to form a section of the newel at one end and to tail into the wall at the other. The first steps are built upon solid masonry; the others as they rise are supported by the newel, the edge of the step below and the wall, and no vault is required. Later, spiral vaults were again introduced, and the treads built of bricks, as at Nether Hall, Essex, about 1470, and Kirby Muxloe, Leicester, 1480–1484.

By far the greater number of these spiral stairways turn to the right as they ascend, so that while those defending them from above have the greatest space in which to use their sword arm, assailants mounting would be at disadvantage in this respect. But, since in a conflict there must be many occasions when the positions would be reversed, there are generally some stairways turning left as they rise. In the inner bailey at Caerphilly seven stairways turn right and two left. At Conway seven turn right and one left. At Beaumaris out of ten stairways four turn left, and at Caernarvon seven turn right and four left.

GARRISONS

The number of fighting men quartered in a castle varied greatly from time to time, and depended on conditions of peace or war, on the status and means of the commander and on the faithful performance of military obligations. The permanent garrisons provided for the royal castles of Caernarvon and Conway in 1284 were as follows. For Caernarvon, in addition to the constable, there were to be two serjeant horsemen, who had charge of the castle in the absence of the constable, ten serjeant crossbowmen, a smith, a carpenter, a mechanic and twenty-five footmen at arms – forty men in all.[1] For Conway, in addition to the constable and his household, there were to be thirty fencible men in all, consisting of fifteen crossbowmen, a chaplain, a smith, a carpenter, a mason, a mechanic, and ten others – Janitors, watchmen and other ministers of the castle.[2] In 1401–1404 the garrison provided for Caernarvon Castle, in addition to the constable, was a hundred men, consisting of twenty men-at-arms and eighty archers; Conway Castle, seventy-five men, consisting of fifteen men-at-arms and sixty archers; Harlech Castle, ten men-at-arms and thirty archers; and Beaumaris Castle, fifteen men-at-arms and one hundred and forty archers.[3]

NOTES

1. Welsh Roll Chancery, 12 Edw. I, 1284, Memb. 5; Cal. Rot. Wall. 288, Memb. 2; Ibid., 292.
2. *Ibid.*
3. 'Acts of the Privy Council, Vol. II, Henry IV, pp. 64–66.

Chapter 16
Development of the Tower-House: Transition Period

In the design of castles from the latter part of the fourteenth to the end of the fifteenth century the military and domestic factors come more and more into sharp contrast; for, while there is a general tendency towards the strengthening of the curtain and the outer defences, there is also an ever-increasing desire to extend the hall, the living rooms and offices, and to place these domestic buildings in convenient relation to each other.

During the latter part of the fourteenth century castles built on hills, as Pierrefonds in France, and Cesena in Italy, differ as much in plan as the sites they occupy vary in physical character. Those on level ground were normally rectangular, were defended by corner, and sometimes by intermediate, towers and were surrounded by moats, as the castles at Ferrara and Mantua in Italy, Vincennes in France, and

Bodiam in Britain. But in all cases, whether on the hill or on the plain, great attention was paid to the approaches, which were made as difficult, dangerous and exposed to attack from the castle as possible.

Castello della Rocca at Cesena near Forii, dating about 1380, is built on a hill on the south-west side of the city. It consists of a polygonal inner bailey, standing on the top of the hill, and an outer bailey which runs down its south-eastern slopes. The inner bailey is surrounded by powerful walls, with towers at the angles, and the principal structures within it are a large rectangular building of three storeys and near it a square tower, both standing clear of the walls. The gatehouse, projecting within the curtain, is on the north side of the bailey, and there is a postern on the south side, both opening on to the outer bailey.

Cesena: Castello della Rocca

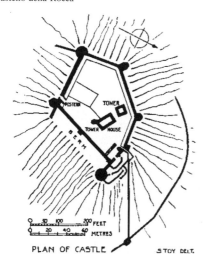

PLAN OF CASTLE

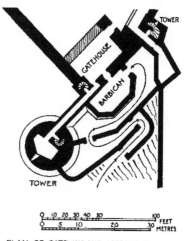

PLAN OF GATEWAY AND APPROACHES

The gatehouse is strongly defended. It is flanked on one side by a large circular tower (built outside the bailey, but joined to it by a short wall) and on the other by a smaller tower and by the curtain wall of the outer bailey, which runs down the hill parallel with the line of approach. In front of the gatehouse there is a small barbican, with its entrance at right angles to the main gateway; and the approach to the barbican is intercepted by a series of cross-walls, built between the circular tower and the curtain, and forming a serpentine passage with gateways at the turning points. Here an enemy, even after he had climbed the hill in the teeth of attack from the battlements of the outer curtain, and before he had reached the barbican, must negotiate this sinuous passage, exposing each flank in turn, and open to enfilade throughout the whole course.

Tantallon Castle, East Lothian, built probably during the third quarter of the fourteenth century, stands upon a bold promontory jutting out into the sea, and is protected on three sides by precipitous cliffs. On the fourth, the land side, the castle was defended by two baileys, and (though the outer ditch may be the result of siege operations) by three lines of ditches, all drawn across the promontory from the cliff on the north to the cliff or a deep ravine on the south. The approach to the middle bailey was further defended by a ravelin which projected into the outer bailey.

The inner bailey is at the head of the promontory, and is cut off from the rest of the works by a massive screen wall, built across from cliff to cliff, the wall having a gatehouse in the middle and a round tower at either end. Along the edge of the cliff, on the other sides of the bailey, domestic and military quarters were built. Of these buildings the north range, containing a large hall, a kitchen and other offices, all in ruins, is all that remains, the other ranges having been destroyed or fallen down. The outer portions of the towers flanking the screen wall have also been demolished; and the gatehouse, which was defended by a barbican, has been subjected to alterations and additions. But the wall itself, which is over 12 ft. thick, remains to the height of the wall-walk, and retains portions of the parapet.

The strength of Tantallon lay largely in its inaccessibility, being defended on the land side

Tantallon castle from the south-east. Bass rock on right

Troyenstein: after Otto Piper

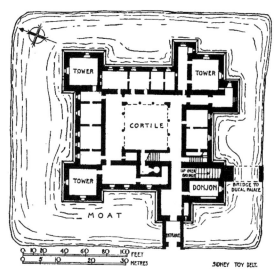

Mantua: plan of the Castello di Corte

circuit of the path, from the gateway to the upper platform. Arrived at this point, the entrance doorway to the tower stands so high above the platform that it is only to be reached by means of a rope and basket let down from the staging above the doorway. Finally, as a last resource, if all these obstacles had been overcome and the enemy had got possession of the tower, its occupants could escape by

Ferrara: plan of Castello d'Este

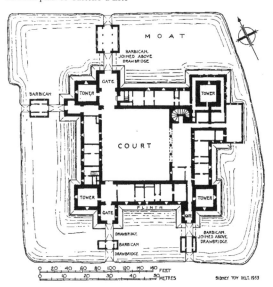

by its powerful screen wall and its outworks, and on the other sides by precipitous cliffs rising sheer out of the sea.

In mountainous countries the castle often consisted of a single tower, perched on the top of a hill and surrounded by defensive works so designed as to make the tower as inaccessible, and its approaches as dangerous, as possible, as at Troyenstein in the Austrian Tyrol, dating from the latter part of the fourteenth century.

Here the tower is surrounded at the base by a spiral path, enclosed by walls on either side and defended by battlements which stand high above the path, so that an enemy who had rushed the entrance gate, in face of fire from three tiers of battlements, would be exposed to attack on both sides during the whole

173

way of an underground passage at the base of the tower.

Castello d'Este at Ferrara, built 1385, and Castello di Corte at Mantua, 1395–1406, are both built on level ground, and are surrounded by wide moats. They are rectangular castles, with a square tower at each corner; and their living quarters and offices are built round an internal courtyard. Since they each stand within the walls of an important city, their approach works are restricted; but even here the approach, as originally disposed, was so designed as to make access to the castle as difficult and open to attack as possible. Both castles have the widely-spread, high plinths common in Italy; and the walls and towers were originally defended all round by machicolated parapets. At Mantua much of the crenellation remains, with V-shaped notches at the head of the merlons – a device very prevalent in Italy and the Austrian Tyrol at this period.

The Castello d'Este, Ferrara has four entrances, each defended by a barbican standing in the moat, with a drawbridge both

Château de Vincennes: the Donjon from the north-west

Plan of Bodiam castle

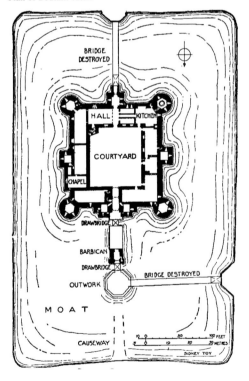

at the outer and inner ends. Two of the barbicans are completely isolated, while those at the north-west and south-east are each connected overhead to the main building by a stone bridge thrown across the moat above the inner drawbridge. The northeast tower is the strongest of the four corner towers, and was the donjon of the castle. There is no gate immediately beside it, but it commands completely the gateways of the north-west entrance, both that into the barbican and that into the main building. It is defended all round by a chemise.

One of the most powerful fortifications of this period was the Bastille at Paris, built 1370–1383 on the site of the Porte, or Bastide, Saint-Antoine, and destroyed in 1789. It was an oblong structure with eight wall-towers, bearing some resemblance in plan to Conway Castle. It was of great strength and height all round, its walls rising up to the same level as the towers, and the whole crowned by a continuous machicolated parapet. It was surrounded by a wide moat. Originally there were two gates, one at each end, defended by the adjacent towers and approached from across the moat by drawbridges. Later one of

174

Ferrara: Castello d'Este from the south-west. Crenellations removed and renaissance storeys added to walls and towers

the gates was blocked. Here the continuous wall-walk and flat roofs formed a very spacious fighting platform, commanding the city on the west as well as the field on the east, on which troops and engines could be rushed from point to point with the greatest facility.

Bodiam Castle, begun in 1386 and finished probably about 1390, stands on level ground on the banks of the River Rother. It has a rectangular plan with a round tower at each corner, a gatehouse flanked by square towers in the middle of the north side and a square tower in the middle of each of the other sides. There is a postern in the middle tower on the south.

The castle stands in a large rectangular moat, and is defended on the north by two advanced works, a barbican and an octagonal outwork, both standing isolated from each other in the same moat as the castle. Contact between them was by means of drawbridges. Approach to the castle was by way of a timber bridge which spanned the moat between an abutment on the west bank and an octagonal outwork. So placed, the bridge was at right angles to the gateway, and was exposed to flank fire from the walls of the castle. It was entered from the bank by a drawbridge. To reach the barbican from

the octagon it was necessary to turn to the right and cross a second drawbridge, and from the barbican a third drawbridge led to the main gateway of the castle. From the postern another long timber bridge, with probably a drawbridge at either end, led across the moat to the south bank. Both bridges have been destroyed, and the castle is now approached by a causeway, built probably in the sixteenth century, which juts out towards the octagon from the north bank of the moat.

The gateway is defended by machicolations at parapet level and by loopholes with oilets. Within the passage there were three sets of barriers, one at either end and one in the middle, each set consisting of a portcullis and a door, the set at the inner end being arranged against attack from the bailey. One of the mediaeval portcullises, made of oak, plated and shod with iron, still remains. In the vaulting both of the main gateway and the postern the stone bosses are pierced with holes about 6 in. in diameter, the undersurfaces of the bosses being about 2 ft. 6 in. below the level of the floor above. These holes, dispersed all over the vault and camouflaged by the bosses, were for attack on enemies entering the gateway. The

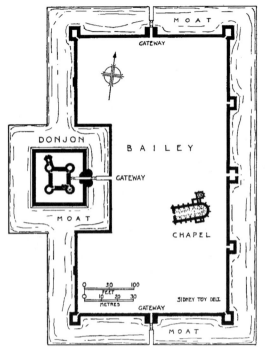

Plan of the Château de Vincennes

Already at Vincennes, begun in the first half of the fourteenth century, the donjon containing the royal quarters was isolated from the other parts of the castle, surrounded by its own wall of enceinte and wide moat and strongly fortified; and at Dudley the residential keep built at this period was an independent structure, defended as well against the bailey as the field.

The Château de Vincennes, built by Charles V on the site of one founded by Philip Auguste, clearly illustrates this new development. It has a large rectangular bailey surrounded by a wide moat with towers at the corners and along the east side. Originally there were only two gateways from without; the gateway through the middle tower on the east appears to be of later date. The Tower House, or donjon, projects out towards the city from the middle of the west side, has only one gate of entrance and is completely isolated from the bailey by its own encircling moat. It is a tall square tower with round turrets at each corner, is of six storeys, is 170 ft. high and is defended all round by a chemise. A square turret, surmounted by twin tourelles, projects out obliquely from the tower towards the chemise. A drawbridge from a postern at second storey level connects the tower with the covered wall-walk on the chemise. This Tower House is a complete unit, both defensive and residential, and in this respect, though the reasons for its design differed, strongly recalls the keeps of an earlier period. The defence was from the wall-walk on the chemise and the two tiers of battlements on the summit of the tower; all storeys are vaulted, the vault on the top being particularly thick and strong. As a dwelling the design befitted a royal residence. The second and third storeys were royal apartments, and, in addition to the spiral staircase which ascended from base to summit of the tower, the two storeys were connected by a grand stairway in the south-east turret; there was also an oratory in the square turret at third storey level. The fourth storey was occupied by the lords in attendance, the fifth by the servants and the sixth was reserved for the defence. The original kitchen was on the ground floor. The keep of Warkworth Castle, Northumberland, built on a mound on the opposite side of the

towers of the gateway and postern have machicolated parapets: elsewhere the parapets are simply crenellated.

Within the castle the domestic quarters were ranged against the walls round a rectangular courtyard. On the south are the great hall, the buttery, pantry and kitchen; on the east, opening from the great hall, the private and guest halls and chambers and the chapel; on the west, adjoining the kitchen, the servants' rooms and other domestic offices; and on the north the military quarters. The postern opened from the screens in the great hall.

The freedom now exercised in the disposition of the domestic buildings within a castle became a source of danger. At Bodiam none of these buildings could be held against an enemy who had penetrated into the courtyard, or against mercenaries (often employed by leaders at this period and lodged within their castles) who had become disaffected or treacherous. It soon became obvious (probably from painful experience) that greater security to the principal dwelling rooms was essential.

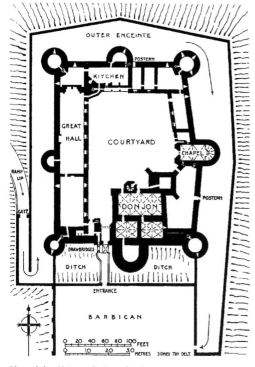

Plan of the Château de Pierrefonds

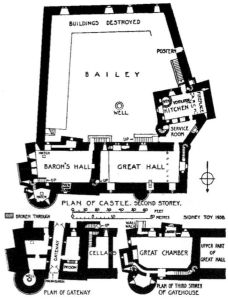

Plans of Doune castle

bailey from the gatehouse, about 1390, is also an independent fortified residence, standing apart from the other buildings and commanding the field on the north and the bailey on the south.

At Pierrefonds, built 1390–1400, the quarters of the retainers and garrison are ranged round a large courtyard against the

strong inner curtain, and, as became the powerful prince who built them, the Duke of Valois, they are designed on a palatial scale, with tiers of handsome halls and rooms. But the particular residence of the Duke is a tall structure of many storeys near the gateway, completely separated from the other buildings, and capable of independent defence. The castle has a rectangular plan with round towers at the corners and at the middle of each side, the middle tower on the south, adjoining the donjon and defending the gateway, being much

Mantua: Castello di Corte. Original crenellations retained and roofed over

Pierrefonds from the north-east

stronger and larger than the others. The approach route, above referred to, is particularly interesting and strong. The castle stands on a land promontory, jutting northward, and is protected on the east, north and west sides by natural escarpments. There was an outer wall carried all round these three sides, and the entrance was by a gate at the head of the ramp on the south-west. The approach to the gateway into the castle from this point involved the transit of the whole of the narrow terrace, or outer enceinte, between the two walls and the crossing of the barbican and ditch on the south. During the whole of this course an enemy would be under direct attack from the walls and towers of the castle.

This castle was dismantled in 1622, and for many years remained in a very ruinous state, with wide gaps ascending to the full height of its towers, until restored and largely rebuilt under the direction of Viollet-le-Duc in the latter part of the last century.

Doune Castle, Perthshire, about 1395, is designed on principles similar to those of the inner bailey at Pierrefonds, though on a more modest scale. The analogy is all the more striking in that the entrance gateway in both castles is defended by a half-round tower incorporated in the tower-house, though at Pierrefonds the gateway passes beside the tower-house, while at Doune it passes through it. The tower-house at Doune is at the north-east corner of the bailey, which is roughly rectangular in plan, the great hall extending west from it, and the kitchen and offices opening from the south-west of the great hall. Other buildings, since destroyed, were ranged round the east and south walls of the bailey, and there is a well in the courtyard.

The ground floor rooms of the tower open off from the gateway, and were for the use of the guard. They also contain a prison and a well chamber. The entrance to the upper rooms was by way of a flight of steps up from the courtyard to a doorway on the second storey. Another flight of steps led to the great hall and offices. At present a way has been broken through between the second storey of the tower, called the Baron's hall, and the great hall. Originally there was no direct contact between these two rooms, but there was a means of approach to the great hall from the third storey of the tower, by a spiral stairway. The door

leading from the tower to this stairway, however, was set to close and bolt against the great hall, so that while normally the lord of the castle probably used the great hall for dining (since otherwise his service would be much restricted) in case of necessity the door at the head of the stair could be closed and barred on the inside, and the tower isolated from the rest of the castle.

In many castles built during the fifteenth century the domestic quarters are contained in large rectangular towers, which were either incorporated in the curtain wall or stood isolated within the bailey. Generally these towers could be defended independently; and some of them, particularly those in Spain and Scotland, are of great strength. Many of them were well lit and conveniently planned dwelling houses. Borthwick Castle, Midlothian; Tattershall Castle, Lincoln; and Castello de Fuensaldano, Valladolid, are examples.

At Borthwick the residential quarters are all contained in a great stone tower which stands isolated within the bailey (above). The castle was built 1430–1440, and stands on a promontory at the junction of two streams. It has a wedge-shaped plan, with the long sides meeting at the point of the promontory. The gateway, now rebuilt, is at the south end of the west wall, which forms the base of the wedge,

Borthwick castle: the tower from the north-west

and was defended by a round tower of great projection at the comer.

The tower within the bailey, while designed as a convenient residence, is also a very powerfully-built structure, vaulted at various storeys and at the summit. It consists of a main rectangular body and two wings, both wings projecting out from the west side, and rising to the full height of the tower. There are two entrances. One of them is at second storey level, and is approached by a bridge thrown across from the wall-walk of the curtain, the wall-walk being reached by a flight of steps up from the courtyard. The other entrance is immediately below the first, and leads by a flight of steps down to the basement, or first storey. The first and second storeys arc connected by two spiral stairways.

The second storey contains the great hall, the parlour and the kitchen, the parlour opening from the dais at one end of the hall and the kitchen from the "screens" at the other end. Spiral stairways from the parlour and from one end of the screens rise to the upper floors and the battlements. In the kitchen wing there is a special service stairway. On one side of the screens there is a beautiful lavabo, with a carved canopy and a wall-shaft below the basin, similar in design to the piscinae in churches. At the dais end of the great hall there is a fine fireplace, with a tall pointed hood which rises up to within a few feet of the lofty vault; and in the wall on the right of the dais there is a wide recess with moulded edges and a sculptured head. The recess doubtless formed a sideboard, and has grooves at the sides and back for a shelf. The tower is surmounted by a machicolatcd parapet with round turrets at the comers.

The tower-house at Tattershall was built in 1433–1443 on the west side of the inner bailey of a thirteenth century castle. The old curtain wall was taken down at this point, and the tower, constructed of brick with a stone base and stone dressings, was built projecting out into the moat, with the inner long side in line with the curtain. Of the fortifications of the bailey stretching eastward from the tower-house little of the original masonry remains, save foundations and fragments in line with the curtain, including those of two round towers. Foundations of kitchens, added in the fifteenth

Tattershall: the tower house from the south-west

century, are also to be seen to the south of the tower-house.

Tattershall Tower consists of a vaulted basement, or first storey, and four upper storeys, the second storey being at ground floor level. At each comer there is an octagonal turret, which rises from the base to a level high above the walls. Each storey above the first (which was used for stores and contained a well) has a large central hall with chambers opening out of it, the hall being lighted by large windows. There are three entrance doorways, all at ground level and all opening originally from a forebuilding, now destroyed, on the bailey side of the tower. One doorway leads by a flight of steps down to the first storey, the second straight in to the floor of the second storey and the third to a turret stairway ascending to the upper floors and battlements. The second storey was the great hall. There is no direct contact, within the tower, between this storey and that below or that above, so communication must have been through the forebuilding. The three uppermost storeys, with direct contact with the kitchens, were the

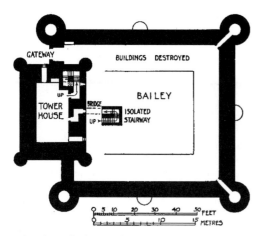

Plan of Castello de Fuensaldano

partitions and to bring the kitchen into more convenient relationship with the great hall. Elphinstone, East Lothian, and Newark, Selkirkshire (both rectangular buildings without wings and both dating from the fifteenth century) are examples.

Elphinstone Tower is of four storeys, the second and third being vaulted and the fourth covered by a timber roof. Both the third and fourth storeys are lofty, well lit halls with mural chambers at the corners and sides. A portion of one end of the third storey, with a wide fireplace, is partitioned off from the great hall to form a kitchen, and the fourth storey was also divided into two rooms by a partition. The entrance doorway is placed at a level between the first and second storeys, only a few steps from the ground. The doorway gives direct access to the two lower storeys only; but from the doorway passage a flight of steps, commanded from above by an opening in the wall of the great hall, ascends to the upper floors. From the great hall spiral stairways in the corners of the tower rise to the upper floor, and one of them to the battlements.

Newark Castle, standing on the crest of a steep bank of the Yarrow Water, consists of a large tower, built in the early years of the fifteenth century, standing in a courtyard which was probably enclosed in the sixteenth century. The tower measures 65 ft. by 40 ft. externally, and is of six storeys, the top storey being formed partly in the gabled roof. The second storey only is vaulted. Here the original entrance was at the third storey, and gave direct access to the great hall. The present entrance at ground floor level was broken through later. The entrance was defended by a guardroom, formed in the wall and opening out of the entrance passage. A spiral stairway at one corner of the tower led from the great hall down to the first storey and a stairway in the opposite corner down to the second storey, both stairs rising to the battlements and each terminating in a turret or caphouse. The kitchen, with an enormous fireplace, is formed at one end of the great hall, and was probably separated from it by a partition, now destroyed. The upper floors also appear to have been divided by partitions, each into two rooms.

private apartments, handsomely decorated with traceried windows, ribbed vaults and wide sculptured fireplaces. The battlements are in two tiers, the lower tier having machicolations and openings in the parapet for wood shutters.

Though this tower-house has strong defences at the summit, personal comfort rather than military strength is the dominating factor in its design. Its windows are large, all the floors above the basement are (and always were) of timber, and the defences at the entrance doorways must have been remarkably weak.

Castello de Fuensaldano in Spain, built in the fifteenth century, has a large tower-house which projects outside the curtain at one end of a rectangular bailey. The bailey has a round tower of great projection at each corner. The gateway into the bailey passes between the tower-house and a corner tower, and is commanded by both of them. Here also the tower-house could be defended independently of the rest of the castle. It is approached through a rectangular stairway which is built isolated from it in the bailey. At the head of the stairs the space between the stairway building and the entrance to the tower-house was spanned by a drawbridge.

Many towers with no other outer defences than the walled courtyard in which they stood, and differing little in character from those of the previous century, were built in Scotland at this period. In these towers there is now a tendency to increase the number of mural chambers, to divide the upper rooms by

Large numbers of these towers, called peels, were built in the Border counties during the sixteenth century. Constant raids for cattle and goods among the inhabitants of those regions made the provision of places of refuge for person and property a dire necessity. On warning being given, the people went to the nearest peel, made their cattle secure within the courtyard and themselves within the tower. Smailholm Tower, Roxburgh, is a typical example of these towers.

In the development of the tower-house in Scotland during the sixteenth century there were wings at the corners or sides of a rectangular main body, producing Z, T and E shaped plans.

DOMESTIC BUILDINGS

The disposition of the domestic buildings, the living rooms and chapel at one end of the great hall and the service quarters at the other, was, with minor variations, common throughout the whole mediaeval period. Where the buildings were elaborate and extensive, as at Pierrefonds, the kitchen stood near the dining hall. Generally the great hall was a lofty one-storey building having large windows to the courtyard and an open timber roof. The wide and tall windows were not originally so

vulnerable as many of them appear to-day after they have lost the strong iron grilles with which they were protected; as in the case of town houses, noted above, those in exposed positions had powerful iron grilles on the outer faces. The fireplace was normally in one of the end or side walls; sometimes on a hearth in the middle of the hall. In the latter case the hearth was provided with a reredos, and probably with a hood, and the smoke escaped through a louvre in the roof. It could never have been a satisfactory arrangement, and was certainly rare. At one end of the hall there was a raised platform, or dais, on which stood the high table. At the other end a passage, called the screens, was formed between the end wall and a partition, either of stone or wood, which stretched across the end of the hall and supported a minstrels' gallery over the passage. The main doorway to the hall, often entered through a porch, was at one end of the screens and a doorway to the postern at the other. The great hall was often constructed on a magnificent scale, with large traceried windows and wide fireplaces, as at Pierrefonds and Kenilworth.

Poitiers: fireplace, Palais des Comtes

Among the finest mediaeval fireplaces, best retaining their original form and stonework, is that at the south end of the Salle des PasPerdus, the great hall, of the Palais des Comtes at Poitiers: it dates about 1400. There are three distinct openings and three flues; the jambs between the openings are decorated with attached shafts, and the tall heads above are enriched with heraldic sculpture. Immediately above the fireplace there is a gallery, corbelled forward for greater width, and having a richly traceried parapet. The end wall of the hall, behind the gallery, is pierced by double windows, those facing the hall being each of four lights, with traceried heads, and those facing outwards being tall single lights, formed between the buttresses and the flues. The flues pass up behind the inner and between the outer windows, and are then deflected back into the end wall to terminate in chimneys above the gable.

In each of four of the tiers of halls in the tower-house at Tattershall, 1433–1443, there is an original wide stone fireplace elaborately moulded and carved. They have high panelled heads of varied design, with traceried and heraldic sculpture.

There were generally two doorways leading from the screens through the partition into the hall, and three doors in the end wall on the other side of the screens. Of the latter, one opened to the pantry, one to the buttery and the third (the middle one) to a passage leading to the kitchen. The well was near the kitchen, often in the courtyard, and embellished with elaborate ironwork at the head.

Chapels were now often large and elegant, either incorporated in a range of buildings or standing isolated in the courtyard. La Sainte-Chapelle in the Palais de Justice, formerly a royal chateau, at Paris is one of the most beautiful of all chapels built within a castle. It was built in 1245–1248. It is a lofty apsidal structure, with ribbed vaulting springing from tall clustered wall-shafts, its large mullioned windows rising from wall-arcades and soaring up to a great height to geometrical tracery at the head. The windows are filled with coloured glass, much of which is contemporary with the building. The chapel stands on a crypt of exceptionally fine and scientific vaulting. The chapel in the Chateau de Vincennes, standing isolated in the bailey, is an apsidal and vaulted edifice of somewhat similar character to the Sainte-Chapelle. It was begun in 1379, but was not completed until 1552. At Amboise there is a fine little transeptal chapel, which stands perched upon a massive substructure overlooking the Loire, at the far end of the bailey from the chateau. It was built about 1491, but has been much restored. In the courtyard of the castle of Ashby-de-la-Zouch, Leicestershire, there is a well-designed chapel of about 1480, with large tall-windows, the perpendicular tracery of which has been destroyed.

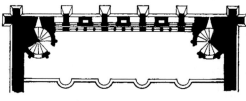

Poitiers: fireplace, Palais des Comtes

PLAN AT GALLERY LEVEL

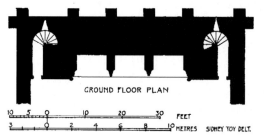

GROUND FLOOR PLAN

FEET
METRES   SIDNEY TOY DELT.

PRISONS

Though the name prison is often misapplied to ill lit rooms which were actually store-rooms, or even latrines, there was usually one prison, and in large castles two or more prisons. Some have been already noted. The basement of the south-east tower of Skenfrith Castle was a prison, entered through a trap-door in the room above, and having no other outlet than a ventilation shaft, which passed up steeply through the wall to a small opening on its outer face. There are similar cells in the basement of two of the towers at Conway Castle, though here the openings are larger, pass more directly through the wall, and admitted a dim light as well as air.

The basement of Caesar's tower, Warwick Castle, was a prison, It has no contact with the upper floors of the tower, but is approached by a flight of steps down from the courtyard to the prison door. From this point another flight of steps led up to a gallery between a small window and an opening (originally closed by a grille) to the prison, so that the warder could overlook the prisoners from the gallery without himself entering the chamber. The prison is paved partly by stone slabs and partly by bricks. It is provided with a latrine, and is ventilated by an airshaft passing up to the courtyard.

At Pierrefonds the two lower storeys of four of the towers are prisons, all circular cells about 13 ft. in diameter with stone vaults. In each case the upper cell is reached by a spiral stairway, descending from the higher floors, and a passage with two doors between the stairs and the chamber. It is lit by two loopholes, placed high in the wall and well out of reach, and has a latrine. A circular hole in the centre of the floor, with a stone cover, forms the only entrance to the lower chamber. This latter, a bottle-shaped cell, is provided with a latrine, but has neither light nor ventilation. When the cover was replaced over the hole in its roof it was little other than a living tomb. About the

time of the restorations carried out under Viollet-le-Duc, in 1862, the skeleton of a woman, crouched in the latrine, was found in one of these lower chambers.

At Dalhousie Castle, Midlothian, built in the fifteenth century, the prison is approached by a mural stairway down from the second storey of the tower, and is entered by a small doorway, only 6ft. wide by 3 ft. 4 in. high. It has a latrine, with the cesspit below the timber floor of the prison, and is ventilated by an airshaft, but has no window. At Crichton Castle, in the same county, the entrance doorway to the prison is only 1 ft. 11 in. wide by 2 ft. 5 in. high, and the sill of the doorway is 6 ft. above the floor of the cell. This prison also is unlit, but has a ventilating airshaft. The cell at Warwick measures 19 ft. 3 in. by 13 ft. 4 in.; that at Dalhousie 10 ft. 10 in. by 10 ft. 3 in.; and that at Crichton 7 ft. 2 in. by 6 ft. 8 in. All three are covered by stone vaults.

TRANSITION PERIOD

In building new military works the general form of mediaeval defences was followed long after the introduction of fire-arms. The radical changes in design required to render the new

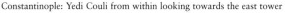

Constantinople: Yedi Couli from within looking towards the east tower

building suitable for defence against artillery took some time to develop, and the fortifications built by the Turks following their capture of Constantinople are conspicuous examples of the survival of old forms.

Although the Turks had used heavy artillery in their recent conquest, there was no provision for defence by fire-arms either at Roumeli Hissar, on the Bosporus, built about 1454–1456, or at Yedi Couli, at the walls of Constantinople, built about 1458; though guns, trained on the Straits, were doubtless mounted on the sea wall of the former at a later period. At Yedi Couli[1] the walls and towers are of great height, and the whole building is of mediaeval character, with loopholes and battlements suitable only for defence by the weapons of the Middle Ages.

There can be no question, however, but that Yedi Couli was designed as a powerful fortress. It shows an astonishing advance in plan, and in this respect is a prototype of the forts developed in Italy some seventy years later. It adjoins the great land walls of the city, built AD413, and the section of the walls enclosed, suitably refortified, contains the Golden Gate, built about A.D. 390. The castle extends within the city in star-shaped plan, with large round towers projecting well out from the points of the star. Thus planned, the towers fully commanded not only the outside faces of the adjacent but also those of the far sections of the curtain. At the re-entering angles of the walls there are small redans, and in each of the sections adjoining the old land walls there is a turret with an open back.

As developed in Italy in the sixteenth century the walls of these star-shaped fortifications were relatively low, and were backed by revetments. The bastions at the angles of the star were also low, and constructed as gun emplacements. At Yedi Couli the curtains are 54 ft. high and 16 ft. 6 in. thick, while the towers at the points of the star are 100 ft. high, and (as noted above) there is no provision for defence by artillery throughout the castle.

The three great towers at the points of the walls of Yedi Couli are each 63 ft. in external and 30 ft. 6 in. in internal diameter. Two of them are circular within and without, while the third is circular within and polygonal without. They are divided into several storeys, dimly lit by loopholes, and have fireplaces and latrines in the upper storeys. They are all entered at ground level from the bailey and also from the wall-walk on the curtain. Stairways are formed in the thickness of their walls. In one case the stairway is concentric with the tower, and in the other two it rises in zigzag form. In the south tower, in place of flights of steps, the ascent is by a series of ramps. At a level 80 ft. above the ground, in each tower, there is a wide wall-walk behind which, greatly diminished in diameter, the tower rises a further 20 ft. The south tower

The Bosporus: Roumeli Hissar – plan of the castle

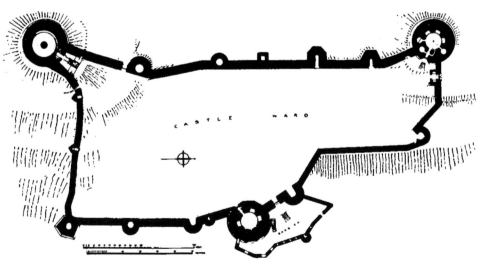

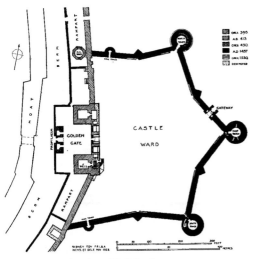

Constantinople: plan of Yedi Couli

curtain, rise from the level of the bailey to the wall-walk.

The Kremlin, or citadel, in the heart of Moscow, built 1480-1490, is another fortress of this character. It is triangular shaped with sides about 750 yds. long and stands on rising ground at the junction of the river Moskva with its tributary Neglinka, one side running along beside the river and another, on the west, along the east bank of the stream. It is surrounded by a powerful wall, built of brickwork, varying in thickness from 14 ft. to 20 ft., and in height from 30 ft. to 70 ft. The wall is surmounted by an embattled parapet, is strengthened at intervals by square towers, and is pierced by four gates with carriageways and a postern for pedestrians only. The postern had a secret passage to the river bank.

Originally the gateways were defended by drawbridges, and from without the Kremlin must have presented a formidable appearance. But, as at Roumeli Hissar and Yedi Couli, the defensive system provided for mediaeval weapons only; and here at the Kremlin the battlements, with their narrow notched merlons of the same width as the embrasures, appear to be designed more for ornament than defence. The steeples and pyramidal structures built on the gates and towers were added in the seventeenth century when defence was no longer a major consideration. The clock tower,

has a domed vault at the summit; the east tower is now roofless and the north tower has lost its upper extension.

The gateway into the castle from the city passes through the lower storey of a tower, and was defended by a portcullis, a machicolation and double doors. There was no other postern than that through the Golden Gate, which passes through the walls to the open country beyond the city. Straight stairways, built at frequent intervals against the inner face of the

Moscow: the Kremlin, south-east corner from the river.

185

Moscow: the Kremlin, east wall and towers. Gate of the redeemer and clock-tower on the right.

Moscow: plan of the Kremlin

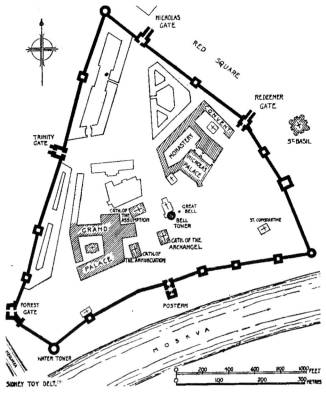

186

one of these additions built above the main gate, the Gate of the Redeemer, is 205 ft. high and contains a fine peal of bells.

Within the Kremlin are three cathedrals, numerous other churches, a monastery, a convent and two palaces, as well as government buildings, offices and barracks. Near the centre is an octagonal bell-tower 325 ft. high, built in 1601, and on a pedestal beside it stands the fractured " Great Bell of Moscow."

NOTE

1. *Vide* "The Castle of Yedi Couli, or the Seven Towers, Constantinople," by Sidney Toy, *Journal of the British Archaologlcal Association*, 1951, pp. 27 *et seq.*

Chapter 17
Fortification for Artillery

While the development of the living quarters was proceeding on the lines of convenience, the effective use of firearms was coming more and more into prominence. Great strides in the design of artillery were made during the fifteenth century. Cannon casting stones and other missiles are said to have been used at the Battle of Crécy in 1356. However this may be (and there is insufficient evidence for it), they were certainly in use before the end of the fourteenth century. Firearms were used by the English at the siege of Berwick in 1405; and they were used with great effect by the French during the second quarter of the fifteenth century. In his treatise on artillery, Prince Louis-Napoleon Bonaparte writes that the French owed their successes during that period as much to their superior artillery as to the heroism of Jeanne d'Arc.[1] At the siege of Constantinople in 1453 the Turks used guns of great calibre. The power and development of the new weapon by the latter years of the fifteenth century was amply demonstrated in its use during the campaigns in Italy of Charles the Eighth of France. In 1494 the French troops marched through Italy, and with their guns reduced castle after castle with astonishing rapidity.

Despite this great progress in the use of artillery in the field, the provision for firearms in military architecture was not made before the gun had become a well developed weapon. Contrary to what one may suppose, the crossbow being the prototype of the hand-gun, small arms were a development from the cannon, and not the cannon from small arms. Cannon in its initial stages could not be mounted on the walls and dipped so as to attack those below; and it was not until the last quarter of the fifteenth century that gun-loops, coeval with the walls, begin to appear, and then only in the bases of walls and towers. Gun-loops such as those in the west gate at Canterbury were adapted from earlier arrow-loops; for the fortifications of towns and castles were being continually adjusted to the defensive requirements of the day.

In the early gun-loops the base of the hole is circular for the mouth of the piece and the upper part a slot for sighting. Sometimes the slot has a circular hole at the head, as at Falaise, Calvados. At Kirby Muxloe, Leicester, 1480–1484, the hole and slot are separated. Later the hole for the gun took various forms, but generally it was widely splayed outward at the sides to give the gun the greatest possible range, right and left, as in the fortifications at Périgueux and Avalon. In situations high in the wall the sills were sloped rapidly downwards to repel hostile operations immediately below, as in the Carlsthor gate at Munich and at Salignano near Otranto.

From the early part of the sixteenth century there is complete disseverance between domestic and military structures. The domestic quarters develop in the palace, mansion-house or hotel, and the military buildings into a fort under the complete control of the king or governing body.

Among the most powerful works of the early Renaissance were the fortifications of the city of Rhodes, built by the Knights of St. John of Jerusalem in the fourteenth century – in some places on ancient foundations, but greatly augmented, strengthened and adapted to defence by artillery towards the end of the fifteenth and in the early years of the sixteenth century.

The city of Rhodes is built on the east shore of the north tip of the island. Three long moles running from the shore out into the sea at this point enclose two well-sheltered harbours,

Gunloops

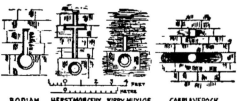

BODIAM   HERSTMONCEUX   KIRBY MUXLOE   CAERLAVEROCK

which were defended by three powerful towers, one at the sea end of each mole. The two pedestals, one for each leg of the Colossus of Rhodes, probably stood on the submerged causeway at the entrance to the Ancient Harbour. The city, stretching south and west from the Grand Harbour, is surrounded by powerful walls and wide moats. The CoDachium, or citadel (containing the palace of the Grand Master, the principal buildings of the Order and the residences of the Knights is at the north side of the city, facing the open country on one side, and having a wall, now destroyed, between it and the city on the other.

The curtain walls (defended at the salient points and at intervals along the sides by towers) were until the latter part of the fifteenth century from 9 ft. to 12 ft. thick and about 30 ft. high, with crenellated parapets of the notched form. On the south and west, the sides toward the land, the walls were protected by a ditch, with a narrow berm between the wall and the ditch.

These fortifications, particularly those on the land side, were very considerably strengthened between 1470 and 1521, and especially under the direction of Pierre d'Aubusson, Grand Master 1470–1503. On the land sides the ditches were widened and deepened, the benns formed into outer galleries along the wall faces, and bulwarks, defended by artillery, were built round the gateways and salient towers. In some places the defences were augmented by an outer rampart and a second ditch. Further, the curtain

Plan of the City of Rhodes

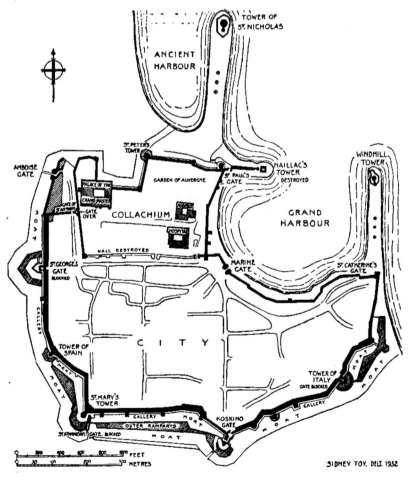

Rhodes: South wall with gallery

was reinforced by building up additional material on the inside, bringing the total thickness to about 40 ft. Many of the towers were lowered to the general height of the curtain, and in places the parapets of the curtains were adapted for artillery. The galleries on the outer face of the curtain, proving in siege operations to be more dangerous than useful to the defenders, were not included in the new works after about 1500, though existing ones were retained (see above).

Originally there were eight gates in the city walls. One of them, St. Anthony's, was later enclosed, and a new one, Amboise gate, built in the outwork. Two gates on the west, those of St. George and St. Athanasius, and the gate of Italy on the south-east were all blocked for greater security in attack. There were also three gates to the citadel, of which that on the west opening on to the wall-walk above St. Anthony's gate still exists. The gates of St. George, St. Athanasius, St. John, or Kosldno, and of Italy, though much altered and

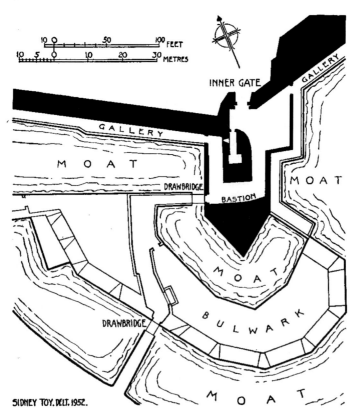

Rhodes: plan of the Koskino gate

SIDNEY TOY. DELT. 1952.

strengthened later, probably date from the fourteenth century. The Marine gate was built in 1478 and the Amboise gate about 1504.

St. George's gate was remodelled about 1430, and blocked about 1478 when the bulwark was added. The bulwark, like others added to these fortifications, is tunnelled by casemates with ventilating holes in their roofs. St. Athanasius' gate, St. Mary's tower, the tower of Spain and the Koskino gate were all strengthened by bulwarks in the latter years of the fifteenth century; and the line of wall between their extreme points was defended by an outer rampart and double ditch at the same time. The passage through St. Athanasius' gate, after crossing the bridges over both ditches, descended by flights of steps to pierce the wall east of St. Mary's tower. It was blocked about 1514.

Koskino gate, as completed about 1480, was defended by three outworks, forming three tiers of battlements; by two ditches; and by a sinuous passage of approach interrupted in succession by two drawbridges. An enemy approaching the outer bridge would be open to direct attack from a battery of heavy guns mounted on the bulwark, as well as from the two tiers of battlements on the bastion above it; while during the whole course of his attempt to reach even the bastion he must cross two ditches and negotiate a sinuous passage in face of deadly fire from all quarters, including the gallery and the battlements of the curtain. Having carried all those defences, he must rush through the passage in the bastion, turn round the inner tower, and finally carry the inner gate, which was defended by a portcullis and a stout door. To provide additional protection on the east side of the bastion, where there was no other outer defence than the ditch, the gallery was extended across the east face of the bastion to the bulwark.

It is pertinent to note at this point that in the case of direct assault on a fortress, especially in the later Middle Ages, the attack was generally made at some point in the walls thought to be the most vulnerable, and not at a gateway, the gateway having powerful defences. When entry by an enemy was made through the gateway it was usually rather by stratagem than by direct assault.

In the siege of Rhodes in 1480 the most vulnerable part of the walls was that stretch,

called the Jews' wall because the Jews' quarters were behind it, running eastward from the Koskino gate to the sea. Having suffered great damage during the siege, this portion was afterwards repaired and strengthened. The wall was reinforced from behind to bring the total thickness to about 40 ft., and the gate of Italy was blocked. Since the section of wall between the gates of Koskino and Italy was commanded by three wall-towers, the outer rampart was omitted here. Later, under the Italian Grand Master Carretto, 1513–1521, the round tower of Italy, which defended the gate, was enlarged, and a wide semi-circular bulwark with emplacement for a battery of heavy artillery was built round it. Further, the stretch of wall to the north of the tower was defended by an outer rampart and a second ditch. The fortifications on the north side of the city, toward the sea, being less open to attack, received less attention, and the walls were not thickened.

The Marine gate is of bold appearance and solid construction, having relatively small chambers and thick walls. It is flanked on either side by tall towers and surmounted by continuous machicolated parapets. The passage is defended by a portcullis and door. The north wall of the citadel was defended by St. Peter's tower, in the middle; the round tower at St. Paul's gate, at the east end; and by the palace of the Grand Master, which was a powerful donjon, on the west.

The three towers at the head of the moles jutting out into the sea formed powerful advanced guards in the defence of the city. Naiilac's tower, a tall square structure surmounted by turrets, all with machicolated parapets, collapsed during an earthquake in 1863. Windmill and St. Nicholas' towers, both circular and surrounded by outer defences, remain substantially complete.

St. Nicholas' tower occupies so important a position in the defences, and was so formidable in itself, as to draw upon it the full force of the Ottoman attack, both by land and sea, in the siege of 1480. It consists of a strong circular tower, with very thick walls enclosing vaulted chambers, a circular chemise round the tower and a polygonal bulwark round the chemise. The original entrance was altered after 1480, but appears to have been first by a gate through the bulwark, then by an isolated newel stairway and a drawbridge to the chemise, by flights of steps up to the wall-walk on the chemise, round the chemise to a point opposite the doorway in the tower, another flight of steps up to the level of that doorway, and finally by a drawbridge across the gap between the chemise and the doorway in the tower. The tower was a complete fortress, containing a well, fireplace, latrines and store-rooms, and was capable of long independent resistance.

The fortifications of Famagusta, on the eastern shore of Cyprus, dating principally from the last decade of the fifteenth century, deserve note as early defences constructed for artillery. At the salient points, and at intervals along the sides of the walls, are strongly built bastions, that at the south-west corner defending the main city gateway, which passes through it. This gateway was protected by an isolated ravelin; and the approach was first by a bridge across the moat to the ravelin, then, after taking a right-angled turn and crossing a second bridge, to the gateway through the bastion. From about the end of the sixteenth century isolated ravelins ceased to be in favour, since in time of siege they proved to be a greater menace to the defence than to the enemy. For, while it was difficult for the defenders to enfilade the moat beyond the ravelin, the enemy's miners found the ravelin a shield for their operations.

Another interesting feature of the fortifications of Famagusta is the triangular-shaped bastion at the north-west corner of the walls, forming part of the works carried out here by Italian engineers about 1560. The bastion is joined to the corner at the middle part of its base so as to leave a recess, called a flanker, on either side. The recesses are closed

at the opening by masonry, pierced with holes for batteries of cannon. They are approached by inclined ways leading down from points within the city walls, and also by flights of steps leading down from the bastion. From these flankers, as well as from the emplacement on the bastion, the outer faces of the curtain on both sides could be thoroughly commanded and raked with gunfire. This form of bastion was introduced in the fortifications of Verona about 1520 by the eminent Italian engineer Michele Sanmichele; and that at Famagusta is a particularly fine and well preserved example of its type, with a ventilated gallery connecting both flankers (see above).

In 1530, eight years after their departure from Rhodes, the Knights of St. John established themselves at Malta, and proceeded to erect military works which are among the most powerful and extensive defences of their period extant. Even now, despite demolition and alteration due to modern military requirements and other less laudable accounts, these structures are still sufficiently complete to be of exceptional historical value. Valetta, the capital city, is built on a tongue of land which runs out seaward between two long harbours, and is flanked and commanded by land on the far sides of the harbours for the whole of its length. It was therefore necessary to defend the high ground on either flank of the city, as well as the promontory on which it stands.

The walls of the city are built on a serrated plan, having triangular bastions with flankers at the salient points and strongly defended gateways. Each of the two bastions flanking the King's gate, which is in the middle of the wall at the land end of the promontory, has a cavalier, that is a small fort, built in the middle

Famagusta: Upper and lower plans of Bastion at N.W. corner of the city

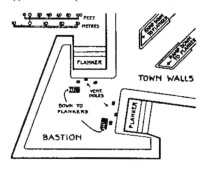

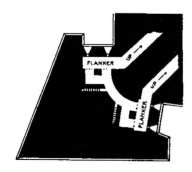

of its emplacement, and commanding not only its immediate surroundings but the trenches beyond. At the head of the promontory, facing seaward, there was a star-shaped citadel called the Fort St. Elmo. The city at first occupied only the seaward half of the promontory, but later the landward half, called Floriana, was incorporated and fortified.

Among the earliest and most perfect examples of large towers added to old fortifications, and designed entirely for defence by artillery, are the Burg Muqattam and the Burg Al-Wustany at Cairo. These towers stand one at either end of a strong wall which, with them and a gateway in the middle, was thrown across one end of the citadel in the first pan of the sixteenth century. Burg Al-Wustany has lost its upper pan above the wall-walk of the curtain, but the other tower is practically complete

Burg Muqattam is a powerful round tower of four storeys, its walls are 22 ft. thick and it

Citadel of Cairo: Burg Muqattam

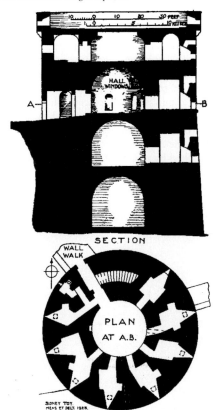

is covered at each storey by a strong domed vault. It is entered from the wall-walk on the curtain by a passage leading straight into the central hall of the third storey. From this level the fourth storey and the battlements are reached by a mural stairway rising concentric with the wall, and opening off from the entrance passage.

In all storeys above the basement mural chambers for the guns open off from all sides of the central hall. Each chamber is pierced on the outer wall by two rectangular openings, one above the other. The lower opening, with widely splayed jambs, was for the gun, and is sufficiently high to permit of sighting above the piece. The upper opening was for the admission of light and the escape of smoke. Ample space is provided in the chambers for ammunition, and there is a latrine on each floor.

In England political events led to further developments of the fort. During the reign of Henry the Eighth many old castles which had been allowed to fall into disrepair were reconditioned and put into defensive order. The use of gunpowder had diminished their value, but had not sufficiently developed to render them obsolete. Even the artillery of a century later when brought by the Parliamentary army against Corfe, a castle of particularly strong masonry, was powerless to reduce it, though the guns battered away at its walls for nine months.

But something more modern was necessary to meet the impending trouble. Henry had broken with the Pope, and was at variance with the Emperor. He might expect an invasion at any moment. He therefore decided to build at various points along the south coast of England a line of forts, designed for artillery and equipped with the latest type of guns. Well preserved examples of these forts, built about 1540, exist at Walmer and Deal in Kent, Camber in Sussex, and St. Mawes and Pendennis in Cornwall.

The principle governing the design of the new forts was that the whole building should be concentrated in one compact block which could be defended all round by artillery, the guns being mounted on platforms rising in tiers one behind the other. This principle was followed in all the castles, though there were variations in plan and detail.

Walmer Castle consists of a quatrefoil-shaped curtain, or chemise, one storey in

Constantinople: Yedi Couli from within, looking towards the east tower

height, and a round tower of two storeys, the space between the chemise and the tower being covered with a flat roof forming a gun emplacement. A circular pier in the centre of the tower contained a spiral stairway by which the emplacement and the upper storey of the tower were approached. The whole building is surrounded by a wide and deep moat, and was entered by a drawbridge over the moat and a doorway in one of the lobes of the chemise.

From the vaulted passage between the chemise and the tower a stairway leads down to a casemate, or mural gallery, which runs all round the walls of the chemise. The gallery is pierced on the outside by numerous loopholes, fifty-six in all, from which the surface of the moat could be raked by gunfire at every point. On one side of the gallery there are large recesses for the accommodation of artillerymen and on the other smaller recesses for their ammunition. Ventilation and outlet for smoke is secured by circular holes in the vault of the gallery, with shafts to loopholes on the outer face of the wall. The larger guns were mounted on the emplacement above the chemise, and commanded the neighbourhood of the castle in all directions.

Deal Castle is much larger than Walmer, and has two tiers of gun emplacements. It consists of a central tower and a sexfoil chemise, the tower being of three storeys and having attached to its outer face six lunettes, or lobes, which rise through two storeys only. The chemise is of one storey, and the space between it and the tower is covered by a flat roof forming the first gun emplacement. The upper floors and battlements are reached by a spiral stairway in the centre of the tower, and, as at Walmer, the castle is surrounded by a moat and approached by a drawbridge.

Deal Castle from the air.

The lobes attached to the tower had flat roofs for the second tier of gun emplacements; and, these lobes being arranged on plan alternately with those of the chemise, the guns mounted on the two tiers were together able to direct concentrated fire from a large number of pieces at any point around the castle within their range. Both Walmer and Deal castles have been altered and added to, but the original walls remain substantially intact.

Sandgate Castle (a large portion of which has been pulled down) consisted of a central tower and two lines of triangular-shaped chemise walls, the inner line having a tower at each angle and the outer being rounded at the angles. It was entered by a D-shaped gate-tower and a stairway between the tower and the outer wall. Here the lower gun emplacements appear to have been at the rounded angles between the towers of the inner chemise and the outer wall. The upper emplacements have been destroyed.

Camber Castle consists of a central round tower and a multangular-shaped chemise, the chemise having a large lobe projecting from each of the cardinal points. A fifth rounded

Deal Castle from the air.

projection, containing an entrance porch and having much thinner walls, was added at a later period.

At St. Mawes there are three lobes with gun emplacements ranged in trefoil round a central tower; and at Pendennis a wide emplacement passes concentrically round a circular tower, except at the point where the emplacement is intercepted by the gateway. In the latter part of the sixteenth century the fort at Pendennis was enclosed within an extensive bailey, defended by a curtain wall and a ditch.

One of the most powerful forts of the sixteenth century is the Chateau Munoth at Schaffhausen, Switzerland, built at a strategic point on the right bank of the Rhine, where the river takes an abrupt bend southwards. The fort is built in the form of a large circular tower, strongly vaulted throughout and with very thick walls. It consists of a basement and ground floor, and guns were mounted on both of them, as well as on the roof. Swift and easy contact between the floors and the roof was assured by the provision of three stairways and a spiral ramp, the ramp being of such width and easy gradient as to permit of the moving of gun carriages through it. The curtain walls radiate from the tower down to the Rhine, enclosing a triangular bailey.

At Nassau, Bahamas, there is an interesting military work of the late eighteenth century called Fort Fincastle, built by the governor of those British possessions and now used as a signal station.

Fort Fincastle stands on an eminence dominating the city of Nassau and the approaches to the harbour east and west. It consists of a circular body, 84 ft. diameter, containing the main gun emplacement, an elevated platform for a second emplacement, and a sharply pointed prow, the whole surrounded by a dry ditch. The entrance is on the south side, and from it a flight of steps leads up to the first emplacement, 9 ft. above. This part is surrounded by a thick parapet over which the heavy guns, working on swivels and pointing west, north-west and south-west, fired. On the platform (which stands 12 ft. above the first emplacement and is reached by a flight of steps) were smaller guns firing through embrasures and pointing north-east and south-east.

The function of the prow was precisely that of the same feature in mediaeval work

Fincastle, Bahamas, from the air

chambers, all entered from the main gun emplacement and ventilated by openings which pierce the walls to the outer face, where they appear as narrow loopholes imperceptible from a distance. A recess, without doorway, opening directly on to the main emplacement was probably for ammunition required for immediate use. The stone roof of the prow slopes away on both sides to discharge the rain-water falling upon it.

Artillery now being powerful enough to destroy masonry at a considerable distance, it was obvious that walk had to be lowered and the line of defence brought nearer to ground level. Lofty walls and towers gave place first to lower structures, then to works half above and half below the ground, and, after the temporary and abortive return to early forms in the *tours modèles* of France and the Martello towers of England, eventually to defences dug out below ground level. The further development of fortifications, however, with their complicated systems of casemates and outworks, belongs to a special field of study, and this work will be concluded with an account of the siege of Rhodes in 1480 when artillery was used both in attack and defence.

described above, namely to deflect the missiles (here cannon balls) fired against it, and, in this particular case, to contain within its thick masonry vaulted chambers for guard-rooms, ammunition and general stores. There are three

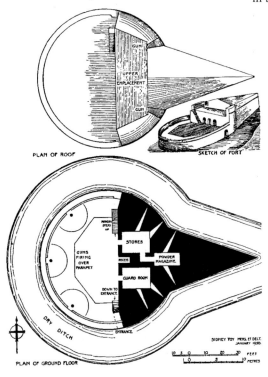

Fort Fincastle, Nassau, Bahamas

196

Chapter 18
Siege of Rhodes in 1480[1]

The siege of Rhodes in 1480 was one of the most moving events of later mediaeval history, and had effects reaching far beyond the island. Under constant menace of attack long before it occurred, the Knights of Rhodes set their defences in order. The Grand Master at that time, Pierre d'Aubusson, was a man of outstanding integrity, wisdom and courage, who before coming to Rhodes had won distinction for his sagacity as a diplomat, as well as for his bravery and success as a soldier, both in the service of the Emperor of Austria and the King of France. Under his command the walls of Rhodes were repaired and strengthened, new defences of the latest design were added and batteries of artillery were mounted on the battlements all round the city. To prevent the enemy from finding provisions and shelter in his assault, the crops and trees in the immediate neighbourhood were cut down and two churches were removed.

The Knights of Rhodes, or Order of St. John of Jerusalem, were divided into eight sections, called Languages; and when the city was placed in state of siege each language was charged with the defence of a particular length of the fortifications. In 1480 the walls facing the Grand Harbour were assigned to the Castile language, those on the north to France, those on the west to Germany, Auvergne and Aragon, and those on the south and south-east to England, Provence and Italy. Able commanders were appointed to the garrisons in St. Peter's tower and in the three isolated towers in the harbour. A chain boom was thrown across the entrance to the Grand Harbour.

Failing in his endeavours to persuade the Knights of Rhodes to purchase immunity from attack by the payment of an annual levy, and determined to subjugate the island, Mohammed the Second fitted out and despatched a powerful expeditionary force under the command of a trusted pasha. The fleet appeared off Rhodes on May 23rd, 1480, and, despite strong resistance, effected a landing on the west shore of the island, near the city. Immediately on arrival, with more impetuosity than wisdom, they rushed towards the west wall of the city, only to be driven off in this and a second more organized attempt.

They then decided, on the advice of a German engineer operating with them,[2] to concentrate all their forces, both on sea and land, in an attack on the tower of St. Nicholas, a strong fort guarding the approach to the city from the sea. It was thought that, this strong point being carried, the other defences of the city would prove relatively easy prey. The Turks set up their artillery on the west side of the Ancient Harbour and, under the protection of timber mantlets, bombarded the tower incessantly. On their side the Knights set up a battery of guns in the Garden of Auvergne, within the walls just south of this position, and directed a constant fire on the enemy. The pasha, using his heaviest guns, some of which were said to cast balls 3 ft. diameter, by constant fire broke down the outer wall of the fort.

Realizing the seriousness of the position, the Grand Master sent picked men to reinforce the garrison, and went there himself to direct operations. Finding that the west wall was reduced to debris, forming a kind of bastion which was beyond damage from cannon fire, Aubusson filled the breach with a strong wood screen constructed of heavy timbers. To prevent the enemy from using the submerged causeway at the entrance to the harbour, which was fordable at low tide, he had spiked planks laid down upon it. Concentrating all efforts on the protection of this part of the city, he prepared for the impending naval attack by placing fire ships in the harbour and by mounting guns on the walls which commanded the approaches to the wall by sea.

On the morning following these preparations the combined attack began, heralded by a great clamour, blowing of trumpets and beating of drums. The Turkish galleys, favoured by a strong breeze, steered directly for the tower, and the land forces, having crossed the harbour, began to scale the walls and attack the garrison behind them. The Turks hurled showers of arrows, stones and fire pots at the defenders, while some of them, armed with iron grabs attached to the end of long cords, threw and retrieved these weapons with great dexterity. They rushed to the fight with intense fury, those put out of action and thrown down from the ladders they had set up being immediately replaced by others, as wave after wave of reinforcements surged forward.

The defence was conducted with great skill and courage. Those in the tower, knowing that they must conquer or perish, fought as brave men do in such straits. Those defending the mole were able to repel with hand-guns attempts to gain a footing there. At sea the fire ships in the harbour, aided by the batteries of artillery on the walls and the use of Greek fire, spread havoc among the enemy's fleet. Seven hundred ships were destroyed, and the rest, drawing off in haste, lost many men drowned in the flight. The close attack on the tower was also repulsed, and both fleet and army retired to their bases round the point of the island. The victory was with the defence.

Following this reverse, the Ottoman commander decided to attack the wall at its weakest point, which was that section on the south-east side of the city called the Jews' wall. Aubusson, observing the preparations for this manoeuvre, and knowing that the Turks with then powerful artillery must soon make a breach here, decided to strengthen this section of the wall by a substantial addition from behind. The work must be done in haste, and every available person was employed in it: men, women and youths, rich and poor alike, those not skilled in building carrying materials for those who were. He also deepened the moat in front of the wall, and pulled down many houses in the city behind it, ordering the women and children to vacate their houses and occupy strong shelters he had built for them.

Owing to the exposed character of the position, the enemy dug trenches for his troops. He set up batteries of his heaviest artillery against the wall, and directed some pieces towards the tower and windmills on the adjacent mole. Having made these preparations, he commenced an incessant and deadly bombardment, using cannon balls of enormous size. Soon breaches were made in the walls. The Turk employed Fifth Column agents and methods, spies in the city working on the fears of the timorous, representing that the position was hopeless, and gunmen without directing their fire on the houses which they thought (wrongly as we have seen) to be occupied by the women and children. The spies within, dilating on the vast Ottoman reinforcements they averred were approaching the island, were joined by some Italians and Spaniards; but these, afterwards deploring their inconstancy, were pardoned, and fought with the same bravery as their fellows.

Seeing that these stratagems were useless, and that the cries of surrender by his troops met with no response, the pasha began to construct a breastwork on the far side of the moat, opposite the wall. Without delay Aubusson, selecting fifty picked men, sent them forth by night to attack the men employed in this operation and destroy their work. This force, issuing from the casemate at the foot of the wall, crossed the moat, climbed the counterscarp by ladders and, sword in hand, fell upon the men they found there, who, taken completely by surprise, were either slain or put to flight. Then, demolishing the structure and spiking the cannon they found, the force returned. The attempt at this point proving fruitless, the pasha decided to return to the attack on the tower of St. Nicholas which, already severely damaged, he thought would now be less difficult to take.

In this second assault on the tower a timber bridge was to be thrown across the water to it from the west side of the Ancient Harbour. The bridge was built on land, and it was constructed so that it could be hauled across by cable, which was to be passed through an iron ring attached to the other side. Secretly by night, an anchor with a ring attached to it was taken across, secured to the rock beneath the tower and a cable passed through the ring and brought back. An English sailor, named Roger, seeing what was going forward, and waiting until the Turk had returned, dived into the sea, unfastened the anchor and left it in such a manner that no interference was apparent. When in the morning the Turks began to haul their bridge across they soon found that something very serious had happened, that their manoeuvre had been detected and countered. Roger received 200 crowns of gold for his exploit. The Turks then endeavoured to carry the far end of the bridge across the water on suitable craft, while they concentrated an incessant artillery fire on the tower and neighbouring walls of the city. Thirty vessels were employed in the task, and by this means the bridge was fixed in position.

Meanwhile the Knights enlarged the ditch around the tower, both in depth and width, employing a thousand miners in the work, and, thinking it probable that a simultaneous attack would be made on the Jews' wall, repaired the damage sustained there in the last engagement. On the completion of their preparations, the Turks, again with great shouting and blowing of trumpets, rushed to the attack. A great enemy force which had arrived at the foot of the fort, and was being reinforced by a constant stream of men crossing the bridge, began a violent attack at the breach which had been made previously in the outer wall. At the same time the enemy's galleys, having arrived in the harbour, joined in the assault, and a desperate struggle fought with great determination on both sides ensued. The first assault was beaten off, but, undeterred by reverse, the enemy came on again with both forces. And now they were to suffer great loss. Cannon fire from the tower and from the walls of the city smashed their bridge in pieces, killing those who were on it and preventing others from passing over; while the fire ships in the harbour, aided by artillery attack from the walls, made devastating execution among the enemy's fleet. So great was their loss, both in men and ships, that the Turks retired and made no further attempt on the tower of St. Nicholas.

On this crushing repulse the pasha flew into a high passion and shut himself up for three days. Then followed the most violent and persistent of all the assaults. The Turk set up his artillery along the whole line of the land walls, with the apparent object of making a concerted attack all round. But, while he opened fire at other points, his main thrust was still at the Jews' wall. Here, on the far side of the moat facing the wall, he built a high rampart, mounting his guns on its summit, and dug mines to enable his troops to enter the bed of the dry moat unobserved. When in the moat the men, aided by others issuing from the mines, built, with the materials they had collected, a sloping rampart against the wall which rose up as high as the bastions. To counter this move, the Grand Master had a very large and powerful *trebuchet* brought to the spot, for these weapons appear to have been still in use. This one could be turned in any direction, and threw enormous stones with great violence and to a great distance. When brought into play, missiles from this weapon not only slew or put to flight those building the rampart, but, breaking into their mines, buried those within them.

Aubusson then ordered the enemy's works to be demolished and its materials to be brought within the city, cutting a hole through the wall at moat level for this purpose. Seeing that the reinforcement of the wall, which was built in haste during the last attack at this point, was not strong enough to resist the enemy's artillery, he decided to strengthen it with the materials brought in. Again every available person, irrespective of age, sex or status, was employed on the task, as well as on that of assembling at this point every kind of missile that could be found, including scraps of iron, sacks of sulphur and pots of boiling oil. The pasha now made a further effort at diplomacy, representing that the Knights would gain great advantage by surrender at this stage, since their case was otherwise hopeless. These efforts having failed, he gave orders that on the city being taken all except infants were to be put to the sword or impaled, setting up a thousand stakes in the neighbourhood for impalement. He ordered his artillery to open fire and to maintain an incessant attack, day and night, on the defences all round the city. This bombardment produced dire effects on the walls and towers, particularly at the Jews* wall where yet again the attack was most fierce and concentrated.

And now, encouraged with hopes of plunder and provided with chains to bind their prisoners, on signal given by the firing of a mortar the Turkish troops, with ear-splitting shouts and yells, rushed in to the great assault. Debris brought down into the moat by the heavy attack on the Jews' wall greatly facilitated the assault at this point. The Turks scaled the wall with irresistible fury, and the defenders, overpowered by numbers, were driven off. The Turks immediately planted seven of their flags on the wall. Then reinforcements from within, having ascended the wall, drove back the enemy; but he returned in such overwhelming force that, after a desperate fight, he held the position. Then Aubusson, with valiant and determined supporters, mounted the wall and fell on the Turks. Realizing that the loss of this post would be fatal, they fought with almost superhuman courage and strength, and after two hours of incessant fight retrieved the position, drove off the Turks and tore down their flags.

This result was only achieved through the strenuous efforts of all within the city. Well knowing what dire fate awaited them in case of defeat, every one who could fight or carry missiles rushed to the walls. Women in men's clothes poured down boiling oil on the enemy, and hurled flints, scraps of iron and even Greek fire (which required skilful handling) at him. The pasha, having selected a body of picked men, ordered them to attack the Grand Master, and him only. About a dozen of these men fought their way through to Aubusson's side; and, though he laid about him with prodigious strength and effect, his weapons being broken, he was wounded in many places. One of his wounds was at first thought to be fatal, and consternation spread throughout the city. Then it was that the defenders fell upon the Turks with the utmost fury and irresistible impetus, and after a hard struggle drove them off the wall. And now the forces attacking other parts of the city, seeing that the assault on the Jews' wall had failed, themselves took to flight. The whole army was then in retreat and, the Rhodians issuing from the city in pursuit, the defeat became a rout. Later it was found that Aubusson's wound was not fatal, and he recovered.

The pasha having failed in every attempt to take the city (though he had carried on a relentless attack for three months), in view of his very heavy losses and desire to save the remainder of his men, raised the siege. During his preparations for departure two Spanish ships, sent to relieve the city, but not arriving until the conflict was over, appeared off the coast. They were immediately attacked by the guns of the defeated enemy, and had to scuttle to the harbour for their own safety. The Ottoman fleet left the island on August 18th, 1480.

NOTES

1. *Histoire de Pierre d'Aubusson*, Dom Bourbours, Paris, 1676.
2. This man afterwards professing repentance and a desire to serve the Knights, was received within the walls but closely watched; proving to be a spy, he was hanged in the city market place.